University of London Classical Studies

VII

THE STAGE
OF ARISTOPHANES

The Stage
of Aristophanes

C. W. DEARDEN

UNIVERSITY OF LONDON
THE ATHLONE PRESS
1976

Published by
THE ATHLONE PRESS
UNIVERSITY OF LONDON
at 4 Gower Street, London WC1
Distributed by Tiptree Book Services Ltd
Tiptree, Essex

U.S.A. and Canada
Humanities Press Inc
New Jersey

© *C. W. Dearden* 1976

0 485 13707 0

Printed in Great Britain by
WESTERN PRINTING SERVICES LTD
BRISTOL

PREFACE

No two people agree on the form that the Fifth Century Athenian theatre took. The paucity of archaeological evidence, the doubtful value of theatrical illustrations on vases, the confused and often contradictory statements of scholiasts and lexicographers make this disparity of view hardly surprising. The result has been a large number of studies of the Athenian theatre: my only excuse for adding to them is that I have tried to approach the problem from a different angle and have concerned myself with a single playwright, Aristophanes, in an attempt to show the kind of theatre that his plays seem to imply and the extent to which this is compatible with the archaeological and other evidence. For a study of this kind the comic playwright is peculiarly helpful for he, unlike his tragic counterpart, is willing to sacrifice the flow of his plot to win a laugh at the expense of the absurdity of the dramatic conventions that surround his performance. While he laughs, we can observe the creaking stage machinery.

As will be immediately apparent, this book owes much to earlier writers on the theatre; and though I have often disagreed with their conclusions I am very conscious that without the stimulus they provided, much of it would have been impossible. It is based largely upon my thesis for Ph.D. submitted to the University of London. In the writing of that thesis I was fortunate enough to be supervised by Professor T. B. L. Webster and to him I am deeply grateful for his unstinted interest in my work and his penetrating criticisms of it: indeed much more grateful than can be acknowledged here. Professor E. W. Handley gave unstintingly of his time to read through the manuscript in draft, made numerous suggestions on it and saved me from many errors: to him also I am deeply indebted. My examiner Professor R. E. Wycherley made many valuable

suggestions and comments as did Professors K. J. Dover and
R. P. Winnington-Ingram, who read parts of the typescript at
various stages in its preparation. Miss E. Mary Cosh, with
enviable skill, improved the manuscript beyond recognition,
my mother typed it time and again without complaint and my
wife lived with it for seven years. This book is an expression of
gratitude to them all.

I should like to record my thanks to the Humanities Research
Council of the Canada Council for funds enabling me to visit
theatres in Greece, Italy, and Sicily and to work in London, to
the New Zealand Universities Grants Committee for money to
purchase books and microfilm and to the delegates of the Henry
Brown Fund of the Institute of Classical Studies for a grant to
help with publication.

I have finally to thank the long-suffering staff of the Athlone
Press for all their help and courtesy.

Victoria University of Wellington   C.W.D.

News of the death of Professor T. B. L. Webster reached New
Zealand while this book was with the publisher. Others have
spoken and written of his qualities both as a scholar and man
more eloquently than I could. Suffice it to say that I owe much
to him, and, as some small token of the respect and affection in
which I held him, I dedicate this book to his memory.

CONTENTS

ABBREVIATIONS   xi

I. THE THEATRICAL BACKGROUND   I
The City Dionysia and the Theatre of Dionysus.   3
The Lenaea and its Theatre   5

II. THE THEATRE   9
The Archaeological Remains   9
Aristophanes on the Theatrical Structure   11
The Raised Stage   13
The Paraskenia   18
The Number of Doors and the Prothyron   20
The Roof   30
The Windows   31
The Parodoi   32

III. THE SKENE   38
Scene Indication and Scene Painting   38
Stage Properties   46

IV. THE EKKYKLEMA   50

V. THE MECHANE   75

VI. THE ACTORS   86
The Three-Actor Rule   86
Mutes and Extras   94
The Chief Character as a Point of Unity   94
Appendix: The Division of Roles between Actors   96

VII. THE CHORUS   101
The Development of the Chorus   101

Size and Arrangement of the Chorus   105
Subsidiary Choruses and Special Dancers   109

VIII.   COSTUME IN OLD COMEDY   111

IX.   THE MASKS   122
Appendix: Allocation of the Masks   126

APPENDIX: THE STAGING OF THE PLAYS   143

NOTES   180

INDEX LOCORUM   191

INDEX OF MONUMENTS   197

GENERAL INDEX   198

ABBREVIATIONS

References to ancient authors are abbreviated as in *LSJ*. Fragments of comedy, unless otherwise stated, are quoted from Th. Kock, *Comicorum Atticorum Fragmenta*, Teubner (1880) except for Menander for whom the edition of A. Koerte, Teubner (1959) is the source. Fragments of tragedy are taken from A. Nauck, *Tragicorum Graecorum Fragmenta*, 2nd edn, Leipzig, (1889) and the supplement to it ed. B. Snell, Hildesheim (1964).

References to periodicals are according to the scheme in *L'Année Philologique*. Texts are quoted from the Oxford Classical Texts (O.C.T.) where such exist; where they do not, the Teubner editions are preferred. Otherwise the name of the editor is given. Aristophanes: reference is made to editions of Aristophanes and to commentaries on his work by the editor's (or commentator's) name alone. English titles for Aristophanes' plays have been preferred throughout: they are abbreviated as follows:

Ach.—Acharnians	*Lys.—Lysistrata*
Knights	*Thesm.—Women at the Thesmophoria*
Clouds	*Frogs*
Wasps	*Ass.—Women in Assembly*
Peace	*Wealth*
Birds	

Most names have been Hellenized e.g. Kleon; especially is this the case where the names are not in general usage; where they are, I have often preferred the better-known Latin form (Socrates rather than Sokrates) to a too pedantic adherence to the above principle. I trust this will not cause confusion or annoyance. Other abbreviations used are as follows:

Arnott	P. Arnott, *Greek Scenic Conventions in the Fifth Century B.C.*, Oxford (1962).

ATL	B. D. Merritt, H. T. Wade-Gery, M. F. McGregor, *The Athenian Tribute Lists*, Cambridge, Mass. (1939–53).
BHT	M. Bieber, *History of the Greek and Roman Theatre*, 2nd edn, Princeton (1962).
Cantarella	R. Cantarella, *Aristophane, Le Comedie Vol. I*, Milan (1949).
Flickinger	R. Flickinger, *The Greek Theatre and its Drama*, Chicago (1918).
GTP	T. B. L. Webster, *Greek Theatre Production*, London (1956).
Hourmouziades	N. C. Hourmouziades, *Production and Imagination in Euripides*, Athens (1965).
IG	*Inscriptiones Graecae.*
LSJ	H. G. Liddell and R. Scott, *A Greek–English Lexicon*, 9th edn, revised by Sir Henry Stuart Jones and R. McKenzie, Oxford (1940).
MNC	T. B. L. Webster, *Monuments Illustrating New Comedy*, 2nd edn, *BICS* sup. 24 (1969).
MOMC	T. B. L. Webster, *Monuments Illustrating Old and Middle Comedy*, 2nd edn, *BICS* sup. 23 (1969).
MTS	T. B. L. Webster, *Monuments Illustrating Tragedy and Satyr Play*, 2nd edn, *BICS* sup. 20 (1967).
Pack	R. A. Pack, *The Greek and Roman Literary Texts from Graeco-Roman Egypt*, 2nd edn. Michigan (1965).
PCDith	A. W. Pickard-Cambridge, *Dithyramb, Tragedy and Comedy*, 2nd edn, revised by T. B. L. Webster, London (1962).
PCF	A. W. Pickard-Cambridge, *The Dramatic Festivals of Athens*, 2nd edn, revised by J. Gould and D. M. Lewis, Oxford (1968).
PCTh	A. W. Pickard-Cambridge, *The Theatre of Dionysus in Athens*, Oxford (1946).
POxy	*The Oxyrhyncus Papyri*, London (1898–).
PSI	*Pubblicazioni della Societa italiana per la*

	ricerca dei papiri greci e latini.
PV	A. D. Trendall, *Phlyax Vases*, 2nd edn, *BICS* sup. 19 (1967).
Russo	C. F. Russo, *Aristophane Autore di Teatro*, Florence (1962).
Sifakis	G. M. Sifakis, *Studies in the History of Hellenistic Drama*, London (1967).
SIG	W. Dittenberger, *Sylloge Inscriptionum Graecarum*, 3rd edn, Leipzig (1915–24).
'Staging'	T. B. L. Webster, '*Staging and Scenery in the Ancient Greek Theatre*', *BRL*, 42 (1959–60), 493ff.
Webster *Tragedies*	T. B. L. Webster, *The Tragedies of Euripides*, London (1967).

CHAPTER I

THE THEATRICAL BACKGROUND

For the study of the Athenian theatre two festivals are of paramount importance, the Lenaea celebrated in January and the City Dionysia in March. At both of them contests of tragic and comic plays were organized but at the City Dionysia tragedy seems to have held pride of place and, indeed, it seems likely that the festival was, in its early days, devoted solely to tragedy, or so the victor lists would lead us to believe, since they record Thespis as the earliest tragic victor in c. 534 B.C. but remain silent for comedy until 486.[1] At the Lenaea the reverse was true. Again according to the victor lists, the festival started off as a solely comic one in 442 and tragedy was added ten years later. As might be expected, the tragic poets seem to have considered it of less importance than the Dionysia—at any rate the great tragic poets seldom exhibited there:[2] comic poets seem to have produced plays at both festivals indiscriminately.[3]

It is difficult to believe that the year 442 B.C. is the actual date at which comic contests at the Lenaea began: more likely the date records the festival's transfer to the theatre of Dionysus and the dramatic festival itself had been in progress for some time. Evidence to support this statement and for an earlier site for the Lenaea is to be found in a tangle of ancient comments on the wooden stands or *ikria*, erected for theatrical performances.[4] From the evidence two strands can be discerned: the first connects the collapse of the *ikria* with Aeschylus and Pratinas, and thereby with tragedy and satyr play, the City Dionysia, and the precinct of Dionysus Eleuthereus. Mention is made of 'seeing from a poplar tree' near the temple, possibly the old temple of Dionysus, south-west of the present theatre, where the *ikria* were built. The second piece of evidence mentions a group of black poplars in the Agora, presumably to be distinguished from the tree near the temple. Coupled with this

is the evidence of Photius (sv. ἴκρια) and others, for a theatre
in the Agora, between which and the Lenaea and Lenaion a
connection, albeit tenuous, can be made out.[5] Furthermore it is
difficult to see what the Dionysian contests in the Agora can
have been if they were not those later transferred to the theatre
of Dionysus, and still further evidence may be seen in the statement of the *Marmor Parium* that Susarion invented comic
choruses, and that they were introduced into Athens between
580 and 560 B.C. Whatever the exact meaning of that affirma-
tion, it is likely that, as comedy played only a secondary part in
the City Dionysia, the performances took place at the Lenaean
festival and that comic performance there is of some antiquity.

The victor lists themselves pose a further problem. The style
of stone cutting of these lists points to a date soon after 346 B.C.,
but there is no evidence of how they were compiled or of the
source on which Aristotle drew for his list of didascaliae.[6]
Hypothesis, and analogy with the practice at Delos,[7] suggests
that originally there may have been two sources of record in
Athens; one a financial account held by the archon, detailing
the amounts paid out for the performances and presumably the
names of the victors, but containing no titles of plays, the other,
a set with the names of producers, victors etc. and the titles of
plays, which was probably dedicated to Dionysus and preserved
in his temple. As tragedy at the City Dionysia was closely
associated with Dionysus Eleuthereus, it would be natural for
the records to be placed in his temple by the theatre: when the
Lenaean festival was transferred to the same place, the fact that
the Dionysia contests were already being recorded could well
have led to the adoption of similar arrangements for the Lenaea.
This further suggests that Aristotle's remark (*Poetics* 1449a 37)
on the obscurity of the early history of comedy may have been
caused by the absence of records before 486 B.C. when those of
the Dionysia commence, for in reflecting that the tragic records
stretched back to 534 he could well have concluded that
comedy had been developing unrecorded during those same
fifty years on which he, therefore, felt unable to comment.

Certainly by 430 B.C., however, the comic poet had the two
festivals available to him, and the hypotheses to Aristophanes'
plays show that he exhibited at both seemingly without dis-

crimination. Nevertheless, a number of scholars have vigorously argued that the two festivals required entirely different theatres and settings for their plays, and that the evidence for the one cannot therefore be used for the other. We must, then, begin by considering the differences between the two festivals.

THE CITY DIONYSIA AND THE THEATRE OF DIONYSUS

The City Dionysia was the main Athenian dramatic festival and an 'effective advertisement of the power and public spirit of Athens, no less than the artistic and literary leadership of her sons'.[8] Held at a time of year when the seas were once again navigable, it brought to the city representatives of the whole Greek world, both on business and pleasure. Its setting was the theatre of Dionysus nestling at the foot of the Acropolis, where the festival's third, fourth and fifth days were given over to tragic and comic contests. During the period of the Peloponnesian War it seems almost certain that comedies were performed in the afternoon, after a morning devoted to tragedies.[9]

I do not intend to discuss here the history and development of the theatre prior to 430 B.C.; it is enough to state that the earliest remaining foundations of the scene building date, seemingly, to about 430 and that there is no evidence of major reconstruction of this, the so-called Periclean theatre, before Lycurgus redesigned it about 330.[10] The main foundations of the theatre were of stone, providing both tragic and comic poets with a single base on which to build the backgrounds for their plays. The question then arises: how far could the poets adapt the theatrical area to their own desires? Could the stage building be changed at the poet's whim with each performance, or was there some semi-permanent shape, which can be recovered from indications in the plays?

The scene building or *skene* was probably of wood, and as a result commentators have been quick to describe it as 'temporary', implying that it could be adapted to whatever form the poet wished it to take, within the limits imposed by the foundations. Theoretically the poet had plenty of scope for adaptation; practically, however, the scope was severely curtailed by the organization of the festival. It has been calculated that the time available between plays at the festivals would

have been at the most half an hour,[11] and while this would be
sufficient for the removal of properties and the changing of
scenery panels if necessary, a complete rebuilding of the *skene*
would be impossible. Indeed Aristotle (*Poetics* 1451a 10ff.)
implies that there was no time limit on a tragedy beyond that
fixed by the nature of the drama itself, and the plays of Euripides vary in length by as much as 700 lines, which would make
no small difference to the time available for changing the *skene*.
The time problem must be even more marked if Webster's
hypothesis is correct, that between 450 and 420 B.C. each tragic
poet produced one of his three plays on three separate days, for
this would have given him no chance to compensate in length
or in the amount of scene changing required for his produc-
tions.[12] The stage background must have remained constant
for the whole day, and if for the whole day, then also for the
whole festival: for one of the few things we do know about the
organization of the competitions is that the order of presentation
was determined by lot at the beginning of the contest.[13] If the
playwright did not know beforehand at which point in the
festival his play was to be performed, he must have planned it
to conform with the normal structure of the *skene* with only
minor variations.

The stage background, then, was constant for the festival, but
in theory it could have been taken down and destroyed between
festivals and rebuilt entirely anew each time. Such a practice
would have been expensive—especially when timber was in
great demand for ships, as during the Peloponnesian War—
but nevertheless possible. Certain points, however, suggest more
permanence in the building. The Lenaean festival was held in
January, and it might be expected that the theatrical structure,
once erected, would have remained in place until the City
Dionysia in March, especially as rehearsals of the plays, co-
ordination of the parts of actors and chorus, and so on, must all
have required use of the theatre, and with fifteen plays to be
thus prepared, the month between the two festivals seems little
enough without the inconvenience of a major rebuilding
programme as well.[14] Furthermore, the poet, when composing
his play, must have required to know what form the theatre was
to take, and major modification could only have taken place

through some interference by the state, or a previous collective decision of all the poets. All this clearly implies a conservative approach to any structural changes, though minor alterations remain perfectly possible. The *skene*, then, is to be imagined as almost constant in structure—a structure sufficiently neutral in form to serve as a background for whatever setting the playwright might wish to convey to his audience, with the possible availability of scenery panels as an additional aid.

Throughout the lifetime of Aristophanes the theatre of Dionysus remained substantially the same, and the plays of this poet can be considered as a homogenous group from which valid deductions about the theatrical structure can be drawn without reference to the chronological sequence of the plays.

THE LENAEA AND ITS THEATRE

A number of Aristophanes' plays were, according to their hypotheses, produced at the Lenaean festival, a festival which Aristophanes himself describes (*Ach.* 504ff.) as purely domestic, since the January storms prevented the presence of strangers and allies. The parochial nature of this occasion is amply illustrated by the permission accorded to aliens to perform in the choruses, and to resident aliens to act as *choregoi*.[15] At this festival comedy was more important than tragedy: both before and after the Peloponnesian War the complement of comic poets competing was five, while only two tragic poets were represented, each with two plays. (For the duration of the war the number of comedies was reduced to three.)[16]

The festival's status is well attested, the theatre in which it was celebrated less so. The generally accepted view is that followed above: that originally the festival was of minor importance, on a level with the production of plays in the deme theatres at the Rural Dionysia, and as it became more ambitious it was transferred to the theatre of Dionysus about 442 B.C. There have inevitably been dissenters from this thesis. Dörpfeld argued that the transfer did not take place until Lycurgus rebuilt the Dionysus theatre in the mid-fourth century, and more support for his view has come from Anti and Russo,[17] though the latter quite rightly dismissed Anti's theories on siting the Lenaion in the trapezoidal area excavated by Dörpfeld to the west of the Acropolis. He argued a distinction, however, between the festivals and the theatres in which they were celebrated, basing his evidence on those of Aristophanes' plays stated in their hypotheses to have been performed at the Lenaea: the *Acharnians*, *Knights*, *Wasps*, and *Frogs*. These arguments we must consider in more detail.

The essential feature of the Lenaean theatre, Russo maintains, was its temporary wooden construction, which leaves no room for the use of the *mechane* which must have needed a strong foundation. Those plays which require a *mechane* are therefore not Lenaean. To this argument it can be objected that the fact that in the four plays that are listed as Lenaean the *mechane* is not used does not necessarily imply that the machine was unavailable; its use is not over-frequent in Dionysian comedies, while it could be justifiably claimed that the *ekkyklema* required an equally firm foundation considering the number of people it occasionally has to carry and that machine certainly was used in a Lenaean comedy, the *Acharnians* (408ff.). Russo's second claim is that in three of the four Lenaean plays an actor entering through the orchestra is invited to 'ascend' (*Ach.* 732, *Knights* 149, *Wasps* 1341) which again distinguishes them from the Dionysian plays (he later uses a reference to 'descending' (*Ass.* 1152) to ascribe the *Women in Assembly* to the Lenaea), on the assumption that the Dionysus theatre had no stage. This assumption, which he makes no attempt to prove, we shall discuss further in the next chapter. Finally, Russo argues that only Dionysian comedies mention the public corridors leading to the theatre, the dressing rooms and the Bouleutic seats,[18] points which must surely be coincidental unless it is assumed that there was no corridor to admit the audience to the Lenaean theatre.

In referring, next, to the internal structure of the plays, Russo attempts to demonstrate a general difference of approach by the poet to the different festivals. While this may be true, it is in itself no proof that separate theatres existed: it could merely reflect a difference in the type of audiences at the two festivals. Turning to more specific points, the argument that the scenery of the Lenaean plays is simple compared with the 'exotic' settings of the Dionysian is belied by the *Frogs*, clearly the most 'exotic' of all if realistic scenery is demanded; and the same play gives the lie to Russo's next argument that the Dionysian comedies show a more concrete and connected setting with careful progression from scene to scene and central characters governed by theatrical unity of place, in contrast with the more loosely knit Lenaean plays. The *Frogs* is probably the most structurally perfect of all the plays. Russo's last point concerns the difference in setting of the plays. The Dionysian are set in Athens, or in the sky and the world of the birds, while the Lenaean take place on the Pnyx, in the Agora, or in the sanctuary of the Limnae. This is an extension of Anti's argument that the Lenaean plays introduce references, sometimes demonstrative, to the Agora and the Pnyx, on the strength of which Anti assigned *Women at the Thesmophoria*, *Women in Assembly* and *Wealth* to that festival. But as Dover has pointed out,[19] it is difficult to see why a performance at the Lenaea should have induced the poet to include references to places visible to the audience, any more than a performance at the Dionysia. It was the subject chosen for the play that influenced the references, and though it is generally true that the Dionysian plays have a wider scope than those intended for the Lenaea, this again is probably an indication of a difference in approach by the poet to the two festivals, but in no way implies that different theatres were used. Russo's arguments for a second theatre are, in short, unconvincing, and in default of any ancient evidence for the existence of two theatres in the time of Aristophanes, it must be accepted that Lenaean performances took place in the theatre of Dionysus.

The signs we have seen of a difference in Aristophanes' approach to the festivals suggests, however, that there may be some criterion for dividing the otherwise unassigned plays between the festivals. Dicaeopolis, in a famous passage in the *Acharnians* (502ff.), claims that as this is the Lenaean festival and no strangers are present, Kleon cannot complain of being disgraced before the allies. The domestic nature of this festival, in other words, allows the poet more freedom of manoeuvre, since in attacking a prominent politician before a local audience only the individual is threatened, not the image of the state which would be involved if such an attack were delivered before the assembled allies at the Dionysia. On this basis a play like the

Knights, with its personal attack on Kleon, might be expected to be for performance at the Lenaea as its hypothesis claims it was; the *Birds*, on the other hand, a fantasy concerned little with the political giants of the day, might be confidently assigned to the Dionysia, as is in fact recorded.

If political attacks on well-known politicians were more easily made at the Lenaea, we might also expect that purely topical attacks on politicians and private citizens, now usually characterized as 'otherwise unknown', would be more prominent at that festival where they would be instantly appreciated, rather than at a cosmopolitan gathering like the Dionysia where much of this abuse would be over the heads of many of the allies.[20] A conservative estimate of such passing references provides the following totals: *Acharnians* 18, *Knights* 26, *Clouds* 4, *Wasps* 24, *Peace* 8, *Birds* 27, *Lysistrata* 5, *Women at the Thesmophoria* 7, *Frogs* 20, *Assembly of Women* 20, *Wealth* 8. Two groups are clearly distinguishable. To the Lenaea can be assigned *Ach.*, *Knights*, *Wasps*, *Frogs* and *Ass.*, the first four of which are also assigned by their hypotheses, to the Dionysia *Clouds*, *Peace*, *Lys.*, *Thesm.*, and *Wealth* the first two of which are confirmed by their hypotheses. The *Birds* is the sole exception. The number of political references suggest it should be Lenaean but hypotheses I and II to the play state that it was performed at the Dionysia.[21]

Whether the plays were performed at the Dionysian or the Lenaean festival however, makes little difference to their stage arrangements, as we have seen. All the evidence points to the use of the theatre of Dionysus for both festivals and all the plays, therefore, can be freely used to shed light on the appearance of the theatre at the end of the fifth century B.C., and the conventions affecting it.

CHAPTER II

THE THEATRE

THE ARCHAEOLOGICAL REMAINS

The meagre remains of the fifth-century theatre of Dionysus require some description (see plan p. 10).[1] Briefly, they consist of a long wall 'H' running some 73.1m east to west and intended to support the whole of the terrace area, directly behind which stands the northern wall of the Hall. The two rest on a common foundation, but the lack of any cross-masonry between them suggests that though part of a single plan, the Hall is slightly later than the wall. A nose of masonry 'T' some 2.74m in depth and 7.9m in length runs north about 20.7m from the west end of 'H' and is clearly contemporaneous with it. 'T' contains two holes connected by a narrow, shallow depression, the westerly hole 67.3cm square, the easterly 67.3cm wide and 121.9cm long, while on either side of 'T', a series of cuttings are visible in the wall at approximately equal distances (labelled 'S1–10', though only eight remain, the two closest to the western edge of 'T' being conjectured). The only other evidence is provided by the line of the auditorium walls which, for some reason, does not lie symmetrically on the north–south axis of the auditorium.

Controversy has centred on the means of approach to 'T' from the Hall. Pickard-Cambridge maintained that an opening existed in the rear wall of the Hall itself, and thereby gave the actors easy access to 'T' by means of a staircase. But Webster has shown[2] that there is no evidence for the staircase, that in any case the number of steps required for ascent from Hall level to that of the door in the *skene* front would demand two thirds of the depth of 'T' and make 'T' unusable for anything else, and that, as is patently clear, the alleged threshold is not symmetrical with 'T', and only half of it could be used if the large hole in 'T' was not to be fouled. Clearly the theory is

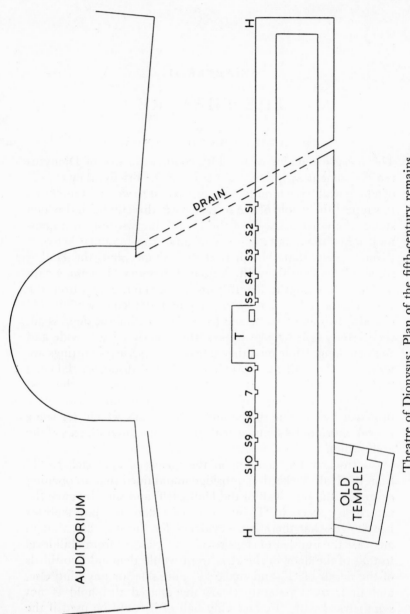

Theatre of Dionysus: Plan of the fifth-century remains

untenable, and an entrance through the *skene* door must have required a previous approach by the side of 'H'.

'T' itself has been suggested as the site for the theatrical machines, notably the *mechane*, but perhaps the *ekkyklema* also, on the plausible assumption that the holes have some connexion with the machines. The stage or acting area must clearly be adjacent, and an assumed duplication of the shape of 'H' and 'T' in front of the actual foundations has found many supporters, though without any explanation being offered of why the foundations themselves were not made larger to take in the whole area. The more economical hypothesis is to suppose with Webster that 'T' served not only as a foundation for the mechanical devices but as acting area as well and that on it was built the *skene* front. This unfortunately drastically limits the amount of space available for such lively scenes as the battle between Lysistrata and her women and the Magistrate and his Archers (*Lys.* 437ff.). Webster calculated an available depth of 1.3m, if the *ekkyklema*, when withdrawn, filled the area between the two holes: even this seems little enough space, and it is possible that 'T' simply represented the fullest potential extent of the *ekkyklema* and that the acting area could be extended forward into the ten feet or so separating 'T' from the edge of the orchestra.

ARISTOPHANES ON THE THEATRICAL STRUCTURE

If the archaeological remains themselves are inconclusive, such direct references as Aristophanes makes to the parts of the theatre add little of importance. His concern is naturally with the audience, whose rows and the wooden benches on which they sit are referred to in *Knights* 163 and *Thesm.* 395, the word *ikria* used in the latter being presumably a technical term. The seat of the priest of Dionysus in the front row amongst the dignitaries is noticed in *Frogs* 297, and it is obvious that special seats were allocated to other honoured members of the community, hence the singling out of the members of the *Boulē* in *Birds* 793–5 and the confirmatory reference in *Peace* 871, where Trygaeus apparently presents *Theoria* to the *Boulē* and leaves her with them.[3] Of other parts of the theatre, the poet three times (*Clouds* 326, *Birds* 296, frag 388) refers to the passages leading into the orchestra, used as entrance and exit by the audience, chorus and actors alike, using the term *eisodoi* rather than the later name *parodoi*.[4]

A less obvious reference occurs in *Frogs* 193–5. Xanthias is ordered to wait for his master,

$$\pi\alpha\rho\grave{\alpha}\ \tau\grave{o}\nu\ A\grave{\upsilon}\alpha\acute{\iota}\nu o\upsilon\ \lambda\acute{\iota}\theta o\nu$$
$$\grave{\epsilon}\pi\grave{\iota}\ \tau\alpha\~{\iota}\varsigma\ \grave{\alpha}\nu\alpha\pi\alpha\acute{\upsilon}\lambda\alpha\iota\varsigma.$$

'beside the stone of Withering (?) at the resting places'—an allusion that has confounded scholiasts and commentators alike. Explanations have usually tried to fix one of these terms without reference to the other; but the two are clearly an entity, and when we remember Aristophanes' fondness for remarks that shatter the dramatic illusion and make fun of the theatrical conventions[5] it seems reasonable to seek their origin in the theatre, even though they may have secondary application to a religious festival or a slang expression, as has been suggested.[6] A stone in the theatre may be what the scholiast has in mind when he claims that a 'Stone of Withering' was supposed to exist somewhere in Athens.

Tucker[7] interpreted the ἀναπαύλαις as a resting place for the chorus to which they retired when not engaged in performance, but the lack of literary or archaeological evidence for such a place, coupled with the frequent necessity for the chorus or its leader to join in the iambic dialogue with the actors and therefore to be in position in the orchestra, make this theory untenable. A reference might however be seen to the retaining walls of the auditorium, the *analemmata*,[8] and the seats, 'resting places', they support. The relevance of the stone then comes into question. Again, the explanations, that some connexion is implied with the Stone Bearer who had a seat in the theatre, or that Αὐαίνου is to be considered as an imperative, are none too convincing.[9] Clearly there is some connexion with 'dryness' and if the above argument is correct, with a stone placed near the retaining walls. The plan of the theatre reveals a drain running from the north-east corner of the orchestra by the foot of the *analemma*, intended to carry away rain water from the theatre. It is not impossible that this area might be referred to as the Αὐαίνου λίθον and the meaning made obvious to the audience by a gesture.

Such is the evidence of direct reference by Aristophanes to the theatre in which his plays were produced, and though useful, it is very limited. It is, therefore, from a subjective interpretation of his comedies that evidence must now be elicited.

THE RAISED STAGE

The long-standing argument between the supporters of a high stage and the protagonists of no stage at all has now been resolved into a discussion of the relative merits of a low stage, providing reasonable access between orchestra and acting area while allowing actors to be easily distinguished from the chorus, and of a theatre without any stage.

The external evidence for a stage amounts to a single Attic vase of c. 420 B.C., which depicts a comic actor playing the part of Perseus[10] on a low wooden stage approached by four steps. Two men look on from what is presumably the orchestra. Pickard-Cambridge unjustifiably dismisses this as a private performance which has no bearing on the Theatre of Dionysus, despite the number of Phlyax vases which depict almost identical stages and thereby offer strong confirmatory evidence. Although these vases are from South Italy, it has been shown that the scenes depicted have strong ties with Athenian comedies and can be used (with caution) to indicate conditions in the Athenian theatre of the fifth century.[11] Three main types of stage are catalogued by A. D. Trendall as appearing on these vases, their chief characteristic being a simple wooden construction and a flight of steps—number seems to vary with the whim of the painter. The steps are interesting because the vases nowhere suggest the presence of a chorus in the plays, so presumably the ladder is for the use of actors who enter through the *parodoi* and subsequently climb on to the stage—possibly Athenian theatrical practice is to be seen as an influence here. The insistence on a stage, however, on these vases and on the Perseus vase does suggest that such a structure was a feature of the theatre. The literary evidence of Aristotle, which is dependant on his distinguishing between ἀπὸ σκηνῆς and χοροῦ carries us little further: though Hourmouziades argues plausibly enough that its tone does suggest a distinction in level between actors and chorus.[12]

There remains the internal evidence of the plays, which is necessarily the most telling though it must be to some extent subjective. Before going on to consider this, however, one proviso must be made. Too often references in the plays to 'up' and 'down' have been quoted uncritically as 'proving' the existence of a stage, whereas their primary purpose is to suggest a setting to the audience: in other words, the playwright does not specifically aim at providing clues to the theatrical conditions of his own day, those that are present are inherent in the scheme of the play itself. A good illustration of the methods employed is to be found in the *Lysistrata* 286ff. where the Old Men complain of the steepness of the road up to the Propylaea. Those who argued against the existence of a stage referred this to the *parodoi* that sloped up to the orchestra. Arnott[13] rightly invalidated this argument by the simple expedient of showing that by the time they are visible the chorus must already be up the *parodoi*, but he himself continues, 'their goal is the Acropolis and so we must say that between this and their point of entrance in the orchestra was some erection which had to be mounted'. But the point of the Old Men's remark is, first, that the way up to the Propylaea is steep, a fact of which it is dramatically relevant to remind the audience, and, secondly, that they are old and their old age has to be emphasized.[14] There is nothing here that need be construed as referring to the actual theatre, for with only limited scenery available, words and descriptions are necessary to establish the setting.

Of the passages in Aristophanes referring to 'up' and 'down' and frequently cited to 'prove' the existence of a stage, the most important are *Ach.* 732, *Knights* 149, 169, *Wasps* 1341, and *Ass.* 1152. Of these *Ass.* 1152 can be immediately excluded for it refers to the *parodos*, while *Wasps* 1341 can be interpreted in an obscene sense and cannot therefore be used independently as evidence. *Knights* 169 seems to refer to the table which the Sausage-Seller is carrying rather than to the stage and so this too must be rejected, likewise *Ach.* 732 which is spoken before the Megarian and his daughters approach the acting area, for the Megarian's intention is to keep his actions secret for the moment. *Knights* 149 and its accompanying scholium are usefully discussed by Arnott[15] but no reliable conclusion can be drawn from the reference. Another reference, in *Birds* 49ff. seems hitherto to have escaped notice. Euelpides and Peisthetairus enter through the *parodos* at the beginning of the play, and enquire of their birds which way they should go. The birds indicate that the way is 'up', and at 57 the two knock at the door in the *skene*. In the dramatic context it is best to see this 'up' as an allusion to flying, though at this point a climb from *parodos* to stage would be plausible. There is little here, then, to indicate the presence or absence of a stage; but the staging arrangements of two scenes furnish more cogent evidence.

In the *Lysistrata*, the appearance of the semi-chorus of men (254) and the semi-chorus of women (319) shortly leads to a fight between the two and a dousing for the Old Men. The arrival of the Magistrate and his archers (387) effectively halts the scuffle, but leads to a second battle in which their attempt on the Acropolis is vigorously repelled by Lysistrata and her women. At this point comes a song from the Old Men—not that they have just been routed, but that, some hundred lines before, they were doused with water. Clearly they have taken no part in the second battle, for the sight of the chorus standing idly by while right beside them the Magistrate and his men were being discomfited would have made an awkward piece of theatre, and it is more reasonable to assume that the two battles took place at different heights, with the actors distinguished from the chorus.

The appearance of Charon and his boat in the *Frogs* (173ff.) offers further support for the presence of a stage. It will be argued later on that the *ekkyklema* was used in this scene,[16] but whatever the method of staging was some preparation is required for the surprise arrival of Charon at 180 in the centre of the acting area, and the audience's attention must be distracted for just the vital moment of final preparation. The scene from 173 is the perfect answer, the arrival of the corpse through the *parodos*, his refusal of the offer of a job, and his disappearance down the other *parodos*. If both Charon and the corpse appeared on the same level, the distraction would be less successful and largely self-defeating. But given two levels the scene becomes as purposeful as it is funny.[17]

The argument so far has been based on the tacit assumption

that close contact between actors and chorus in the acting area (as distinct from the orchestra) is an important feature of the Greek theatre and that anything that interferes with it, such as a stage, cannot be countenanced as part of the theatre. We must consider, therefore, how close the contact between actors and chorus in the acting area actually is: if it is close, then we must reject the stage.

Among Aristophanes' plays the *Peace* produces the closest contact. The chorus first appears at 296, when Trygaeus summons the 'Men of Hellas' to help him rescue the statue of Peace from the cave in which it is buried (presumably the *skene*), and they, overjoyed at the prospect, sing and dance happily. When they turn to their task, Hermes appears and forbids them, but the chorus persuades him to soften his heart and eventually he remarks (426), 'The job is yours, men. Quick, in you go with your shovels and drag out the stones.' The chorus, it seems, are to enter the acting area and remove the stones. Immediately a libation is poured, and a prayer, in which the chorus partake, offered to the Gods. At the end of the prayer (457), and without further mention of the stones, Trygaeus bids all set to and heave on the ropes, and during the next sixty lines the statue is gradually pulled out, probably on the *ekkyklema*.[18]

What part have the chorus taken in the action? There are two possibilities. It might be claimed that the pouring of the libation and the inclusion of the chorus in the prayer were intended to prevent the chorus from entering the acting area at all, and that the order to do so was simply intended to suggest to the audience that when the time came for the statue to be pulled out, the stones had already been removed; but, more probably, the libation scene was designed to cover the hiatus while preparations were made for the appearance of the statue— presumably ropes had to be attached to the *ekkyklema* before it could be dragged out. Nevertheless, even on this hypothesis it is evident that some of the chorus take part in the libation ceremony, probably allowing only a few actually to enter the acting area—where, it should be noted, there is no question of any concerted action together with the actors. The remainder of the play suggests the more usual lack of close contact between chorus and actors in the acting area.

'Proof' of the absence of a stage has been found in a somewhat similar scene in the *Wasps*.[19] The chorus of Wasps, in
order to help Philokleon, prepare to attack Bdelykleon (403ff.)
and thus to invade the acting area: but the text gives no grounds
for supposing that they actually attack, they simply dance in the
orchestra in a threatening fashion, as do the Birds in a similar
situation (343ff.) when they discover men present in their
kingdom.

In a play where the chorus are identified as a group with the
actors, as in the *Women at the Thesmophoria*, we might expect
more conspicuous evidence of contact between the two in the
acting area. The chorus enter (279ff.) when the scene changes
to the Thesmophorion. Mnesilochus describes their approach,
and clearly actors and chorus come on together, for the moment
the 'Heraldess'—probably the chorus leader—has finished leading the chorus in prayer, one of the actors addresses the meeting.
So far, then, actors and chorus are indistinguishable. But after
the speech of the first woman, the remarks of the chorus
(434-42ff.) imply complete detachment from the scene, and
they continue in the same vein acting as commentator on both
the speech of the second woman (459-65) and on Mnesilochus'
discourse (520-32). The arrival of Kleisthenes (574) with the
news that there is a man in their midst leads to the demand for
a search, which the chorus begs Kleisthenes to undertake (601).
Significantly, he searches only among the actors, taking no
notice of the chorus, and discovers and exposes Mnesilochus,
who remains guarded by a single woman when the stage is
cleared. Thereupon the chorus sings an ode (655-87) and
begins its own search for intruders, reversing the above procedure, for their search is carried out without the actors and
with no indication that it covers the acting area. The next
episode, in which Mnesilochus seizes what he supposes to be a
child and threatens to sacrifice it on the altar, reveals the same
distinction in spheres of activity: for the chorus, though horrified, bid their comrades (the actors) collect wood and burn
Mnesilochus off the altar (699-727), but take no part in the
action themselves. Again, actors and chorus plainly have little
contact in the acting area though together they form a corporate
body. Similarly in the *Women in Assembly* 279, actors and chorus

form one body and both depart for the same place, but the actors leave the scene ahead of the chorus.

The evidence clearly belies any theory of close chorus/actor relationship in the acting area, and indeed suggests a strong distinction between their performing areas. No argument against a stage can, then, rely on this; rather its negative force helps reinforce the evidence discussed earlier, to confirm that a low stage was most probably an integral part of the theatre of Dionysus. It is reasonable to connect this with the area 'T' and to conjecture its height as perhaps four feet, sufficient to raise the actors a little over the chorus without destroying the rapport between them.

THE PARASKENIA

The existence of *paraskenia* in the fifth-century theatre is proved by a speech of Demosthenes, when he accuses Meidias (*Meid.* 17—dated to 347 B.C.) of having 'nailed up the *paraskenia* without public authority although they were public property', in an attempt to stop him producing his play at the festival. What he means by *paraskenia* is less clear, but the *Suda* interprets the word as the place 'by the *skene*' (παρὰ τὴν σκηνὴν) reserved for the properties used in dramatic contests (*Peace* 731 may well be the source of this explanation), and further maintains that Didymus considered the *eisodoi* on either side of the orchestra were called *paraskenia*. This interpretation would make Demosthenes' remark intelligible if there was some construction by the side of 'T' which ran along the wall 'H', and at the same time would allow the hypothesis of 'T' as the stage area to stand.

It has been more usual however, to consider the *paraskenia* as forward-projecting wings such as would normally surround a stage—a reconstruction far from likely if a stage only the size of 'T' is to be accepted. In fact there is no archaeological evidence for such wings, though this need not in itself be suspicious for they could well have been of wood and have left no trace. Such evidence as there is, is derived largely from the fact that they seem to have had a place in the later Lycurgan reconstruction of the theatre of Dionysus, and that the fragments of a South Italian krater in Wurzburg apparently depict a colonnade with a projecting structure at either end, in which doors are evident.[20]

The interpretation of these structures as wings was challenged by Rumpf, and has come under attack again from Jongkees, who argues first that the scene is unlikely to be theatrical, as no central door is pictured, and second that it could not in any sense be construed as a realistic picture of the *scaenae frons*. Furthermore, reconstructions of the theatre that depict the *paraskenia* projecting out into the orchestra[21] usually serve only to strengthen the argument against their presence in the fifth century for they make it plain that large numbers of the audience unfortunate enough to be seated in the vicinity of the retaining walls of the auditorium would be totally unable to see the plays because of these projections. To be sure, the point holds equally true for the Lycurgan theatre, but there the problem is associated with the rebuilding of the theatre: it is unlikely that, when auditorium and stage buildings were constructed to one plan, as they seem to have been for the theatre of Dionysus, the design should deliberately include seats from which vision was impossible. Similarly improbable are reconstructions that provide for doors in the wings facing each other, since scenes produced before them would be invisible to the majority of the audience: doors in the ends of the wings facing the audience are more plausible, but for the fact that parts of the audience would then be denied sight of the central and most important door.[22]

The evidence, then, points against forward-projecting wings, so that whatever Demosthenes means by *paraskenia* (and its significance will be examined more closely in discussing the *parodoi*), its use does not invalidate the earlier arguments for a small stage.

THE NUMBER OF DOORS AND THE PROTHYRON

The stage building and the *skene* front which stood on 'T' were probably built of wood, and may have reached a height of about 5m if Xenophon's remark (*Cyr.* VI i 52–4) that Cyrus' fortresses on wheels were three fathoms high with their wheels, and had beams the thickness of the tragic *skene*, can be taken to refer to the columns on 'H' and 'T'. Such a height would seem not unreasonable in comparison with the known heights of later Hellenistic theatres.[23] The only direct connexion with the stage (as distinct from approaching it through the orchestra) was through the *skene* front, and the plays show that the playwright had available to him at least one practicable door. The acceptance of 'T' as the stage area makes it difficult to suppose more than one door on 'T' in the space available, but provision of doors on either side of 'T' in the wooden walls which, it will be argued, stood in front of 'H', would be possible though difficult, because of the difference in height between these and the one on the stage.

The problem of how many doors the plays of Aristophanes actually require has exercised scholars in recent years but without any generally acceptable solution appearing. Tragedy has been shown, however, to require only a single door for its performance and if comedy required extra side doors, tragedy chose to ignore their existence completely. This thesis has been supported by Dover[24] on the grounds that when a building is constructed for two different purposes, one of which requires greater resources than the other, it is normal, and commonsense, to meet the purposes for which the requirements are more numerous. This unfortunately overlooks the fact that it was the tragic contests that began first, about 534 B.C., whereas comedy was not introduced into the festival until 486, and if Dover is right, it must be assumed that the writers of comedy felt a necessity to write plays requiring three doors even though the theatre in which they were to be performed provided only one.

The necessity for more than one door for comedy has, however, been generally accepted, and a fragment of Eupolis' *Autolycus* (42K) is quoted to support the existence of three. The statement that 'Here they dwell in three huts, each with his own dwelling' appears to be a portion of the prologue, but torn from its context the quotation is of uncertain value as evidence, and needs more telling support to be decisive. Further evidence has therefore been culled from Aristophanes' plays, often on the assumption that each change of location and scene required a new door—a thesis rightly challenged by A. M. Dale, who argued that there was nothing to be gained by staging consecutive scenes in front of different doors, and that a single door was sufficient.[25] The latter part of her case has won little general acceptance, but it is obvious that the question now to be considered is not primarily whether the plays could be performed before a single door, but whether they can be performed in any other manner that can apply consistently to all.

Scholars generally agree that certain plays require no more than a single door, and thus conform to the tragic pattern. In the *Wealth* for example, all the action takes place before the house of Chremylus, external matter being reported by messenger; and in the *Wasps* the action is limited to the area in front of Philokleon's house, the only apparent difficulty occurring when Bdelykleon descends from the roof and appears on the stage (153). The central door, which is supposedly bolted to restrain Philokleon, cannot here be used as there is no reason to break the logic of the scene: an appearance through a side door or in the *parodos* is therefore necessary. It has never been suggested that if two doors existed they might belong to the same house, and without clear indication by the poet this would be a difficult assumption for the audience to make, especially if the doors were at different heights. Miss Dale's suggestion of an appearance by the *parodos* is surely right, and the play then requires only a single door. A similar pattern is discernable in the *Birds*, a play generally assumed to need only one door, without allowing for the difficulties attendant on this. Here the central door is identified from line 56 as that of the Hoopoe's house yet, without any indication of scene change, at 1708 the chorus of Birds prepare to welcome Peisthetairus to *his* halls. The change in ownership is made imperceptibly at 675, as the Hoopoe, Peisthetairus and Euelpides go in together through the door while the *parabasis* is sung. At its conclusion, only the two mortals return to take up again the theme of the preceding scene. This logical connexion between the two scenes, and the fact that the departure of a character is almost invariably followed by his return the same way,[26] make it difficult to suppose that the two reappear, without explanation, through a different door. The two settings in fact are telescoped into a single door. A similar method is used in the *Knights*, usually accepted as a single-door play, but one which in logic demands at least two. It begins before the house of Demus, then moves to the Pnyx (749); the victory of the Sausage-Seller leads to the boiling and rejuvenation of Demus and his reappearance through the gates of the Propylaea (1326), while, in the final scene, Demus

summons the Sausage-Seller to the *Prytaneion*. Three separate
settings are thus identifiable: the *Prytaneion*, Pnyx and Propylaea.
I will be arguing later that the Pnyx was represented on the
ekkyklema and therefore must have required the central door;
Demus' entrance through the Propylaea requires this same door
again, since the poet is in earnest over the advice Demus is to
offer to the Athenian people, and having carefully established
an almost divine aura around his entry he can hardly be expected to plunge into anticlimax by permitting him entrance
through a side door. At 1249 Kleon is rolled back through the
central door on the *ekkyklema*. Unless we are told otherwise, we
must expect him to reappear through that door; but when he
does, it is announced that he is being carried out from the
Prytaneion (1407). The same door, then, does service as Pnyx,
Propylaea and *Prytaneion*.

Rapid changes in the ownership of the door are clearly a
prominent feature of production, so that staging consecutive
scenes set in different places before a single door is no problem.
Hence the *Lysistrata*, commonly regarded as requiring two or
even three doors, in fact needs no more than one. The main
action takes place before the gates of the Acropolis, represented
by the central opening. Separate doors are usually allotted to
Lysistrata and Kalonike, on the evidence of the first six lines.
But at this point the central door is still anonymous, not being
identified as the Acropolis until 253; it can, therefore, be used
for Kalonike's entrance, while Lysistrata herself walks impatiently up the *parodos* before breaking into her opening speech.
To assign a side door to Kalonike for a single line would be an
extraordinary waste of stage resources. The Budé editor per-
versely demands a second door for the grotto of Pan (904ff.),
but Kinesias' seduction, one of the funniest scenes in the play,
cannot be left to take place out of sight of the audience and
must be performed on the stage.

The argument for the use of a single door in consecutive
scenes can be carried a stage further, for certain of them suggest
that the poet was quite willing to suspend the logical relationship between a character and his house represented by the stage
door—scenes in which anomalies arise over the ownership of
doors because there *is* only one: for example, *Women in Assembly*

877ff., where the Young Girl and the Old Hag fight for the favours of the Youth. [27] As the Youth arrives, the Girl tricks the Hag into leaving the windows from which they are keeping watch, and then invites him to come up to her. He hammers on the door, the Girl disappears from the window, and the Hag opens the door to ask the Youth if he is looking for her. He is horrified, and denies even knocking. The situation seems to depend on the exploitation of the single door, without which the scene could hardly be intelligible. Professor Dover[28] objects, however, that 989 and 990 are evidence for two doors, maintaining that the words κρουστέον and κρούσῃς which have an obscene connotation, can refer equally to knocking at two doors (especially in 990).

In the knocking scene, adds Professor Dover, somebody is not telling the truth: either the Young Man's denial is a falsehood, if he has knocked on the single door and the wrong person has appeared, or the Hag must have darted out of her own door pretending he had knocked on that and she is therefore lying when she accuses him. Logically, he argues, the Young Man does not need to knock at all, as the Girl is coming down to him, and as her family cannot be expected to welcome him with open arms, secrecy is essential: 'Comic effect is enhanced if he (the Youth) is standing expectantly (i.e. not having knocked) at the Girl's door and jumps out of his skin when the Old Woman seizes him and pretends with shameless determination that he has knocked at *her* door'. But the point is that the Youth *has* knocked at a door, otherwise the whole scene becomes unintelligible. The Youth knocked, not for any logical reason but in an attempt to impress on the audience his understandable eagerness to get to the Girl, and when he then finds himself in a tight corner it is he who lies, trying to escape by claiming not to have knocked. The whole scene, in this interpretation, depends on the fact that there is only one door. There remains the problem of τηνδεδί in 989, which could mean either 'this door' or 'this girl'. Probably it is intentionally vague, covering both meanings, and is accompanied by a wave of the hand to the 'half' of the house which the Young Girl seems to be occupying. The following scene, in which the Hag and the Girl both try to drag the Youth into the house and thus through the same door, causes no logical difficulty, for as neither are successful a simple struggle over the stage is all that is necessary.

A similar scene is to be found in the *Clouds*. At 1321 Strepsiades rushes out of the door seeking to escape the blows his son Pheidippides is raining on him. The latter returns inside (1475) and Strepsiades, exasperated by Socrates' teaching and its effect on Pheidippides, determines to put an end to it. He summons Xanthias from the house, and together they attack the roof of the Reflectory. Earlier scenes have introduced Strepsiades' house and the Reflectory to the audience in turn: here they seem to be required almost simultaneously—the slave runs out of the door, turns round, and the two attack the roof, while Socrates' disciples rush out through the door. Miss Dale claimed that the attack on the *roof* of the Reflectory was intended to ease the difficulty of the single door, since the central door has just been identified as Strepsiades'; Dover, on the other hand, argues there is nothing strange in an attack on the roof if the intention is to burn the house down. He may well be right, but even so the possibility remains that the attack is made on the roof because there is only one door. If the latter hypothesis is correct, then certainly the rapid change of ownership, from Strepsiades to Socrates and his disciples within twenty lines is difficult though not impossible, thanks, first, to the hero's known intention to attack Socrates' house and secondly to the disciples' heads appearing at the window shouting for help as Xanthias attacks the roof. Either of these points is quite sufficient to emphasize the setting in a scene of fast and furious fun. Strepsiades probably climbs down the ladder again at the end to drive the disciples off stage from the door, as Dover suggests. Dover further argues that the reference to 'this pot' (1473) and the subsequent address to Hermes (1478) imply that both pot and Herm are visible on stage, each standing by its own door. But there is no evidence that a Herm was present on the stage, Strepsiades may simply have looked to heaven and addressed the god (despite the seeming analogy with *Peace* 661ff.) while there is no difficulty in supposing the presence of the pot by the door throughout most of the play, with attention directed to it as required. It is not impossible anyway that both Herm and pot could have stood outside a single door. The scenes from these two plays, therefore, while not providing proof of a single door hypothesis do not argue against the theory, and may provide some indications that this was the arrangement in the theatre.

The flexibility of the door convention is further exemplified in a number of scenes in which the logic implied by already established settings is blatantly ignored. The prime example is the *Knights*, when Kleon and the Sausage-Seller seek to win the favour of Demus on the Pnyx by fetching first oracles and then gifts. Both bring these out through the same door (997/8), then rush back in (1110), to return (1151) fighting to be out first. While it is acceptable to have Kleon rushing in if the door is assumed to remain under its original identification as Demus' house despite the change of scene to the Pnyx, the Sausage-Seller originally entered through the *parodos* on his way to the Agora (146/7), yet at this point he can simply run indoors along with Kleon—into the same door. Logically the latter cannot use this door, but Aristophanes is interested in good theatre, and as it is excellent comic business to have the two scrambling to get in and out of the same door at the same time, he employs that door without any regard for the logical spatial ideas of the scene.

The *Women in Assembly* contains two scenes which show a similar disregard. At the conclusion of the scene between the Young Girl, the Youth, and the Hag discussed above, the departure of the first Hag is the signal for a struggle over the Youth between two more hags. A cry of woe eventually escapes him (1093) 'I've been dragged almost to the very door', but this, the third Hag asserts, will not save him from her clutches. The Youth's cry presumably indicates that he is dragged through the door a few moments later: yet the two Hags, like the Sausage-Seller, originally entered through the *parodoi*. A second, less likely, instance in this play concerns the man who says (728/9) that he will go in and fetch his goods to conform with the new laws. If he is in fact Chremes, as most editors have assumed, then he too entered in the first place from off stage and disappeared the same way (372, 477) but now, apparently, he can enter what must originally have been the house of Blepyrus' neighbour. Difficulties over the manuscript attributions, and the point at which this man makes his appearance, however, render this less compelling. In the *Women at the Thesmophoria* 929ff. the implication is again clear. The Magistrate and the Scythian Archer enter via the *parodos*, summoned by the women to deal with Mnesilochus. The Scythian receives his orders, namely to take the man *inside* and bind him to a plank, and the reappearance of the archer and his remarks to his captive (1001) show that he, at any rate, did go in through the door. A final though more debatable example occurs in the *Peace* (728), where Trygaeus, anxious to return to earth after the rescue of the statue, is told to pass 'Here by the goddess'. The most attractive interpretation suggests that Trygaeus walks past the statue and into the central doorway.

There is clear evidence therefore that one door can accommodate different characters at consecutive moments, that certain scenes are more easily explicable on a one-door hypothesis, and that Aristophanes was not averse to completely ignoring all spatial logic whenever it suited his purpose, even to the extent of letting two unrelated characters use the same door at the same time. So flexible a convention suggests that a single door was all that the playwright required; but the problem of those scenes which appear to contain allusions to two houses on stage simultaneously occupied, must now be faced.

The relevant scenes are few, the most important occurring in the *Acharnians* (1070ff.). Dicaeopolis is on stage when a messenger appears to summon Lamachus to war. Lamachus runs out of a door, thus identifying it as his; but, Dover argues, its identification as Dicaeopolis' kitchen has already been made plain (1007ff.) by all the references to cooking, while the summons of Lamachus to war is not couched in such terms as to prepare the audience for a change in the door's function to that of Lamachus' house. He therefore infers two doors. Alternatively, it can be maintained that Dicaeopolis, on stage from 1007, simply delivers his orders to a closed door, the activity of the slaves behind them being imagined. The scene with the Bridesmaid (1047ff.) then provides sufficient interruption to distract the audience from the kitchen concept, even granted Dicaeopolis' return to his preparations for the feast for a further two lines at its close, and the arrival of the messenger confirms positively the change of scene. Lamachus can then rush out through the single door, exclaiming a paratragic line that immediately identifies the house as his. A moment later a second messenger hurries in (1084) and summons Dicaeopolis to a feast. During the following scene both men send their slaves 'in' to fetch articles suitable for their various enterprises—a scene again apparently requiring two doors simultaneously. Unfortunately such a hypothesis creates more difficulties than it solves, for at least one of these doors must be a side door; yet the whole point of the scene is the humour of the quick-fire orders and the simultaneous darts of the slaves: in short, speed is the key. To have the slaves running to widely separated doors, perhaps even at different levels, would lose much of the point. The strongest argument against separate doors, however, is the almost perfect analogy with the scene in the *Knights* where Kleon and the Sausage-Seller both enter the same door to obtain their gifts and oracles, even though this is logically impossible. In that case there is no doubt over the arrangement, and no reason why a similar treatment should not work just as effectively here.

Two scenes at the beginning of the *Women in Assembly* may contain another example of the simultaneous use of two houses. Blepyrus' neighbour appears at the window in the *skene* (327) to address Blepyrus, who himself first entered through the door and thus presumably identified the scene as his house. The window ought logically to belong to Blepyrus' house, but the later scene between the Hag and the Girl who abuse each other from the windows on either side of the door, shows similar disregard for logic in respect of windows and door alike. It seems probable that Aristophanes, having hit on this scenic expedient used it twice in the same play.

A more substantial difficulty occurs in the *Clouds* during the transitional passage between the first scene, set at Strepsiades' home in the country, and the second at the Reflectory in Athens. Strepsiades and Pheidippides step off the *ekkyklema* (89) as it is withdrawn,[29] and Strepsiades proceeds to point out the now closed door to his son, identifying it as the Reflectory and bidding him go along and join the disciples there. Pheidippides refuses, threatens to leave home and go to his uncle Megacles, who will not leave him without a horse (ἄνιππον) he claims. He departs with the words ἀλλ' εἴσειμι (125) 'I will go in'. Here Miss Dale suggested substituting a reading proposed by Cobet from an Oxford manuscript, so that the line reads, ἄνιππον ὄντ'. ἀλλ' εἶμι 'I will go'. This reading has the advantage of regularizing the Greek by providing ἄνιππον with a participle. Dover[30] dismisses this manuscript as worthless, and maintains that Pheidippides goes into Strepsiades' house. If we are to accept this, it must be supposed that for a moment the scene change is ignored as he enters the central door—a difficult but not impossible supposition. But sense so militates against the reading εἴσειμι after Strepsiades has a moment before threatened to throw his son out, that the alternative reading, although from an inferior manuscript, seems preferable. The youth then simply walks off through the *parodos*.

If we accept the hypothesis of a single door, the interpretation of certain points in the plays can be seen to favour it. As we have seen, in the *Acharnians* Lamachus' rushing out of the door at 1072 identifies it as his home, yet in his earlier appearance (572) he apparently arrives and departs through the *parodos*,[31] while his servant's plea for eels (959) seems to imply that Lamachus' house is off stage. Yet if more than one door was available, one might have expected his house to be identified from the beginning, and a possible reason for its not being identified is that there *was* no second door. The same situation arises at the end of the play. Lamachus appears at 1190 through one *parodos*, Dicaeopolis seven lines later at the other. The herald has already identified the door as Lamachus' (1174ff.), but if there were two doors Lamachus and Dicaeopolis would each be expected to enter their own as they are both returning from a 'night out'. In fact Dicaeopolis simply walks across the orchestra and out through the opposite *parodos*; Lamachus approaches his door, decides instead to visit the doctor, and is carried out through the *parodos*—thus preserving the parallelism with Dicaeopolis' entry and exit. Here again the action points to a single door, as also in the *Clouds* when Strepsiades, ignominiously rejected by Socrates, decides to bring his son in his place and bids Socrates wait for him inside (803). The obvious place for him to go is the house in which he appeared in the earlier scene, but the text gives no indication that he does other than simply walk out of the *parodos*.

Finally, the use of a single door greatly simplifies the scene setting, for the audience can easily grasp the changing location of consecutive scenes if only one door is involved, whereas a multiplicity of doors inevitably produces a more static environment, creates difficulties over setting, and leads to such absurdities as Wilamowitz' supposition[32] that the chorus of Acharnians had to be considered absent during Dicaeopolis' celebration of the Rural Dionysia in the country because they were notionally in Athens. The manoeuvring with localities implied in this play, with Dicaeopolis' house apparently in the country at the beginning but later on next to Lamachus' in Athens, is greatly simplified by an abstract setting based on a single door, and the more doors there are available, the more complicated it will become.

The most satisfactory conclusion from the evidence seems to be that only a single door was available to the tragic playwright and his comic counterpart. The three-door *skene* demanded by the plays of Menander results partly from a change of climate in comedy from fantasy to a more realistic setting, and partly from the introduction of the romantic element in the plots, and the joining of two families in marriage. A door for each family becomes a necessity if the audience are to follow the machinations of this kind of plot.

Vase paintings indicate that the two-leaved door opened inwards, that is into the *skene*, as the majority of house doors seem to have done.[33] The scene in the *Wasps* 136ff. has been taken to prove the opposite, but Miss Dale has convincingly shown that this is a piece of comic business, aimed at creating the impression of a struggle and ignoring the realities of stage procedure. As for the width of the door, Webster is probably right in suggesting approximately 2.60m, sufficient to permit the passage of the *ekkyklema* and the tableau it carried. In tragedy the door is frequently referred to as surrounded by columns supporting a pedimental structure, triglyphs and cornices,[34] and a number of South Italian vases illustrating scenes from tragedy suggest such a structure, portraying an *aedicula* or *prothyron* as their central point.[35] On these the structure seems to be a conventional form used to indicate a theatrical scene, and it is unlikely that such a convention, acceptable to artists and pot purchasers alike, would come from outside the theatre. As the scenes portrayed are taken from fifth-century Attic tragedy and also show connexions with the Phlyax vases,[36] it is likely they represent an actual feature of the Athenian theatre. Comedy itself pays scant attention to the door surrounds, doubtless because an architectural style of this kind was more appropriate to tragedy than to private houses. A single scene in the *Wasps* 198ff. may, however, require the use of the pedimented structure. Bdelykleon orders his slave to blockade the door, but before he can do so a clod of earth falls on him from the tiling (206), and Philokleon is discovered trying to escape. The latter's previous attempt via the roof has already been blocked by Bdelykleon and that route barred, which suggests that now he appears elsewhere, perhaps somewhere on the pediment. The whole structure of columns and pediment seems likely to have been an integral part of the *skene* front, jutting forward slightly in front of the single door.

THE ROOF

The use of the roof of the *skene* building is well attested for scenes in both tragedy and comedy. Action there is usually fairly static, though the occasional lively scene like Strepsiades' and Xanthias' attack on the Reflectory (*Clouds* 1485ff.) suggests that a flat roof would be an advantage. The first few scenes of the *Wasps* demonstrate the need for some connexion between the roof and the interior of the *skene* building, for in that play, as we saw above, Bdelykleon, on the roof, foils Philokleon's attempt to escape through the 'smoke hole' (140ff.) by slamming back the cover and bolting it with a log. This 'smoke hole' is probably the exit that normally provided access to the roof from inside the *skene*, here appropriated as scenery, the same exit used by Bdelykleon himself a few moments later when he descends to help his slave. That communication with the roof was easy is obvious from the *Lysistrata*, where the *skene* roof represents the walls of the Acropolis (cf. 873, 883-4) on which Lysistrata and at least two other women appear (829). Kinesias arrives and persuades Lysistrata to summon his wife Myrrhine, who eventually agrees (884) to go down from the walls to her husband and baby. She appears on stage at 889—a rapid re-appearance even allowing for a little comic business on the part of Kinesias, and one that presupposes easy communication between roof and *skene* interior.

THE WINDOWS

The plays themselves and a number of South Italian vases prove the existence of windows in the *skene* front. Some of the scenes, for instance the ending of the *Clouds*, where the cries of Socrates' pupils would be inaudible unless delivered at a window, have been discussed in other connexions. *Wasps* 379ff. provides an interesting example of the use of windows, when Philokleon's attempt to escape from the house moves the chorus to suggest the window. Bdelykleon is too quick for him, and bids the slave climb on to the other window-frame (398) and beat the escaper with the wreath. This suggests two windows set close together, if the two men are to come to blows, or possibly a double win-dow of the type illustrated on a non-theatrical vase that may reflect contemporary house windows.[37]

This type of window would certainly be an advantage in the scene from the *Clouds* where at least three people seem to be involved.[38] A single window is however sufficient for the scene in *Women in Assembly* (327ff.) when Blepyrus is mocked by his neighbour for his appearance in female attire. The neighbour admits to having also lost all his clothes, so obviously either he too must come on in his wife's clothes and thereby detract from the fun poked at Blepyrus or more probably appear at the window.[39] On the other hand, windows on either side of the door seem necessary later in the play in the scene between the Hag and the Young Girl (877),[40] and some idea of how it may have appeared on stage may be gained from a vase from Lipari (*PV.* Ph 80), which depicts two windows occupied by women who are turning towards each other. The general impression given by these and other vases is of a solidly made window between five and six feet above the level of the stage, which would easily fill the requirements of the plays.

THE PARODOI

The slots cut in the wall 'H' on either side of 'T' give the only clue to the form of the buildings that may have existed in the *parodoi* (in the sense of all the theatrical space between the side of the stage and the theatre entrance). These slots, it has been argued, were intended to hold wooden beams, which by some system of ties supported other beams some distance in front of the wall, between which wooden panels could be inserted to form a corridor on either side of 'T'. Though there is no archaeological evidence for this second set of beams, a construction of this kind would offer an intelligible explanation of the *paraskenia* referred to by Demosthenes (see p. 18). If Meidias were to nail up the ends of this corridor, access to the central door on 'T' would be barred and the performance effectively sabotaged, especially as these corridors would also provide storage space for properties and the changing rooms as indicated in *Peace* 731. Furthermore, the fact that a corridor ran along either side of 'T' would account for the surprising use of the plural in that reference.

Other evidence suggests that curtains made of skin played some part in the theatre, though they were certainly not curtains across the front of 'T'. The references are here printed in full:

(a) Aristotle, *Eth. Nic.* 1123a, 23

οἷον...κωμῳδοῖς χορηγῶν ἐν τῇ παρόδῳ πορφύραν εἰσφέρων, ὥσπερ οἱ Μεγαρεῖς.

for example...in comedy the *choregus* introducing purple into the *parodos* as the Megarians do.

Schol. Ald. ad loc.

σύνηθες ἐν κωμῳδίᾳ παραπετάσματα δέρρεις ποιεῖν, οὐ πορφυρίδας

it was customary in comedy to use skin curtains, not purple ones.

Schol. Par. ad loc.

ἐν ταῖς κωμῳδίαις ἀντὶ κωδίων, ἃ παραπετάσματα ἦν ἐπὶ τῆς σκηνῆς, πορφυρίδας ἔχει, καθάπερ οἱ Μεγαρεῖς.

in the comedies instead of sheepskins, which were the curtains for the *skene*, he used purple, like the Megarians do.

(b) *The Suda* on Phormis (a Syracusan comic poet of the fifth century B.C.)

ἐχρήσατο δὲ πρῶτος ἐνδύματι ποδήρει καὶ σκηνῇ δερμάτων* φοινικῶν

he was the first to employ long cloaks and a *skene* of red skins.

(c) Gregory of Nyssa, *ep.* ix

τοιοῦτον τι θαῦμα ἐν τοῖς θεάτροις τοὺς θαυματοποιοῦντας τεχνά-ζεσθαι: μῦθον ἐξ ἱστορίας ἤ τινα τῶν ἀρχαίων διηγημάτων ὑπόθεσιν τῆς θαυματοποίας λαβόντες ἔργῳ τοῖς θεαταῖς διηγοῦνται τὴν ἱστορίαν, ὑποδύντες σχήματά τε καὶ πρόσωπα, καὶ πόλιν ἐκ παρα-πετασμάτων ἐπὶ τῆς ὀρχήστρας δι' ὁμοιότητός τινος σχηματίσαντες, καὶ τέως ψιλὸν τόπον τῇ ἐνάργει μιμήσει τῶν πραγμάτων οἰκειώσαν-τες, θαῦμα τοῖς θεωμένοις γίγνονται, αὐτοί τε οἱ μιμηταὶ τῶν ἐν τῇ ἱστορίᾳ πραγμάτων καί τὰ παραπετάσματα, ἡ πόλις δή.

(it is said that) conjurors produce this kind of marvel in the theatres: they take as the theme for their amazing display a subject from history or from one of the ancient tales and set forth their story for the spectators in the form of action, putting on costumes and masks and producing by means of curtains the likeness of a city in the orchestra. By adapting the bare space for the time being to the display of their story they win the spectators' admiration.

(d) *Anon de Comoedia* (Kaibel pp. 17ff. V, 33)

ἐν ἐαρινῷ καιρῷ πολυτέλεσι δαπάναις κατασκευάζετο ἡ σκηνὴ τριωρόφοις οἰκοδομήμασι, πεποικιλμένη παραπετάσμασι καὶ ὀθόναις λευκαίναις καὶ μελαίναις βύρσαις τε παταγούσαις καὶ χειροτινάκτῳ πυρί...

at the appropriate time in spring the *skene* was equipped at great expense with a three-storey structure; it was decorated with white and black linen curtains, with booming hides and a hand-turned lightning flash...

(e) Cosmas Indicopleustes, *top. Christ.* V 204a

ἔτι αὐλαίας τὰς κορτίνας καλεῖ, οὕτως δὲ καλοῦσιν αὐτὰς καὶ οἱ ἔξωθεν Ἀττικοὶ λέγοντες αὐλαία τὸ μέγα καὶ ποικίλον παραπέτασμα.

Ὑπερίδης ὁ ῥήτωρ ἐν τῷ κατά Πατροκλέους λόγῳ, οἱ δὲ ἐννέα ἄρχοντες εἱστιῶντο ἐν τῇ Στοᾷ περιφραξαμενοί τι μέρος αὐτῆς αὐλαίαις. ὁμοίως καὶ Μένανδρος στυππεῖον, ἐλέφαντ᾽, οἶνον, αὐλαίαν, μύρον.

aulaias (curtains) he calls kortinas (s.v. cortina, Lewis and Short, A Latin Dictionary) as do the expatriate Athenians when they mean aulaia, that is the large multicoloured curtain. The orator Hyperides in his speech against Patrokles (says): 'the nine archors were banqueting in the Stoa, having partitioned off part of it with curtains'. Similarly Menander: 'tow, ivory, wine, curtain, perfume'.

Schol. ad loc. on αὐλαία

τὰ ὀπίσθια τῆς σκηνῆς...τοῦτο τὸ πλάτος τῆς σκηνῆς...

the back parts of the skene...that is the breadth of the skene...

(f) Pollux IV, 122 (περὶ θεάτρου καὶ τῶν περὶ αὐτὸ)

ἔξεστι δὲ τὸ παραπετάσμα αὐλαίαν καλεῖν. Ὑπερίδου εἴποντος... see (e) above...αὐλαίαις

it is possible to call the curtain αὐλαία, Hyperides in his speech...

Aristotle's evidence would be wholly convincing were it not for the ambiguous meaning of parodos (which may refer either to the entrance of the chorus as defined in Poetics 1452b, 22 or to the place where the chorus entered), and for the problematic dating of the Nicomaecean Ethics. Aristotle died in 322 B.C. and the work is to be dated to the end of his life, certainly after 335; but this is precisely the period in which Lycurgus had control of public finances at Athens (c. 338–326) and presumably when he began rebuilding the theatre. It cannot therefore be proven that Aristotle's remarks are directed at the Periclean theatre. His statement seemingly finds some support in the Suda's assertion on Phormis, but the text is corrupt, the interpretation of skene is of paramount importance, and anyway the Suda is notoriously unreliable. Reliability is also in doubt with the statement of the anonymous writer on comedy, many of whose affirmations have little to commend them, but who may be preserving some half-memory of the use of skins. As for the other evidence, Gregory of Nyssa seems to have in mind an ad hoc

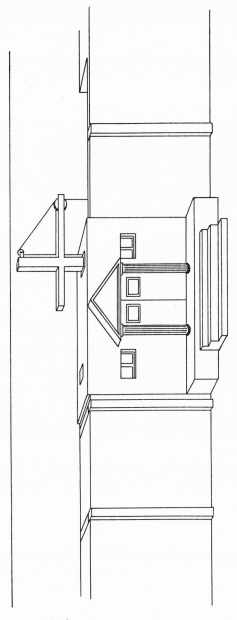

Possible reconstruction of the appearance of the Skene in the theatre of Dionysus

construction, probably of travelling actors, while Pollux' remarks are clearly based on those of Cosmas, a sixth-century Christian writer. It is probably correct to see here the hand of Arretias, Archbishop of Caesarea in the tenth century A.D., who is well known for his interpolations of Pollux' work. However, the line of Menander quoted by Cosmas (frag. 684K) has been accepted by the authors of the Greek Lexicon as evidence that αὐλαία referred especially to a curtain in the theatre. Cosmas has, in fact, no concern with the theatre; he is discussing the *skene* or tent of Moses, and the Menander fragment simply describes the equipment for a symposium.

The literary evidence rests therefore, mainly on Aristotle and the scholiasts, but it is considerably strengthened by the Attic vase (*PV.* Ph 1 see p. 13) depicting a comic actor rehearsing the part of Perseus. By the side of the stage is painted a billowing curtain of some fairly heavy material. What part such curtains may have played is less easy to define. Clearly they were not a permanent feature, for the evidence itself attests the substitution of purple for the more normal skin hangings, while there is nothing to connect their use with tragedy, which suggests that they were peculiar to comedy and easily introduced and removed.

The remarks of Pollux IV, 126, on the significance of the *parodoi*, seemingly distinguish one as leading to the city, the other to the country or the harbour, but this is a convention totally alien to the spirit of Aristophanic comedy, in which the play's setting only exists in so far as it is stated to exist, and the playwright has no interest in identifying off stage areas with no dramatic relevance to the plot. Such conventions are essentially those of New Comedy, where people habitually go for long periods to the country or overseas, or for a short time to the Agora.

Our conclusions on the theatrical area are then as follows. The area 'T' formed the foundation of a permanent low stage, approached by steps from the orchestra, and on it stood a wooden stage building pierced by a single doorway, framed by columns and topped by a pediment. Windows that could be utilized by the comic poet were provided in the *skene* front, as was a flat roof accessible from the inside of the stage building.

On either side of 'T' ran a wooden corridor, providing access to the stage from the side as well as storage space and dressing rooms during the performances, and along this wall curtains may have been hung.

CHAPTER III

THE SKENE

SCENE INDICATION AND SCENE PAINTING

It has been shown that the *skene* front provided an architectural background for the plays; yet the plays themselves, tragic or comic, are in no way confined to such a background—they demand rustic settings, rocks, caves, even the seashore, and the question naturally arises whether this semi-permanent *skene* could be in any way adapted to reflect more faithfully the setting of the plays.

A complete reconstruction of the *skene* in the thirty minutes or so which, it has been calculated, were available between performances, is out of the question; but the substitution of scenery panels either by sliding them between the pillars or fastening them to the *skene* front by pegs, as later done in Delos, would have occasioned no difficulty and would certainly have helped clarify the setting.[1] It is precisely in this period, furthermore, according to the evidence, that scene painting and the use of perspective were being developed. The spearhead of the movement, as Vitruvius VII praef., 11 records, appears to have been Agatharchus who made a tragic *scaena* when Aeschylus was producing a play, and left a commentary on it. Aristotle attributes the introduction of *skenographia* (literally 'scene painting') to Sophocles, and though Else[2] has shown this to be an intrusion into Aristotle's argument it is not certain that the remark is a later interpolation. Setting a precise date for the introduction of scene painting from these statements is made difficult by further testimony (pseud. Andoc. *Alcibiad.* 17) which claims that Alcibiades kept Agatharchus as a prisoner in his house until he had finished the wall paintings there. As this can hardly have been before 430 B.C. and Aeschylus died in 456, either we must accept the unlikely possibility that Agatharchus discovered the art of perspective painting early in his

career, or Vitruvius' reference must be to a revival of a play by
Aeschylus.[3] If the latter is true, scene painting would be date-
able to about 430 and would consequently have been available
to Aristophanes, though in fact none of the evidence of the early
years connects the art with comedy. The date perhaps suggests
that the introduction of scene painting represents an exploitation of the resources of the recently completed Periclean
Theatre. Subsequently Democritus and Anaxagoras are said by
Vitruvius to have read and followed the precepts of Agatharchus
in his book on perspective, and Zeuxis, a younger contemporary,
is recorded as depicting grapes with such graphic success that
birds flew *in scaenam*.[4]

Literary evidence for some kind of scene painting is clearly
strong, but in the absence of the survival of actual scenery
panels the state it had reached must be judged from outdoor
scenes painted on vases, and it is immediately apparent that the
literary and visual evidence is at variance. One of the best
painters of the period (as Rumpf notes) is content to portray
Mount Helicon simply as a rock on which a muse is seated, and
throughout Greek art a similar indifference to nature can be
seen: the masterly picture of Alexander the Great preserved in a
mosaic copy in Pompeii, for example, depicts as background
'three stones on the ground, a miserable plant, a dry gnarled
tree', the *Odyssey* frescoes (170–70 B.C.), despite their representational landscape pictures, also include a personification of the
landscape with a title to render it intelligible.[5] Yet it might have
been expected that the introduction of scenery in the theatre
would have provided the necessary impulse to vase painters to
include realistic details of naturalistic scenes in their paintings.
On the other hand the fact that the scene painter made an
impression of a landscape or a town scene his sole aim, rather
than making it merely the background for the main group, as is
normally the case in vase painting, may have encouraged artists
to be freer in their representations in scene painting. Certainly
Zeuxis' grapes seem to have been realistically portrayed, though
much naturally depends on the general standard of painting of
the time in comparison with which his grapes appeared so
realistic. Furthermore, if the Athenian public were used to
identifying landscapes on vases from the presence of a muse or

some such personification, similar indication on the theatrical
skene would presumably enable them to conjure up a realistic
scene for themselves. A possible indication of theatrical scenery
may be found on the South Italian krater of 380–370 B.C.
(*PV*. Ph 37) known as 'Chiron's cure' where, it has been
plausibly suggested, the Nymphs who peep round the rocks are
in fact looking through the disguised *skene* window. There is,
however, no means of telling whether the painter was accurately
portraying what he saw on the stage or was interpreting the
scene.

If scenery existed, it seems unlikely that it would be used for
a single performance and then discarded. The expense of providing it, especially if the top artists of the day were to work on
it, would doubtless have been too great for the normal play
producer, which suggests that the scenery consisted of 'stock
sets' sufficiently unspecific to be appropriate to a whole range
of plays. The later accounts from Delos show the provision of
scenery to have been a state charge—and no wonder, when in
282 B.C. the painting of four panels cost 400 drachmae, while in
274 the painting of the *skenai* and *paraskenia* produced a bill for
2500 drachmae, though admittedly in the Hellenistic theatre
the area to be covered was greater than in the Periclean.[6] That
stock sets were used in the later theatre is evident from Vitruvius'
description (V. vi. 9) of tragic, comic and satyric scenery, implying a set for each *type* of play rather than for individual plays,
and the argument from cost suggests an analogous situation in
the fifth century. However, the form of the sets described by
Vitruvius, and seemingly illustrated in the Boscoreale paintings,[7] is unlikely to have been that of the fifth century where the
settings of comedy, at least, are usually far removed from the
backcloth of private houses with windows and balconies that
the characters of New Comedy inhabit.

Literary evidence, then, for scenery in the fifth century is
plentiful, though the scenery itself was probably generalized.
But did the comic poet in fact set out to provide the audience
with a realistic comedy in a realistic setting, which might call
for representational scenery? To dismiss the plays as unrealistic
because they depend on such seemingly unrealistic elements as
the *mechane*, the *ekkyklema*, the use of masks, the wearing of the

phallus etc. is to over-simplify. These accessories to the performance were hallowed by convention, and as A. C. Schlesinger rightly warns,[8] 'dramatic logic depends on dramatic
convention: there are some things that an audience will accept
immediately on presentation because these things are usual,
whereas other things may be open to question.' That the Greek
audience did accept such things as the *ekkyklema* as conventional
and not totally unrealistic is obvious from the way that Aristophanes' humour is frequently based on incongruity caused by a
character stepping outside the framework of the play for a
moment to mock these very conventions.[9] If the audience had
not felt caught up in the play's action and uncritical of these
features such allusions would have been pointless. The play's
realism therefore, depends on the logical working of the plot
within the conventions, not from the point of view of the
scholar who has the text before him and can compare the action
at different points and spot the illogicalities, but from the
position of the audience without these advantages, who are
simply watching a play unfold before them. It is in this context
that we must consider the play's logical unity.

An unrealistic use of time in his plots is a charge frequently
flung at Aristophanes.[10] For example, when in *Acharnians* 729
Dicaeopolis begins his trade with Megara, it is claimed that
insufficient time has elapsed during the play's action to allow
news of his recently concluded treaty to reach that city. Logically this is true enough but, for the audience in the theatre,
between the making of peace and the arrival of the Megarian
the *parabasis* delivered by the chorus diverts attention to the
current Athenian political situation; when the dramatic threads
are picked up again the audience accept a lapse of time without
question, and probably without even being aware of it. The
question of realistic time sequence does not exist, any more than
it does when Dicaeopolis and Lamachus leave at 1142, one for
dinner and the other for war, but return from their expeditions
almost simultaneously (1190 and 1198). Once again the choral
ode (1143–73) is used to gloss over the lapse of time. Not so,
however, with Amphitheus' journey to Sparta and back, begun
at *Ach.* 133 and completed by 175, which seems rather to be a
deliberate attempt to make fun of the theatrical convention for

telescoping time. The *Birds* employs a different technique for obscuring the passage of time. The action appears to be encompassed within a single day, though this is not precisely stated, until at 922 we are suddenly informed that the tenth day feast of the city, founded earlier in the play, is at hand, and shortly afterwards Prometheus (1514ff.) announces that the gods are starving through lack of sacrifices. Again dramatic time may be assumed to have elapsed during the *parabasis*, but the audience might be forgiven for considering the scene following the chorus' remarks to be as near in time as in thought to what precedes them. It is simply the hazy, unspecific concept of time throughout most of the play that permits unhesitating acceptance of the tenth day feast as a fixed point. In such an atmosphere the unity of time is as meaningless as are questions about its realistic use.

The unity of place receives similarly cavalier treatment, though here perhaps the term 'unrealistic' has more meaning. The difficulties and consequent illogicalities caused by the sudden switch from setting to setting have been a constant irritant to scholars and have driven one at least to cry, 'Wo spielen diese Szenen: auf der Erde? In Himmel? Sie spielen auf dem Theater...'[11] Two general points about the setting can, however, be made at once. First, the scene is set out of doors, a fact kept constantly before the audience by the use of 'in' and 'out' in referring to the *skene* building, though the *ekkyklema* frequently ignores or glosses over this distinction; secondly, as a natural consequence of the festival's being Athenian, and the poet's claiming to be teacher of the Athenians, the action takes place in or concerns Athens. Much of the time this remains a subconscious undercurrent to the play, only occasionally being made more explicit. These two points excepted, however, Aristophanes in setting the scene frequently exploits the same techniques he uses with time: that is he gives his scenes no particular identification, they simply 'take place'. By thus ignoring the problem of setting and hurrying on the action, he carries the audience with him and avoids any awkward questions. The *Acharnians* exemplifies the technique. Dicaeopolis celebrates the Rural Dionysia, presumably in the country, then visits Euripides' house (in Athens?), and is finally joined somewhere by Lamachus (572). The scenes follow one another without pause, and the question of setting is never mentioned by the actors or permitted to be raised by the audience. In the same way the corpse scene in the *Frogs* (170–9) may be presumed to take place on the way to the Underworld, but the scene itself is too short and too comic for logical questions about setting to be raised. The *Lysistrata* takes the method a further step forward. At the beginning of the play the setting is vague, but may be considered to take place in front of Kalonike's house. Thereafter the scene shifts to the Acropolis, but even here, where the context is apparently firmly fixed, the hazy conception of the setting is apparent in the fact that the gates of the Acropolis, presumably represented by the stage door, and naturally referred to as πύλαι in lines 250 and 428, are described in the intervening scene by the more normal word for a door, θύρα. In the play's final scene (1216–322) revellers come out of a building, perhaps the Acropolis, but the scene is defined no further than that, and the audience must simply accept it.

On occasion, however, the poet needs to be explicit in locating his scene. A direct statement at or near the beginning of the actual scene, or even before it begins, is the easiest method and allows immediate identification. So Dicaeopolis (*Ach.* 20) states firmly 'The Pnyx here is empty', and again (202), 'I shall go in and celebrate the Rural Dionysia': so that on his reappearance (241) the scene should be recognizable from the previous statement and from the ritual cry indicating the beginning of the ceremonial. The only exception to this method occurs when Praxagora and her women indicate that they are going to the Pnyx (*Ass.* 283), yet the next scene takes place not on the hill but in front of Praxagora's house. Here, however, the departure of the chorus is an indication to the audience of a special situation.

A second method is the use of implicit information that a speaker is connected with the setting.[12] Thus when Aristophanes brings on Strepsiades, he has only to remark 'the slaves are snoring' (*Clouds* 5) for the audience to assume he is master of the house on the stage, while the slaves who appear at the beginning of the *Wasps* are immediately identified as belonging to the household, subsequent identification being carried little further.

The setting remains general, but sufficient for the poet's purpose.

The question of the logic of the scene setting, then, if it is
important to the poet at all, should arise when a definitely
established setting is changed. In fact, however, Aristophanes
does not allow the question to be raised any more than in his
treatment of time, because even after a setting has been positively identified, he rarely makes any further reference to it. For
example, in the *Knights*, Demus demands that the coming contest takes place on the Pnyx (751), and the Sausage-Seller
agrees. After a short choral ode the contest begins and the
setting, presumed to be the Pnyx, is confirmed at 783—the
change perhaps being emphasized by use of the *ekkyklema*.
During the remainder of the scene, however, apart from two
passing references to the hill (1109, 1136), neither of them
emphasized as a scene indication, no attempt is made to keep
the setting before the audience, and it is allowed to fade from
their memory. The process is made easier by the lack of any
detailed scenic description by the poet. The play continues with
the *parabasis*, until the Sausage-Seller reappears with the news
that he has boiled Demus back to youth again. When the chorus
begs to see him, the Sausage-Seller replies, 'See him you shall.
Listen, the gates of the Propylaea are opening' (1326). Another
setting is thus established, only to fade and change again when
Demus summons his new-found friend to the *Prytaneion* (1404).
The scenic identification of the Propylaea is only important for
the moment of Demus' appearance, giving him the necessary
status for the part he is to play in the next few lines; its importance thereafter diminishes and it is ignored.

The choral ode, too, is used to engineer a change in scene.
The *Acharnians* begins on the Pnyx (20), a setting reinforced by
references to Prytanies, (23, 40, 54, 56, 173) to various officials
(43, 54) and by use of the arrangements and formulae of public
business (43, 61, 124, 133, 172). The assembly is dissolved (173)
and the officials disappear, and while the Amphitheus scene
which follows might be considered to take place on the Pnyx,
it is perhaps better to say that it simply 'takes place'. Dicaeopolis announces his intention of going in and celebrating the
Rural Dionysia (202), and the subsequent choral ode is suffi-

cient completely to destroy any idea that we are still on the Pnyx. Similarly, the *parabasis* in the *Peace* provides sufficient break for the audience to understand that what was the heavens has now become earth again, an assumption confirmed by Trygaeus' reappearance through the *parodos* and his address to his slave. The same play provides an example of the use of stage machines for this purpose, in the original scene change from earth to heaven. Trygaeus' flight on the beetle, his monologue and the otherwise empty stage combine to make it obvious that the scene is changing, and the astronaut's remark (178), 'I see Zeus' house', confirms the change. In the *Thesm.* 265ff. the withdrawal and reappearance of the *ekkyklema* provide the clue to the scene change described by Mnesilochus. Obviously realism has little meaning in the setting of the plays, for only when the setting is dramatically relevant to the plot does the poet identify it, and even then he will subsequently ignore it if there is no further reason for emphasis. As Fraenkel admirably observes, 'generally speaking in early comedy the background did not exist for the audience unless it was specifically mentioned'.[13] It is this that makes possible the total fluidity of setting and time that the plays demonstrate; a fluidity which in its turn makes it impossible that they were ever produced before a realistic background, since realism would clearly be too limiting for the multiplicity of action and setting. The requirement is rather an anonymous background capable of being transformed by the audience's imagination to whatever scene the poet suggests. A play like the *Frogs*, with scenes at Heracles' house, on the road to the Underworld, on Charon's boat in Acheron, in a region of 'darkness and mud', among the Initiates, and finally in Pluto's halls all within 450 lines, thus becomes a feasible production proposition: realistically it would be a nightmare even to a modern stage manager.

Some slight evidence of the audience's ability to make the imaginative effort required to conjure up the setting can be seen in Aristophanes choosing to set certain scenes before daybreak or at night, despite the impossibility of darkening the theatre. Clearly he considered the audience capable of imagining the stage in darkness even in the glaring sunlight of a March afternoon, granted a few helpful indications such as the presence of lamps, characters falling asleep or in bed, and verbal intimations to the same effect. Thus Praxagora at the beginning of *Women in Assembly* apostrophizes her lamp, in the *Clouds* Strepsiades appears in bed and calls for a light, the chorus of Wasps are guided by their sons lighting their way, and so forth. The audience's imagination, possibly helped out by a little scene painting, was the main weapon in the poet's armoury for producing the setting he desired.[14] The use of more realistic settings implies the establishment of fixed conventions concerning time and place within which the action proceeds logically, a condition foreshadowed in the *Wealth* and brought to fruition in New Comedy.

STAGE PROPERTIES

It is recorded that in one of his plays Aeschylus so roused his audience's fury by seeming to reveal the Mysteries that he was forced to flee for sanctuary to the theatre altar.[15] The story provides evidence both for the altar's existence and for its sanctity. The discovery of altar bases (though of a later date than the fifth century) in the centre of the orchestra in a number of theatres confirms the story. It is unlikely, however, that this was the altar so frequently required in the plays, which seems to have stood on the stage.

Debate has centred round whether this altar was a permanent scenic feature or an *ad hoc* property. External evidence suggests the former: Pollux IV, 123 explicitly states that an altar, called the *Agyieus*, stood on the stage before the doors, as well as a table bearing cakes termed *Theoris* or *Thyoris*. The second half of the statement unfortunately suggests that he has in mind the production of a specific play, and this naturally diminishes the authority of the first part. However, the scholiast on *Wasps* 875 picks up the information with the remark that the *Agyieus* is the conical pillar before the house door, sacred to Apollo and itself a god, though this suggests a statue rather than an altar. Harpocration in a note on ἀγυιᾶς adds that the altar was thus referred to by Cratinus and Menander (frag. 811K) as well as by Sophocles in his *Laocoon* (frag. 370 Pearson). He might have quoted further references both in tragedy and comedy, especially *Thesm.* 748 where Mnesilochus, seated on the altar, swears by 'this Apollo' (cf. Men. *Dyskolos* 659, *Samia* 444 (Austin), frag. 801K). The fact that the majority of references in the plays are to Apollo suggests that the altar was dedicated to that god and was probably permanent: a portable one would surely have attracted a wider range of divine attributions to the most appropriate god or goddess for the play.[16]

The occasional scenes in Aristophanes where the presence of an altar is taken for granted reinforce this argument: such as *Frogs* 830ff. where, without specific reference, Dionysus tells Euripides to 'throw on the incense' (888). More frequently however, reference to the altar is specific—in both the *Peace* (938ff.) and the *Birds* (859ff.) preparations are made for a sacrifice on the altar, and similar mention is made of it in the *Danaides* (frag. 245) and the *Lemnian Women* (frag. 365).[17] Its most extensive use occurs in the *Women at the Thesmophoria*, first as an altar on which Mnesilochus threatens to sacrifice the 'baby' he has seized, then as a place of refuge. The parody of Euripides' *Helen* 437ff. (*Thesm.* 885), that this scene includes, shows clearly that the tragedians also made use of the altar for a tomb, since Mnesilochus here plays the role of Helen, seated on King Proteus' tomb, to his would-be rescuer Euripides' role of Menelaus. Some plays, on the other hand, contain no reference to an altar at all, but this is not an argument against its presence for, as we have seen, when a particular feature was not mentioned then it ceased to exist for the audience. Two scenes suggest that the altar was only temporary. At *Peace* 937 Trygaeus, preparing to sacrifice a sheep, says to his slave, 'Right, quick, take the sheep. I'll provide an altar for the sacrifice', which seems to imply that he intends to go and fetch one. Arnott[18] argues convincingly, however, that Trygaeus at 942 merely points to the altar beside the door as if surprised to find it there and hence exemplifies the intervening comments of the chorus that 'Everything that God and fortune wish to go well does so'. The second scene occurs in the *Lysistrata* 185ff. where the women decide to seal their oath with a sacrifice. They suggest that the sacrifice be performed over a shield, thus implying, it has been argued, that there was no altar. In fact the scene is a parody of Aeschylus' *Seven against Thebes* (42ff.) where the messenger reports the sacrifice of a bull into a black shield

by the seven warriors, and it in no way invalidates the hypothesis of a permanent altar.

Later evidence that the altar's upkeep was the responsibility
of the state also tends to the conclusion that it was a permanent
fixture. It cannot have stood in the centre of the stage, as
Arnott proposes (p. 53), because it would then block the steps
leading up from the orchestra and interfere with the use of the
ekkyklema, which Arnott himself (p. 80) claims ran from the
central doorway to the edge of the stage. It probably stood back
from the front of the stage, as suggested in *Peace* 942 and confirmed by the *Andromache* and the *Suppliant Women* of Euripides.
In the former play, Andromache, in search of sanctuary at the
altar of Thetis, is described as πάροικον (43), while in the
Suppliant Women, Theseus refers to Adrastus (104) lying beside
Aethra who is sitting on the altar as 'lying at the gates'.[19]

There seems to have been some convention that this altar
should not be used for sacrifice. This may have been due simply
to the difficulties inherent in performing a sacrifice on stage and
the resultant mess, but possibly it also implies some taboo. Thus
in the *Peace*, for example, when Trygaeus and the Chorus
decide to sacrifice the sheep (937), after a good deal of work
preparatory to the actual sacrifice, the slave eventually hands
the knife to his master for him to cut the victim's throat, only to
be informed that 'it is not right'. The slave surprised, questions
further and is told 'Peace does not like sacrifices, her altar isn't
red with blood. Take it inside and sacrifice it there, then bring
the thighs back. That way the *choregos* will be saved a sheep.'
The joke about the expense is evidently to cover Aristophanes'
desire to avoid the sacrifice. In the *Birds*, too, Peisthetairus
states his intention of sacrificing (848), but preparations are
interrupted by the appearance of a string of characters who
gradually exhaust Peisthetairus' patience until he cries (1056),
'Let's go in here quick, and sacrifice the goat inside to the
Gods.' The motivation for departure is stronger, the effect
identical.

The presence of statues on the stage (as distinct from in the
parodoi[20]) is a more complex problem. Their appearance is well
attested in tragedy,[21] where it seems likely that individual
statues were introduced in individual plays rather than being a

permanent stage feature. For comedy the evidence is less conclusive. The scholion on *Wasps* 875 seems to suggest that the
reference to *Agyieus* is to a statue by the doorway but the strong
connexion between Apollo and the altar that we noted before
makes it likely that Bdelykleon pointed to that. The *Clouds*
provides two further references: Pheidippides' oath 'By Poseidon, this one, the god of horses' (83) has frequently been taken
to imply a statue on the stage. But as the scene is set 'indoors',
probably making use of the *ekkyklema*, it is more likely that he
points to a clay tablet of Poseidon by his bedside. The presence
of a statue of Hermes at 1478ff. has already been discussed.[22]
Dover suggests that it would be natural to find one by the stage
door, as by a house door, but there is no absolute necessity to
suppose it here: Strepsiades may simply look to heaven and
address the gods. It is certainly wrong to suppose, as a number
of manuscripts assert,[23] that Hermes spoke 1508ff. and deduce
his presence from this. That a *dinos* stood outside the house in
this play is evident from 1473. This may well have been introduced at 1146 when Strepsiades brings some gift to Socrates; he
promised the sophists barley at 669, and a *dinos* would seem an
appropriate utensil in which to carry it.

Finally, Arnott (p. 67) quotes *Peace* 726ff. as valuable evidence for the presence of a statue. Trygaeus, having rescued
Peace, asks how to return to earth and Hermes replies 'Here,
by the goddess.' The most obvious explanation is that he goes
by the side of the statue through the *skene* door, but the scholiast
has another view, as Arnott notes: 'He refers this line to a statue
of Athena in the theatre. When one interpretation is so obvious,
to give another presupposes special knowledge and the scholiast
is therefore more likely to be correct.' In fact the scholiast gives
both explanations, this latter seeming to be a conjecture on his
part from the text and therefore it presupposes no special
knowledge, while his subsequent remarks completely ignore his
own conclusions here as to whether Peace stays in heaven or not.
The scholiast's reliability, in short, is not proven, and without
other evidence it must be assumed that statues did not have a
permanent place on the comic stage.

CHAPTER IV

THE EKKYKLEMA

Aeschylus, in the *Eumenides* (34ff.) with startling technique, confronts the audience with the Pythian priestess crawling on all fours out of the central door of the *skene*. She is in a state of shock, but manages to relate in some detail what she has just seen inside the temple. At line 64 the scene is presented a second time, with Apollo standing by Orestes who sits as suppliant on the altar surrounded by the sleeping Furies. This time, however, the god's words to Orestes indicate that the scene is visible to the audience and on the stage, despite the fact that the setting is stressed as being inside the temple. Such an indoor setting is clearly unusual: the vast majority of scenes in tragedy and comedy are firmly fixed as taking place in front of the house or palace that the *skene* represents. In a similar scene in Sophocles' *Ajax* Tecmessa describes Ajax seated amongst the cattle he has slaughtered, and then, at the chorus' bidding (344ff.) she agrees to open the door and Ajax is revealed. The messenger in Euripides' *Heracles* (1028ff.) details the hero's madness and the consequent murder of his sons and wife, the intervention of Athene, Heracles' slumber and the attempt by his father and the messenger to tie him down to a broken column in the house. The chorus sing of parallel disasters, then describe the opening of the doors and Heracles asleep and bound, and around him the bodies of his children.

Such examples demonstrate the feasibility of producing interior scenes on the fifth-century Greek stage though the whole atmosphere of that theatre seems to demand an exterior setting. More than this, the number of these scenes in both tragedy and comedy indicate that some simple yet effective means of producing them was readily available.

Of the explanations that have been offered for their method of production, the most straightforward (by Pickard-Cambridge) postulates a direct or implicit statement by the poet that an indoor scene is being represented. The theory suffers from formidable defects, notably as regards the representation of tableaux—the form that these scenes most frequently take, as the examples cited above illustrate—for it is difficult to see how such a scene could be convincingly represented if the actors are first required to walk on and take their places, and even more so if they represent sleeping figures or corpses. The effect, far from being startling or tragic, would be merely ludicrous.

A variation of this theory was expounded by Kelley Rees,[1] who argued that the *prothyron*, the area between the columns in front of the door, was the setting for the indoor scenes, and solved the difficulty of actors walking on to take their positions by inventing a curtain hung from the columns of the *prothyron*, that could be drawn aside to display a tableau. The problems of this conjecture are no less troublesome, for it implies a door that would be virtually unusable until the *prothyron* scene had been disclosed, and an unusable door cannot be countenanced. Even more important is the limitation on the audience's view caused by the narrowness of the *prothyron*, especially as, in the theatre of Dionysus, the sun would be shining in the audience's eyes. On this theory the opening of the *Clouds*, for example, could only be considered as the work of an inept playwright gifted with little theatrical *savoir-faire*, for an audience would be unlikely to give its undivided attention to a play that opened with an almost invisible indoor scene crammed into a narrow doorway. Such a technique would constitute an open invitation to an audience to hiss the play off the stage.

Ancient scholars in commenting on such scenes frequently assert the use of the *ekkyklema* for their production: modern scholars, on the whole, have been less ready to accept it, though opinions have varied from Bieber, 'no device is better attested as belonging to the fifth century than the *ekkyklema*', to Bethe, 'das *ekkyklema* gibt es also im 5.jahrhundert überhaupt nicht'.[2] The evidence has been much discussed, but the most important points bear reconsideration, and here the testimony of Aristophanes of Byzantium is pre-eminent. As the Alexandrian editor of the texts of Euripides he probably consulted all available manuscripts, both actor's texts and library copies, and

his evidence is therefore of some value when he criticizes Euripides' use of the *ekkyklema* in *Hippolytus* 171: for, in spite of its
use at this point in the play being highly doubtful, his statement
shows that he considered the device to have been in use in that
poet's lifetime. To this evidence can be added the *parepigraphe*
to *Women at the Thesmophoria* 277, which states τὸ ἱερὸν ὠθεῖται
'the temple is pushed out' suggesting the Thesmophorion
appeared on the *ekkyklema* (a suggestion amplified by the
scholion ἐκκυκλεῖται ἐπὶ τὸ ἔξω τὸ Θεσμοφόριον). This remark,
preserved in the Ravenna codex, is not incorporated in the
main body of the scholia but inserted between the lines of
the text, suggesting that it may well be an interlinear note ante-
dating the scholia. Further, unlike the majority of scholiastic
notes, as, for example, the scholion on *Peace* 726 discussed
earlier,[3] this statement cannot be deduced from the text. Those
factors taken together suggest that it originated in an actor's
copy of the play, possibly contemporary with Aristophanes, and
therefore constitutes strong argument for a machine of some
kind.

Further evidence, though less explicit and intelligible, is provided by the lexicographers.[4] Pollux (IV, 128) explains that
'the *ekkyklema* is a high platform on beams, on which stands a
chair. It displays the dreadful deeds done indoors behind the
skene, and for this operation employs the term *eiskyklein*. It must
be assumed that one stands beside each door'. One scholiast on
Clement of Alexandria repeats this remark almost verbatim;
however, another says that the *ekkyklema* was some kind of
wheeled device, which by turning (στρεφομένου) showed an
interior scene, and in this he is in agreement on the one hand
with the scholiast on Aeschylus' *Eumenides* 64, who refers to
στραφέντα...μηχανήματα on the other with Eustathius (II, 976,
15) who mentions a machine on wheels; while the scholiast on
Aristophanes' *Acharnians* 408 also speaks of a wheeled platform,
and is in turn echoed by the *Suda*. A major problem here is
confusion over terminology, attributable to late scribes attempt-
ing to interpret the remarks of earlier scholars whose readers
understood the *ekkyklema* for people who did not. Besides, the
meaning of the words employed has changed over a period of
time,[5] while the transference of terms and use by later scholars

of false terminology appropriate to other machines (στρεφέσθαι for example, seems to be more reasonably applied to the later *periaktoi*) has further clouded the issue. One tradition, indeed, confuses the *ekkyklema* with the *mechane*. More weight attaches to the evidence of a Delian inscription recording the sum paid for the upkeep of the *exostra*,[6] a term which is also found in the scholia apparently as a synonym for *ekkyklema*. Its derivation from ὠθεῖν may be compared with the *parepigraphe* on *Thesm.* 277, discussed above. Here again reasonable proof is provided for a machine. Indeed, the conflicting accounts of the actual workings should not divert attention from the strong tradition in favour of some kind of machine, for which the very existence of the word '*ekkyklema*' is a strong argument, since it is hard to imagine why scholiasts and lexicographers should have invented the term out of thin air. To argue further that the machine was an invention of the later theatre when so much of the evidence is concerned with the fifth century B.C. would be mere pedantry: there seems no reason for Aristophanes to have picked on the word in his plays if it had no current significance in their production.

If there was a device, then we must examine the form it took and the ends it served. The scholia, for all their divergence of opinion, seem to agree on three points: it was a kind of platform, it rolled on wheels, and it exhibited interior scenes. The discovery in Eretria of marble tracks running to the front of the stage, possibly intended for the *ekkyklema*,[7] seemed to support a machine of this kind, but their subsequent loss make any certainty difficult, and such tracks would certainly have made for an uneven and awkward stage surface when the machine was in the back position. Other descriptions have been offered, notably by Exon and Mahr:[8] Exon argued for a machine in which part of the *skene* made a semi-circular turn on a pivot and was fitted with a platform displaying the interior scene; Mahr suggested a platform coming forward through the central door, with a back wall the size of the opening through which it appeared. The drawback to both these explanations is that, by not allowing for a rear entrance door to the *ekkyklema*, they make the staging of many of the scenes impossible.

The simplest form for the machine consistent with the

demands of the plays seems to be a platform that can be rolled from the central door of the *skene* to the edge of the stage, and when withdrawn forms the threshold of the *skene* building and thus necessitates a step up into it, while when displayed it stands a few inches above the height of the stage. The height could not have been very great, for it was still possible, when the device was extended, to use the ladder connecting the orchestra and stage, as *Women at the Thesmophoria* 279ff. illustrates; and any serious difference of height would have made this hazardous. The chief problem posed by a device of this kind is how to open the *skene* doors to exhibit a tableau, for the space required for the swing of the doors would necessitate placing the tableau at the rear of the *ekkyklema*, and would thus be open to the same objections that were directed at the proposals of Kelley Rees. A pause during which the tableau could be arranged, between the opening of the doors and the exhibition of the scene, would clearly be an advantage, so it is interesting that those supposed *ekkyklema* scenes which do demand the whole of the platform seem to allow just such a pause before the scene is displayed. In *Acharnians* 395ff., for example, Dicaeopolis talks with the slave for some time before Euripides appears, and the doors when they are once opened by the slave presumably remain open, allowing the scene to be prepared (this will also be useful if Euripides' remarks before his actual appearance on stage are to be readily audible). Similarly, the appearance of Agathon (*Thesm.* 95) is heralded by the arrival of his slave, whose address from the doorway (39–70) permits the requisite arrangements to be made. The slave goes in at 70, but there is no reason to think that the door is closed again before Agathon appears.

A low, wheeled platform, then, as suggested by the scholiasts, seems to be sufficient: as to its size, T. B. L. Webster has suggested[9] as a maximum 2.55m by 1.30m, to enable it to fit between the holes in 'T', and this seems not unreasonable for the requirements of tragedy and comedy. We shall now consider in more detail the individual scenes of Aristophanes which require the use of this machine, beginning with the best attested examples.

Acharnians 395–479

Here Dicaeopolis at 393 announces his intention of consulting Euripides, and approaches and knocks on the central door of the *skene*. A slave answers the door and when asked if Euripides is in, replies 'within and not within, if you see what I mean' (396). Such a typically Euripidean statement, amplified in the following few lines, would immediately suggest to the audience that they were to be treated to a parody of the poet and his style. The slave is asked to call Euripides forth, he replies it is impossible; Dicaeopolis persists and summons him notwithstanding, and Euripides answers, 'I've no time'; Dicaeopolis counters with ἀλλ' ἐκκυκλήθητ' (408), and the poet agrees. The scholiast notes that at this point the *ekkyklema* was employed, but Pickard-Cambridge[10] denies it, asserting that the only thing required for this and the parallel scene in the *Women at the Thesmophoria* (95ff.) is the pushing out of a couch: that is, he accepts the principle of the *ekkyklema* but disputes its actual structure.

Yet the evidence for the use of the *ekkyklema* here is explicit. Euripides is introduced into the play (it becomes apparent) to provide Dicaeopolis with rags in which he can plead his case before the Acharnians—though before he actually speaks to them he finds it necessary to apologize for these very rags (498). The whole scene is an obvious and elaborate parody of the spirit of Euripides' plays and in particular of his realism in dressing his heroes in rags[11] and it can hardly be claimed that providing the rags is the main object: they are, rather, the means of satirizing elements of his tragedies. The fun poked at Euripides' style and his weakness for sophisms has been noted above, and when, in this context, a point is emphasized, as is the ἐκκυκλήθητ' repeated in the next line in the form ἐκκυκλήσομαι and given the evidence that a machine of this name existed it can hardly be doubted that Aristophanes is also parodying some favourite Euripidean production method. Its acceptance, moreover, gives special significance to the slave's statement that Euripides is 'within and not within', for the *ekkyklema*, presenting as it does an inside scene outside, reinforces the remark and allows Euripides to continue his work without interruption, being theoretically inside though actually out. A scenic convention accepted unquestioningly by the audience is always a good subject for laughter if the incongruity of the convention is momentarily emphasized. However, the opponents of the *ekkyklema* throw away these opportunities and thereby remove much of the scene's force.

Even the advocates of its use have, nevertheless, raised several questions about this scene. Euripides says that he has no time to καταβαίνειν 'to come down', to which Dicaeopolis replies

...ἀναβάδην ποιεῖς
ἐξὸν καταβάδην; οὐκ ἐτὸς χωλοὺς ποιεῖς (410)

'Do you write *up there* (?), when you could write *down here* (?)? No wonder you produce lame heroes.' A variety of interpretations of this remark have been offered; plainly there is some contrast between 'up' and 'down' but the precise application is not so clear. On the authority of the scholiast, who remarks φαίνεται γὰρ ἐπὶ τῆς σκηνῆς μετέωρος. τὸ δὲ ἀναβάδην ἀντὶ τοῦ ἄνω τοὺς πόδας ἔχων 'he appears on the *skene* high up. Up there (?) is used instead of "having his feet up" ', it has been suggested that Euripides is composing on the second floor of his house,[12] but such an interpretation is impossible, as the *ekkyklema* has to appear through the door and cannot therefore carry any high structure. In any case, the second storey of a Greek house seems normally to have been reserved for the women's quarters, and though this would be a possible explanation of the scene in the *Women at the Thesmophoria* where Agathon is dressed as a woman and satirized as effeminate, here there is no such connotation. The scholiast's explanation can be taken as a guess, but his second attempt, that ἀναβάδην means 'with his feet up', may be nearer the truth; the joke on χωλός is no more difficult to explain than the claim that the motor-car is causing people to lose the use of their legs—Aristophanes is simply saying that lack of use produces lack of the ability to use, but he adds an extra twist by identifying Euripides with his characters and suggesting that the number of lame men who appear in his plays are a direct result of the poet's own lack of movement. The remark that, because the poet dresses in rags, his characters must also appear in rags (412), displays an identical train of thought.

Pickard-Cambridge maintained that this scene was produced simply using a couch, but was then forced to conclude that the rags and other pieces of tragic equipment which Dicaeopolis borrows were brought on from inside the house, presumably by the slave. The seemingly deictic reference to Bellerophon (427) makes this difficult to accept, and it is far more probable there is some visible reminder of the hero on stage, to which Euripides refers. Editors have been quick to see a reference to a mask of Bellerophon 'hanging up'. But it is difficult to see what there could be on an *ekkyklema* on which a mask might be hung so as to be visible, and a much more likely interpretation is that the remark is directed to a heap of clothes lying beside the couch perhaps with a mask or a label on it, and similar heaps for the other characters mentioned. If this is correct then the staging of the scene requires not simply a couch but a platform of some size.

Throughout the scene the ambiguity of 'inside' and 'out' implied in 398 is exploited with no attempt at logical justification. Euripides is 'outside', having been persuaded to *ekkyklein*, yet the remainder of the scene is depicted indoors (he would surely keep his clothing in his own room), and no effort is made to explain the presence in the orchestra of the chorus, who for the purpose of the play simply cease to exist when Dicaeopolis turns away from them until he returns to address them once again. In short, any logical difficulty is overcome by ignoring it.

The scene continues until 479, with Euripides presumably making some attempt to continue with his writing while indicating to the slave to provide for Dicaeopolis whatever he requests from the bundles of clothes. At 479 Euripides loses patience, orders the house to be shut up again, and the *ekkyklema* is withdrawn, whereupon Dicaeopolis takes on the character of Telephus and addresses the chorus in paratragic tones.

Women at the Thesmophoria 95–265
Here we have an almost exactly parallel scene. Euripides and his kinsman Mnesilochus are approaching the door of Agathon's house just as a servant comes out and utters a prayer which informs the audience of the imminent arrival of Agathon. The

latter, in the throes of composition, is coming out to warm his *strophes* in the sun to make them easier to mould (67). The poet appears at 95, described by Euripides as οὗτος ὁυκκυκλούμενος and in his feminine dress is immediately mistaken by Mnesilochus for a notorious *hetaira*.

Again Pickard-Cambridge disputes the scholiast's interpretation that Agathon appeared on the *ekkyklema*, arguing that 'there is nothing in the language of the play that need imply more than that the poet is wheeled out on a couch...In the *Thesmophoriazousae* it is clear that what is presented is not an interior scene but a scene outside in the sunshine, concluded by the poet being wheeled back in'. Against this it can be argued that without an *ekkyklema* some other explanation must be found for the reference to οὐκκυκλούμενος, and while Pickard-Cambridge's claim may be valid that it need not necessarily imply the travesty of a stage device but that there could be some topical allusion to poets composing with their feet up, the difference in date between the *Acharnians* and this play would militate strongly against the topical reference, while the parallelism between the two passages increases the probability of the author's parodying a device. Further, Mnesilochus requires a chair to sit on while he is shaved (221), which seems to indicate that something more than just a couch is rolled on. The distinction between inside and out is by no means as simple as is suggested, for the external setting referred to by the slave is at variance with the fact that Agathon has with him all his female trimmings, including his razor, indicative rather of a scene in his room. The setting can be rationalized as the courtyard, but without some help from the poet this would seem rather abstruse for the audience. Instead, Aristophanes should be thought of as once again making fun of the conventional device for showing an indoor scene outdoors.

Arguments against the use of the *ekkyklema* have found support in Van Daele's suggestion in the Budé edition of the play that Agathon is accompanied by a full chorus who are practising his ode whose numbers and weight (it is claimed) would be too great for the device. But the slave has announced that Agathon is still moulding his work into shape, so that the presence of a full chorus to practise it would be unlikely, while the argument that a full complement of chorus members would overcrowd the *ekkyklema* applies equally to the stage. The scholiast suggests that Agathon is simply singing a monody, and this seems the most reasonable explanation.

When Agathon has completed his ode Euripides unsuccessfully attempts to persuade him to go to the Thesmophorion and speak to the women on his behalf. Instead Mnesilochus agrees to help, but finding the shaving process painful he flees 'to the place of the holy gods' (224). Rogers explains this as a reference to the temple of the Erinyes, his imaginary refuge, so that all that is required is an attempt to flee from the stage; more probably a rush to the stage altar is implied. Mnesilochus returns, however, the shaving is completed, and he is disguised as a woman in clothes which Agathon generously provides. If these clothes are a spare set then this too suggests the use of the *ekkyklema*, as in the *Acharnians*. However, it is more likely that Agathon takes off his own clothes to give Mnesilochus. The scene ends, as Agathon says εἴσω τις ὡς τάχιστά μ᾽ ἐσκυκλησάτω —introducing a second joking reference to the machine.

Here again Aristophanes is parodying tragedy and more particularly making fun of Agathon, and scholars, in an attempt to trace the source of the parody, have not failed to note the resemblances to the scene in Euripides' *Hippolytus* 178ff., where Phaedra is wheeled out for the sake of her health.[13] The theme of that play is referred to at 153, but a closer parallel to the dressing scene is to be found in the *Phaedra* of Seneca 387ff., where the heroine comes out of the palace but refuses the dresses that are offered to her. This may well reflect the action in Euripides' first *Hippolytus*, which in turn may have been the mainspring for the parody in *Women at the Thesmophoria*.[14]

Finally the lack of any clear dividing line between what is 'indoors' and what is 'outdoors' places this scene in an interesting midway position in its use of the *ekkyklema*. In most tragic and some comic scenes the machine is employed simply to show, on stage, an indoor scene, but a number of instances in Aristophanes seem to indicate that the *ekkyklema* could also be used, without any indoor connotation at all, to produce otherwise unmanageable scenes. The instances will be discussed shortly.

Women at the Thesmophoria 278–946

The *parepigraphe* on 277, as demonstrated above,[15] provides good evidence for the use of the *ekkyklema* in this scene; with this can be coupled the note incorporated in the text, that 'they cry out and the Hieron is pushed forward'. Russo may be correct in dismissing this as false,[16] in that Euripides leaves the scene on seeing the signal for the Thesmophorion, not on hearing a cry: but although this is the obvious deduction from the text it leaves unexplained the source of the evidence for the cry. Whatever the interpretation here, however, there are other considerations that point to the use of the *ekkyklema*.

First, the change of setting is unusually sudden. Agathon disappears into his house on the *ekkyklema*, leaving Euripides and Mnesilochus on the stage. The latter extracts a promise from the poet that he will not desert him, and Euripides then observes that the 'sign for the *ekklesia* appears in the Thesmophorion' (277/8). Whether or not any sign is visible to the audience the remark indicates a change of scene, and visible confirmation of this is most easily presented by the use of the *ekkyklema*, for Aristophanes makes no attempt to cloud the distinction between the two scenes by employing a choral ode. Later on we get a reference to 'this Thesmophorion' (880), indicating the presence on the stage of some symbol of the festival.

Here again Bethe[17] argued that the use of the *ekkyklema* was impossible, since it would be required to carry a chorus of twenty-four, a chairman (295–310, 331–51), the speakers in the debate (380, 383–432, 443–58), Mnesilochus, a maid (294), Kleisthenes (547ff.), a bench for each company, and finally the Thesmophorion itself. This would indeed be an intolerable weight for the *ekkyklema*, if the machine did in fact carry all these, but only the Thesmophorion and, perhaps, some benches appear on it: the chorus enter in the normal way through the *parodos* (280ff.), following their leader the Heraldess, for by the time they appear the scene change is already completed. The speakers also enter with the chorus, and Kleisthenes appears separately, later on. The symbols most representative of the Hieron or Thesmophorion (presumably the two are alternative terms) would be statues of Demeter and Kore, and perhaps also a small altar, for which the scene at 765ff. may offer some evidence. There Mnesilochus, parodying the *Palamedes* of Euripides, carves a plea for help on a *pinax*, that is, one of the votive tablets normally hung round the statue of a god.[18] This episode requires the presence of a statue, in this case presumably of Demeter and Kore, and further suggests use of the *ekkyklema* for its transport.

It has been suggested that the machine was withdrawn at 784, leaving Mnesilochus sitting on the altar under guard while his plea for help was carried off. Though attractive, this view cannot be maintained in the face of 880, which definitely demands the continued presence of the statue, and withdrawal must therefore be delayed until 946 when the archer is ordered to take Mnesilochus inside and bind him to a plank. The stage is thereby effectively cleared to allow the chorus to address the audience.

The scene at 698–759 is an ingenious parody of Euripides' *Telephus*,[19] in which, on the advice of Clytemnestra, Telephus seizes the baby Orestes as the means for an appeal to Agamemnon. It is uncertain whether the original scene was actually portrayed on the *ekkyklema*, and there is no necessity to assume that it was, as the opening scene of the *Helen*, also parodied here (846–924), was certainly not performed on the machine. Its employment here however marks the logical change from the earlier scene, for there is now no hint of an indoor setting: the machine is used for the poet's own purpose, with no suggestion of parody or mention of its actual working. From this it might be conjectured that reference to the machine in the text is to be taken as an indication of parody of the use of the device in tragedy. The length of this scene, and its two sister scenes in the play, plainly show that no production difficulties arose in the use of the stage when the *ekkyklema* was extended, and that the setting established by its appearance could easily be enlarged to take in the whole of the stage.

Women at the Thesmophoria 1001–1231

In Euripides' play *Andromeda* the heroine appeared at the beginning fastened to a rock,[20] which must imply the use of the *ekkyklema*: in this direct parody (*Thesm.* 1012ff.), the Scythian archer has been ordered to take Mnesilochus inside, fasten him to a plank (931) and guard him, and thus fettered (cf. 940ff.) the prisoner can hardly walk back on stage when he returns at 1001. The *ekkyklema* is here indispensable, and completes the parallel with the *Andromeda*; the parallel can perhaps be extended to the tying of Mnesilochus to the plank, for a number of South Italian vases depict a production of Euripides' *Andromeda* in which the heroine appeared tied to a column, presumably intended to symbolize a rock.[21] Her unusual position may perhaps reflect the conditions of the original stage production rather more closely than the more orthodox scenes on other artistic interpretations of the stage production.[22]

Here there is no connotation of an indoor scene, as the first words of the archer, as he and Mnesilochus appear, 'Now get your moaning done to the sky', make abundantly clear. The *ekkyklema* must remain out until the end of the play, for it is not until then that Euripides manages to rescue Mnesilochus.

Peace 289–728

The production on stage of the statue of Peace with its attendant figures of *Opora* and *Theoria*, all supposedly hauled up from out of a cave, can be paralleled by a scene from the fragmentary satyr play of Aeschylus, the *Diktyoulkoi*. In that play Dictys, using words almost exactly echoed by Trygaeus in the *Peace*[23] summoned the farmers to help him draw from the sea his net, containing a chest inside which Danae and Perseus were subsequently revealed. The argument in both these cases for the use of the *ekkyklema* rests on the ease it would impart to the production of the scenes. That the parallelism was intended by Aristophanes to be read as parody is, however, unlikely; certainly he gives no indication of any such intention and the question presents itself of why he should want to parody a satyr play. A more reasonable hypothesis would suggest a recent revival of an Aeschylean tetralogy, providing the comic poet with inspiration for his own scene.

Inevitably, disputes over the staging have been frequent. Platnauer[24] in the latest edition of the play agrees that the statue of the goddess could be pulled forward, but objects that 'it is more likely that she is pulled *up* from a basement room, in which case there must have been some sort of trap door and ladder arrangement to make her ascent possible'; while Pickard-Cambridge suggests that the statue was hauled up from below the banked-up orchestra terrace.[25] The difficulty with both these arrangements is, of course, the unmanageability of a statue of the size the scholiast on Plato *Apology* 19c seems to have in mind when he refers to it as a κολοσσικὸν ἄγαλμα. For the chorus to raise a statue invisible to them, through a stage trap door would be extremely hazardous, even granted the availability of a pulley mechanism; then there is the difficulty of managing the production of the two attendants *Opora* and *Theoria*, who should appear as a group with Peace; thirdly, there remains the problem of later removing from the stage a statue that, when on stage, would doubtless block the central door (and it is interesting that between the appearance of the statue at 520 and its conjectured withdrawal at 728, no character enters or leaves the stage through the door, while after 728 it is frequently in use). All these problems require satisfactory solution if the arguments of those who reject the *ekkyklema* are to be convincing.

The objection that the audience would find it inappropriate that the statue be pulled out of the door, when it is allegedly drawn from an underground cave covered with stones, is unconvincing; Danae's chest, ostensibly dragged from the sea must have been similarly positioned on the *ekkyklema*, and it is clear that the audience did not require or expect a realistic portrayal of the scene, but relied on the poet's exegesis for identification. The ingenious compromise suggested by Buschor,[26] however, eases the problem; he pictured the figure as a bust only, with the rest of the figure considered as still underground. The same suggestion has been put forward, on other grounds, by a number of scholars, for Hermes is required to whisper in the ear of the statue, which a large-scale figure would make impossible. Nor can a protest against the withdrawal of the *ekkyklema* at 728 on grounds of the demonstrative reference to the statue at 923 be sustained, for the audience, by this time completely familiar with the figure, no longer required it on stage. A close parallel, equally unrealistic, is to be found in the *Ichneutae* of Sophocles where the Satyrs (or perhaps only

Silenus) dance on the roof of the cave until Cyllene comes out to enquire what is happening. The dance can hardly take place on the roof of the *skene*: it must be performed in the orchestra or on the stage, and Cyllene must appear through the door.[27] If Cyllene's cavern can be presumed to have its mouth in the *skene* front, then there seems no reason for supposing that this cannot equally apply to the *Peace*.

The scene therefore runs as follows. At 224 Hermes tells Trygaeus that Peace is buried in a cave beneath his feet, and points to the stones as evidence—presumably these are lying on the stage by the side of the door. Hermes goes in, and Trygaeus hides while *Polemos* holds the stage, but comes out on the latter's departure, examines the stones and summons the chorus, who thereupon dance for joy in the orchestra. The rescue attempt is about to be mounted when Hermes reappears (362) and is only prevented from restraining them by a bribe. While some of the chorus remove the stones, others pour a libation, and during this scene the stage door must be opened (if it is not left open after Hermes' return). The ropes attached to the front of the *ekkyklema* are given to the chorus, and they haul out the statue of Peace with *Opora* and *Theoria* grouped beside it. At the end of the scene Trygaeus enquires how he is to return home, and Hermes replies, 'Here, by the goddess,' whereupon the mortal, followed by the two women, walks past the statue as the *ekkyklema* is withdrawn. The chorus then turn and address the audience.

Clouds 1–89

Strepsiades and Pheidippides are both asleep in bed (1). After a time Strepsiades rises, calls for his ledger, reckons up his debts, and finally awakens his son. A discussion follows in which he attempts to persuade Pheidippides to accompany him to Socrates' house, but, having failed to win him over, he goes himself. That this scene must be set indoors is undeniable, and the fact that the two are in bed at the beginning would suggest that the *ekkyklema* was used. Nevertheless attempts have been made to do without it: Rees' proposed use of the *prothyron*, examined earlier, can be excluded on the grounds of the difficulty of seeing the scene. Pickard-Cambridge's theory that the actors walked on, climbed into bed and that Strepsiades then sat up and remarked 'Will night never end?' overstretches the bounds of credibility and also leaves unexplained the removal of the beds. Dover prefers the use of removable screens, but his staging is over-complicated and unconvincing. The *ekkyklema* alone offers an easy and acceptable solution and a means later of removing the properties. Facility of production is the most obvious proof of its use, but the speed of the scene change that follows is also a pointer. At 89 Strepsiades and Pheidippides move off, and at 92 the father points out the door, identifying it as the house of Socrates. It is disclosed subsequently that the scene has shifted from Strepsiades' house in the country to Socrates' in Athens, but for the moment (in the three lines between 89 and 92) the audience has to be made aware of the scene change, and withdrawal of the *ekkyklema* at 89 would be a clear and specific confirmation of the fact.

Pickard-Cambridge objects that the command at 19, 'Bring out the ledger', implies an outdoor scene: it could equally refer to bringing something from another part of the house, or from a chest, but the fact that the *ekkyklema* is extended would sufficiently justify the expression—the position of the actors in the theatre, rather than the situation presented, dictates the language used. Possibly the words ἐξαλίσας/ἐξήλικας (32/3) as well as punning on the horse, may also be a joke at the expense of the *ekkyklema*.

The first production of the *Clouds* was in 423 B.C., slightly later than *Cresphontes* of Euripides with its memorable scene in which Merope was prevented, just in time, from killing Cresphontes as he lay asleep in the house. That scene was presented on the *ekkyklema*, and conceivably Aristophanes chose to parody it here, but without a complete text of the lost play certainty is impossible.

Clouds 181–509

At 133 Strepsiades approaches the door of the Reflectory, where his knock is answered by a pupil who, after shutting the door behind him, speaks with Strepsiades on the doorstep. At 181 the latter demands to see the inside of the house and asks that the doors be thrown open—a demand of the kind that frequently, though not invariably, heralds the use of the *ekkyklema*.[28] The remainder of the passage reinforces the possibility.

The necessity that the scene should be clearly visible rules out a simple opening of the door; the *ekkyklema* is the usual means (at least in tragedy) of introducing a tableau, and here we are presented with a tableau of Socrates' disciples, their heads down towards the ground (187) and their behinds sticking in the air. At 198 the now familiar joke on the *ekkyklema* is repeated with the pupil's assertion that 'It is not possible for the disciples to remain long in the open air': at 200 all the other pupils rush back into the *skene*, leaving visible Astronomy and Geometry (perhaps two strange figures), and also a map of the world which the pupil shows to Strepsiades, only to be interrupted by the appearance of Socrates hanging from the *mechane* in a basket. The new arrival bids Strepsiades sit down 'on the holy couch' (254) which, it has been plausibly suggested, might well be Strepsiades' original bed from the first scene—an identification which would doubtless amuse the audience.[29] Unless the bed has remained on the stage from the first scene (and then the question arises of what happened to the other bed) the action of the *ekkyklema* again seems indicated—significantly, when the bed is next mentioned, at 633, Strepsiades is specifically instructed to carry it out of the house. K. J. Dover[30] has objected that the *ekkyklema* would be overcrowded, with at least four students, the figures of Astronomy, Geometry, the map and the bed all on it at once, but there is nothing to indicate that the two strange figures do not appear as the students disappear, and that they bring the map with them. Dover further argues that at no point in the play is there evidence of dramatic motivation for withdrawal of the machine, and A. M. Dale's suggestion that the κατά in καταβαίνων (508) is to be interpreted as Strepsiades stepping off the back of the *ekkyklema* as it is withdrawn, he dismisses by the argument that the context for the use of 'down' appears in the preceding and following words. On the other hand, without the extended *ekkyklema* it would be necessary for anyone entering the door to step *up*, and the line would then be clearly out of context. The argument for the withdrawal of the *ekkyklema* at this point seems, therefore, well grounded.

Dover stages the scene without the *ekkyklema* by supposing a screen over part of the *skene* front, which is carried off by two men standing behind it when Strepsiades cries 'Open the door' (183), to reveal the students in position. Removal of a screen would involve the men descending the ladder from the stage and then walking briskly off through the *parodos* with their screen—a distraction of the audience's attention from the opening of a new and important scene—which makes the supposition implausible. The use of the *ekkyklema*, asserted by the scholiast on the passage and by the author of the Second Hypothesis to the play, provides by far the most successful solution.

Clouds 889–1104
In the codex Venetus a note added by a second hand alongside the text at 889 states that the two *Logoi* appeared on the stage in wicker baskets like fighting cocks. The scholium has been described as worthless and incredible, but it is difficult to imagine a source for such a startling piece of information unless it represents a true tradition for the play at some performance, even if it does not originate with Aristophanes. The information certainly could not be elicited from the text as it now stands, but if it is to be accepted then the transport of the cages to a spot visible to the audience must have required the *ekkyklema*. At some point the *Logoi* would presumably have been released, for continuation of the scene at any length with them confined is impossible; they may have been liberated at 889, but the following lines would well suit a scene between fighting cocks eager to attack each other: a more plausible point might be the interruption by the chorus at 952ff. The *Logoi* vanish without a word at the completion of the scene (1104), and this may point to the *ekkyklema*; but corruption or revision of the text[31] (the scene as now extant requires at least five actors) makes certainty impossible. The loss of a choral ode probably accounts for the abrupt ending.

Frogs 180–270[32]
The explanations that have been offered for the production of Charon's boat are varied and ingenious in the extreme. The

consensus of opinion, however, has favoured a journey across the orchestra, though there have been dissenters who suggest the stage as the setting and Arnott, the latest supporter of this theory, has produced some shrewd arguments for it.[33] The ancient commentators were equally divided and perplexed by the problem.

The text makes it relatively easy to plot the positions of the scene's various characters. Dionysus and Xanthias, after talking with Heracles, return to the orchestra to continue their journey and accost a passing corpse which they try to persuade to carry their luggage down to Hades. The corpse refuses, Xanthias picks up the luggage and presumably approaches the donkey, when Charon suddenly bursts in with his boat. Charon's cry at 180 'put her alongside' metrically completes Dionysus' line, and makes it immediately apparent that the essential requirement of his appearance is speed, so any method of production that cannot supply this must be ruled out. The chief suggestions involve 'rowing' or 'punting' the boat across the orchestra from one *parodos* to the other by some means,[34] but such suggestions overlook the distance and time necessary to move a boat from some point in the *parodos* out of sight of the audience to the centre of the theatre. Obviously the audience's attention ought not to be distracted from the corpse's final line, yet it is difficult to see how this could be avoided since to arrive on cue the boat must either start its journey before the end of that scene or else be made ready in full view of the audience at the edge of the orchestra. Bieber[35] sought to speed the journey by suggesting that the boat was pushed and pulled by the Frogs 'in and out of the orchestra', but the Frogs, if they appear at all, are not introduced before 209.

The alternative of crossing by the stage has certain major advantages. First, the distance is far shorter; secondly, if the stage is Acheron, then Xanthias in his journey round it can simply go out through the *parodos* and behind the *skene*, and return through the other *parodos* without distracting the audience by walking round the orchestra; at the same time, as Arnott saw, he has an opportunity to remove the donkey, which editors usually allow to wander off on its own. Again, as Charon is in all probability played by the same actor who played the part of

Heracles, and as only eight lines separate the two roles, the actor has enough time to change mask and costume but scarcely enough to reappear through the *parodos* after retiring through the central door—an appearance through the same door would be much simpler. Finally, if as suggested earlier[36] the corpse scene was intended to distract the audience while the boat was prepared, it can only be supposed that the two scenes were played on different levels and that as the corpse scene certainly took place in the orchestra, then the boat should appear on the stage.

Those who argue for the stage have, without exception, proposed that the boat sailed from one side of it to the other, but on a stage without wings this would be extremely difficult to produce. A boat plying from the central door to the edge of the stage is far more plausible, and no easier method for this could be found than the *ekkyklema*, whose mechanical details would be familiar to any producer and whose constant use would offer less chance of failure at the critical moment. Any preparations necessary to turn it into a realistic boat could be made inside the *skene* during the corpse scene without detracting from the action. Possibly the boat was presented broadside on, with low sides, so that Dionysus' attempt to sit on his oar (199) was clearly visible. The Frogs, if present, would then enter through the door at 209 and remain singing round the boat, to disappear again as the *ekkyklema* was withdrawn at 270. Dionysus at this point stepped off and summoned Xanthias, who was already waiting by the corner of the *parodos*, and Charon simply disappeared inside the *skene*.

Frogs 830–1481

The structural difficulties of this scene, and the form it originally took, have been the source of much dispute: here I intend simply to discuss the text as it stands. The *agon* is introduced by Aeacus and Xanthias, who establish the setting (738–813) and then retire, with the observation, 'Well, let's go in, for whenever our masters have weighty problems to decide, then there's trouble brewing for us.' This parting remark, unlike the similar one at *Peace* 234, gives no indication that they expect their masters to come outside, and when the *agon* begins the general impression given is that the scene is set inside the palace—though to furnish proof of this is difficult. At the end of the scene Pluto does indeed invite Dionysus to 'go in' with him, but as earlier examples have shown this need not necessarily imply an outdoor scene.

There are certain points in the action that use of the *ekkyklema* would clarify, the most important being the appearance of Pluto. The audience has been informed that the contest is taking place within his halls, but the first indication of his presence comes at 1414, when he speaks without introduction; at 1479 he interrupts again to invite Dionysus into his house, and in neither case would it be easy to assign the lines to another speaker. As he is not given the usual introduction on arrival, it is easiest to assume that Pluto was present from the beginning of the *agon*, recognizable to the audience by the general setting and by his accessories, a crown, throne etc. The production of a throne as well as seats for the contestants and Dionysus might well have required the *ekkyklema*, but there is no absolute necessity for it, since slaves could quite conceivably have run on and off with the various articles.

Knights 763–1252

Some hundred years ago W. Ribbeck[37] was the first to suggest that the Pnyx was represented by the *ekkyklema*, but this won little support and has been ignored by the majority of editors. For a number of reasons we may well suppose that he was correct, not least being the scholiast's remark (1249) where Paphlagon, defeated by the Sausage-Seller, exclaims, κυλίνδετ' εἴσω τόνδε τὸν δυσδαίμονα 'roll in this unhappy man'. The scholiast cites as original for this the *Bellerophon* of Euripides, with κυλίνδετ' substituted for κομίζετ' (frag. 312N). In fact the *Stheneboia* contains the expression κομίζετ' εἴσω τήνδε and it has been suggested that the scholiast confused the two plays, though there is no reason not to believe that Euripides might use a similar expression twice. The change of verb, however, is important. In the *Bellerophon* the main character must have come from off stage through the orchestra, carried on a couch after his fall from Pegasus. Without doubt he made a speech before the door, and was then carried in to die. The substitution of κυλίνδετ' would then suggest some reference to the staging, and the strong possibility that Paphlagon was removed from the stage by the *ekkyklema*. Other indications can be found in the text. At 751 Demus orders off the two contestants, with the words 'Forward all, move to the Pnyx.' The first part of the expression was a ritual cry with no reference to the staging, but after the second half of the line, and even before the choral ode, the setting is already changed; line 754 seems to present confirmation, though it may only refer to the mention of the Pnyx in the preceding line.[38] Certainly there are no further references to the Pnyx after this point, even though a confirmatory mention might have been expected after the choral ode and this would suggest that the new setting was completely obvious and needed no clarification: from which we might infer use of some method of indicating it, such as the *ekkyklema*. Possibly then, at the mention of the Pnyx the device comes forward carrying seats—the arrival of Demus at 728 could have been the point at which the door was left open to allow the properties to be arranged. A seat for Demus is required by 785 and 1153, and it is interesting that he is certainly not seated in the preceding scenes. A further pointer is the number of cumbersome properties featured in this scene: at 993 Paphlagon and the Sausage-Seller go off to fetch their abundant oracles (997ff.), again at 1110 they depart to return with hampers containing titbits for Demus, and all these have eventually to be removed unless they are to remain in evidence for the rest of the play. The withdrawal of the *ekkyklema* at 1252 would provide an excellent opportunity for this, while leaving Demus and the Sausage-Seller still on the stage.

If the *ekkyklema* was used in this play to portray the Pnyx, the question must be raised of whether it was similarly used in the *Acharnians* 20–173. The text provides no useful clues, and the fact that its employment would inevitably detract from the parody of Euripides' use of it, makes it an unlikely possibility.

Birds 92–266
A less than conclusive case can be made out for the use of the *ekkyklema* in this scene, whose latter action (207–66) it will be convenient to consider first.

At 202 the Hoopoe explains how he intends to summon the other birds 'by going into the thicket here and arousing my Nightingale, then together we shall summon them'. Peisthetairus repeats this at 207, as if to impress it on the audience. The Hoopoe sings from 209–22 and again 227–62, and the scholiast remarks that the part of the Nightingale was in fact played by the flute-player, and that it was to his tune that the Hoopoe sang. As the chorus is not yet present, probably the normal *auletes* was called upon to play this part, for the cost of hiring a second to represent the Nightingale[39] would doubtless be prohibitive.

The staging of the scene is full of problems. It is inconceivable that the Hoopoe went inside the *skene* to sing, first because a scene of this length without any stage action is unlikely, and secondly because his song would probably have been inaudible. One possibility is that the Hoopoe remained on the stage, the audience being required to imagine the bush, and that the flute-player played behind the *skene*; an alternative is to suppose that as the Hoopoe was about to enter the door the *ekkyklema* appeared carrying a bush to indicate a thicket, and that both he and the *auletes* came forward on it. The device would be withdrawn at 262 and the Hoopoe return at 270, the demonstrative οὑτοσί marking his re-entry. The problem is, why should the Hoopoe find it necessary to enter the thicket at all to sing? The answer may either be a wish to have the flute-player on the stage in bird costume (though compared with the birds of the chorus Nightingales have a very commonplace plumage), or, as T. B. L. Webster has suggested, the need for a professional singer to sing the summons and consequently for some method of unobtrusively changing actor for singer, a problem considerably simplified by the use of the *ekkyklema*.

If the copse is, at this point, to be represented by a bush on the *ekkyklema*, then we must consider the first appearance of the Hoopoe at 92. Euelpides calls to him to come out, and the bird replies from behind the *skene*, 'Open wide the wood, that I may go forth', the 'wood' being a facile pun on both the thicket and the stage door. However, the expression is parallel to others which seemingly herald the use of the *ekkyklema*, and there is a marked affinity with *Ach.* 408–79 (there Euripides was too busy to be disturbed: here the Hoopoe is enjoying his after-dinner nap (82) and cannot be bothered), but if the *ekkyklema* is used it must either be pushed out only for a moment to enable the audience to recognize the copse later on, or, more probably, it comes forward only a short way sufficient to cover the doorway (the door remains unused between the Hoopoe's appearance and his departure to sing) and remains there throughout the scene. When the Hoopoe enters the thicket (207), he would then step behind the bush as the *ekkyklema* rolled forward to its full extent, carrying the flute-player and the Hoopoe's double.

If it could be satisfactorily demonstrated that the machine was used here, certain features would be noteworthy. During an interval in the song (223–6) Peisthetairus and Euelpides, both on the stage, make comments that imply they are on-lookers, not actually part of the scene; that is, they indicate that the edges of the *ekkyklema* form the boundaries of the thicket and that the remainder of the stage has little connexion with it, in contrast to the scene in the *Women at the Thesmophoria* 278–946. The device would be used, uniquely, to divide one part of the stage from another, a use dictated perhaps by a special set of production circumstances, namely the exchange of parts between Hoopoe and singer.

Wasps 1122–1264

One last, highly doubtful example is this scene where editors generally have agreed with Van Leeuwen (on line 1122) that 'pater et filius foras procedunt': that is that the scene takes place on the stage. The only indication of a possible *ekkyklema* scene is Bdelykleon's advice to his father, 'lie down here and learn' (1208). This should imply a couch on the stage, but it may be a piece of comic business as they practise 'subsiding' into chairs. The presence of a couch would suggest an indoor scene, and Philokleon's remark, 'Come, let us go in now' (1264) would be no obstacle to this.

Conclusions

Even a cursory glance at the plays indicates that the *ekkyklema* was extensively used by Aristophanes, despite his poking fun at Euripides' fondness for it. To do himself what he criticizes in others is a trait frequently observable in Aristophanes, but it is interesting that when he uses the device for his own purposes he quietly passes over its functioning, and only when he wishes to parody it does he call attention to it.

The machine itself must have been simple to use, and when extended, seems not to have interfered with the actor's use of the stage, which indicates that it cannot have been raised much above stage level. It seems to have had no fixed function; we have seen instances where the scene cannot possibly be considered as indoors, from which it can be inferred that the audience did not expect an indoor scene unless it was specifically indicated or the context made it obvious. The tragic poets were evidently far more conservative in their use of the machine,[40] but Aristophanes seems to have treated it as a utility device, unhampered by any set dramatic purpose and capable of infinite adaptation as the poet saw fit.

CHAPTER V

THE MECHANE

Of all the devices that Pollux records as available in the Greek theatre, the best attested is the *mechane* or crane. Plato, in the early years of the fourth century B.C., twice (*Clit.* 407a, *Crat.* 425d) mentions the god on the *mechane*, who appears in order to unravel the knot when the play has reached an impasse; Alexis refers in his *Lebes* (frag. 125, 126K) to the gods suspended from the crane; Aristotle (*Poetics* 1454b, 1) criticizes plots which need a *mechane* scene to complete the action, Antiphanes (frag. 191K) recalls that the tragedians raise the *mechane* like lifting a finger whenever their plots reach a stalemate—and so on. All take for granted that the machine was a part of the theatre, and so familiar to the public that its appearance and function required no explanation.

Pollux (IV, 128ff.) offers a reasonably comprehensive description. 'The *mechane* exhibits the gods and heroes who are in the air, the Bellerophons and Perseuses. It stands by the left *parodos* and overtops the *skene*. What is in tragedy the *mechane*, in comedy is called the κραδή.' The information is echoed by an ancient commentator on an Old Comedy play (perhaps Cratinus' *Seriphoi*) who gives a variety of examples of the use of κραδή from a number of plays.[1] This distinction in name between the tragic and comic machine can hardly signify a difference in actual construction, for the organization of the festival and the short time available makes any rebuilding or modification of the structure unlikely, while so far as it is possible to tell, the action of the two machines was identical. Besides, in parodying *mechane* scenes of tragedy, Aristophanes is unlikely to have used a different machine to work them out.

The position of the *mechane*, according to Pollux, was beside the left *parodos*, though what viewpoint he had in mind in thus describing it is not clear. The holes in 'T' have been suggested

as its base, and if by '*parodos*' Pollux means the whole area
between 'T' and the theatre exit,[2] then the two statements
become reconcilable. It is possible, furthermore, that the missing
cuttings in the wall 'H', S 6 and 7, are not the result of later
mending of the wall, as generally supposed, but were purposely
left free of beams to allow that part of the corridor in front of
'H' to be used for the preparation of the *mechane* scenes. For if
our earlier supposition is correct,[3] that beams in the slots in 'H'
were duplicated in front of the wall, and the two tied at the top
by cross-beams, it would have been difficult to lift loads from
the corridor on to the stage without fouling these cross-beams.
Their absence at this spot might therefore be expected, and this
may well account for the missing slots in 'H'. If this reconstruction is correct, then the more westerly hole in 'T' is more likely
to have held the *mechane*.

How did the machine work? Antiphanes' claim, that the jib
was raised like a finger when an actor was about to be lifted up
to appear over the roof, suggests some kind of counterbalanced
jib fixed sufficiently high above the roof to allow its loads to
clear it. The supporting stock presumably fitted into the hole
in 'T', but as the socket is square the part of the crane which
swung round (περιάγειν —'to rotate' is the word used in *POxy*
2742) must have been fixed on top of the stock and probably
above the roof. Certainly the *mechanopoios* (see pp. 78–9), who
seems to have been the crane operator rather than its builder,
would have had to be in a position where he could see the stage
if he was to perform accurately the delicate task of manoeuvring
the burden on to the stage. The roof would doubtless have provided him with a suitable perch. The jib itself must have been
long enough to give an indication of flight up and down the
stage, but there can be no question of swinging an actor over the
orchestra, as some editors have suggested: in fact the scope of
the device must have been fairly limited. What evidence we
have for crane construction is evidence of the Greeks' proficiency
in this field; unfortunately none of the extant descriptions seem
to correspond with the actual theatre mechanism.[4]

The actor must have attached himself to the *mechane* in the
narrow passage by the stage, by means of the ἄγκυρις or hook
that Hesychius (sv κραδή) mentions. Pollux IV, 131 speaks of

the ropes employed, and Aristophanes frag. 188 mentions τὸν τροχὸν, which may mean the pulley or the drum of the machine. Some sort of harness, too, must have held the actor as he flew through the air—doubtless a pretty uncomfortable experience—and the need to remove this on stage after the flight may have led to the use of mounts for the appearance of people like Bellerophon, since the harness could be disguised round the mount and its removal made less unnatural. The necessity for a harness makes it unlikely that the *mechane* was used to remove from the stage people who had entered by one of the more normal ways, for a poet could hardly expect an audience to sit quietly while the actor strapped himself into position to be hoisted off, nor is it likely that Aristophanes would have missed the opportunity for such a notable parody. Pollux (IV, 130) suggests that the *geranos* was employed for this particular action, but again it is doubtful whether this is anything more than an alternative name for the *mechane*.[5]

Normally the device showed people in flight rather than still, though there are exceptions, and Hourmouziades[6] suggests that the flight was accompanied by anapaests either recited or perhaps sung by the flying person or the chorus. For this a certain amount of supporting evidence may be found in comedy but, for an accurate picture of the performance of the machine we must consider the scenes in detail. Predictably, Aristophanes in his plays takes less trouble to cover its working than do the tragedians, and thereby provides us with a useful store of information on the device.

Peace 82–180
This is the best attested *mechane* scene in drama, and contains many elements common to all scenes in which the *mechane* is employed.

The two slaves whose appearance marks the opening of the play stir the audience's curiosity by their preparations and their remarks about the monstrous dung beetle, which is housed out of sight in the *skene*. The poet acknowledges the audience's curiosity (43) but still continues to tantalize them until one of the slaves begins to explain the 'plot' (54ff.). Even this serves only to excite the audience, especially when Trygaeus is heard to speak behind the *skene* (62/3). The slave peeps in through the door (78), and suddenly the scene bursts into life as Trygaeus appears over the roof sitting astride the beetle. That the *mechane* is employed for this appearance is sufficiently clear from 80/1, and the remarks of the scholiast on V that 'he is raised up in the air on the *mechane*'. Lines 79–81 form an introduction to the actual revelation, and seem intended to cover the working of the *mechane* as it hoisted up rider and mount, while at the same time directing the audience's attention to the roof-top.

Trygaeus' use of anapaests until 101 where, in any case, there is a strong hint that he halts suspended over the stage to conduct a conversation with the slave, lends plausibility to Hourmou-ziades' hypothesis that the metre in such a situation can be taken as indicative of flight. Indeed, after the slave's attempt to stop his master's flight,[7] first by persuasion and then by violence, and the similarly unsuccessful attempts by Trygaeus' daughters to influence him by pointing out the dangers of his journey, the hero reverts once more to the use of anapaests (154), which seem to signify that his flight is resumed. He continues in the metre until 172, during which time he is presumably swung up and down the stage. At 174 he cries out to the *mechanopoios* to take care of him, thus providing the cue for depositing him on the stage, and at 179 knocks at the door of Zeus' house, having by this time clearly dismounted. The parallelism between flight and the use of anapaests is very marked.

When at 720 Trygaeus seeks to return to earth and enquires for his beetle, he is informed that Zeus has commandeered it for his chariot and he will have to walk back 'by the goddess'. The beetle, in other words, has been swung off at some point, presumably fairly soon after its pilot's arrival for it would otherwise obstruct the stage, especially during the rescue of Peace. The violent incursion on to the scene by Hermes (182ff.) offers a suitably dramatic moment that would divert the audience's attention. The necessity for removal, however, points to one of the limitations of the *mechane*: in this case Trygaeus is required to return to earth accompanied by *Opora* and *Theoria*, but other *mechane* scenes all point to a maximum load of two persons—hence the disappearance of the beetle.

Much of the force of this scene derives from the parody of the flight of Bellerophon on his winged horse in the eponymous play by Euripides.[8] Aristophanes goes to great lengths to emphasize this parody: the first hint occurs even before the beetle appears, when at 76 the slave quotes the *Bellerophon* (frag. 308N) and sets the scene for the appearance of Trygaeus; at 126 there is reference to a winged horse (=*Stheneboea* frag. 665N), made explicit at 135 by the mention of Pegasus. The use of anapaests in 154, a parody of *Bellerophon* frag. 309N, suggests that the original was delivered during the horse's flight, and the hero's fall from his mount, mentioned in 146, may be at the back of Trygaeus' mind in his words to the engineer at 174.[9] This laboured identification was possibly necessary because of the length of time that had elapsed between the original production of the Euripidean play before 427 b.c.,[10] and that of the *Peace* in 421 b.c., possibly also because *mechane* scenes, on the evidence of *POxy* 2742, seem to have been relatively common; but it is interesting to compare the technique here with the poet's parodies of Euripides' *ekkyklema* scenes. In the latter the identification, though elucidated at some point, is rarely laboured doubtless because Euripides is himself on the stage when his *ekkyklema* scenes are being parodied so that the parallel is immediately obvious. With the *mechane*, on the other hand, this is not usually the case, and it is correspondingly less easy for the audience to make the identification. The aura surrounding an appearance on the *mechane* is made the subject of further paratragic reference. At 90 the slave addresses Trygaeus as ὦ δέσποτ᾽ ἄναξ, a term normally reserved for address to a god. In tragedy the *mechane* is used almost exclusively by gods and heroes, and the inference is that Trygaeus, simply by appearing on the machine, has taken on a god-like quality.

There remains the problem of Bellerophon's appearance in the original play. He cannot have brought on the horse, fastened it to the *mechane*, mounted and flown off, but, like Trygaeus, must have flown up from behind the *skene* and hung motionless to address the audience,[11] before flying off to disappear again behind the *skene*.

Birds 1198–1261

The appearance of Iris in this play is almost certainly managed

by the *mechane*, and as in the *Peace* careful preparation is made
for the goddess's arrival: the messenger rushing in (1170) with
the news that a god has flown through the city gates into the
air, avoiding the guards; the hurried orders of Peisthetairus for
a bow, a sling and a platoon of guards at the ready (1186); the
theme in the chorus' song of war between birds and gods—all
these serve to create an atmosphere of expectancy as the
audience wait for an unidentified (1176) winged god.

Three lines from the chorus introduce the actual arrival
(1196). 'Glance all around and watch, for the winged sound of
some immortal's flight near at hand comes to my ears.' The
lines, as in the *Peace*, serve to cover the working of the machine
but they also, seemingly, attempt to make dramatic capital out
of its sound by ascribing it to the goddess's wings. Strangely
enough a similar adaptation, though less explicit, is found in
tragedy. In the *Andromache* 1226ff. the chorus introduce Thetis
on the *mechane* with 'What is in motion? What prodigy do
I sense? Look, women, look', and the use of κεκίνηται and
αἰσθάνομαι seem to indicate the impression made on the
chorus by the noise of the machine. The words of the chorus in
the *Birds* as Iris departs (1262ff.) also imply the covering of
noisy machinery, for their dramatic importance is negligible
and they seem intended only to ensure that the clue to the
next actor's identity in the following lines (1269/70) is not
obscured.

Iris' actual appearance was probably designed to be anti-
climactic, though how this was achieved can only be conjectured.[12] She comes to a halt at the order of Peisthetairus, and
apparently hangs motionless from the machine for the whole of
her appearance, judging by the absence of anapaests. After
identifying herself (1204) she listens with increasing anger to
Peisthetairus' denial of sacrifices to the gods, before bursting
into a paratragic speech that perhaps indicates the scene is a
parody of some specific tragedy, though with no clue to its
source (the very fact that Iris appears on the *mechane*, when the
other gods and the birds simply walk on and off, may be
evidence for an intended parody). Iris makes as if to fly off at
1243, but is restrained by Peisthetairus, and forced to hear him
out until he dismisses her (1258) probably, as Rogers suggests,

by clapping his hands to shoo her off. The scene ends at 1261, its brevity perhaps to be explained by the discomfort endured by the actor hanging in mid-air.

If this scene is based on a tragic forerunner, it is legitimate to ask why there is no attempt to make the source plain, and two possible reasons spring to mind. The audience might be expected immediately to recognize a play in which Iris had appeared either if it were very recent or were for some reason exceptionally memorable. In one extant play, the *Hercules* of Euripides, which is almost certainly later than *Birds* (414), Iris appears urging Lyssa to send madness on Heracles (*HF* 822ff.), and she probably also had a part in the *Inachus* of Sophocles, a satyr play.[13] In both these plays however, her role is as servant of Hera, not of Zeus as in Aristophanes, and in the *Inachus* there is no indication that she uses the *mechane*. In short, neither play is a likely source for the parody.

In the *Phaethon* of Euripides, however, a messenger is required to report Phaethon's ride in the chariot of the sun, his subsequent blasting by Zeus' thunderbolt and his fall from heaven, before his still-smoking body is brought on to the stage and carried indoors (*Phaethon* frag. 781N). The identity of the messenger is unknown and has aroused much speculation, but it must certainly be someone in a position to view the whole scene. Iris may well have served in this capacity as messenger of Zeus, a hypothesis that a number of factors tend to support. First, the introduction of the smoking body of Phaethon on the stage would make a scene sufficiently memorable to be easily recollected. As regards dating, on grounds of the number of resolved syllables permitted in the metre, Zielinski ascribed the play definitely to the years 415–409 B.C., while Webster places it earlier but close to the *Trojan Women* in 415, the *Birds* being produced in 414.[14] Thirdly, *Birds* 1238ff., which has caused difficulties of interpretation, if considered as a parody of the *Phaethon* fits neatly into the context of the burning corpse.[15] Further speculation is unprofitable, but the scene may possibly originate in Euripides' *Phaethon*.

Clouds 217–68

The use of the *mechane* for this scene is an undoubted fact, and is evident from lines 217, 226, 229 and 237. Its employment illustrates a number of points previously discussed.

Strepsiades, who is anxious to join the Reflectory, on approaching the door is greeted by a pupil, who explains what the other students are doing and shows him various strange figures. The two are then engaged in the study of a map when Strepsiades suddenly notices a man hung up in a 'basket'[16] whom he discovers to be Socrates (218). He questions Socrates on his purpose in hanging up in the air, then begs him to descend while he explains his own reason in coming to the Reflectory. It must be assumed that Socrates does descend (238), for at the end of the scene he leads Strepsiades into the house (505). At some point, though exactly when is not indicated, the 'basket' must have been removed.

Here again the working of the *mechane* is masked, this time by diverting our attention to the map scene—maps being presumably something of a rarity in contemporary Athens. The use of the basket or sling obviates the need for complicated harness, so that Socrates' descent from the basket presents no problem as he could simply step out of it. Aristophanes makes fun of Socrates throughout the scene by equating him with the gods, and again the tragic influence can be seen with his appearance on the *mechane* automatically giving him a divine air. It seems likely that Socrates simply hangs in the air until he is lowered, (which the lack of anapaests may reflect) and in this it departs from the pattern of the other plays discussed, in which the main function of the *mechane* seems to have been to convey the impression of flight. It is noticeable too that attention is not specifically directed to the device, suggesting that, as with the *ekkyklema*, when the poet is using it for a dramatic purpose as distinct from parody he finds it more effective not to call the audience's attention to it.

Women at the Thesmophoria 1010ff.
The scene is part of an ingenious parody of the *Andromeda* of Euripides, and its use of the *mechane* presents a complex problem.

Mnesilochus and the archer enter through the central door on the *ekkyklema* (1001ff.). The archer goes inside for a moment to find a mat to sit on while guarding his prisoner, and in his absence Euripides appears and makes a sign of encouragement to his kinsman. Mnesilochus observes 'It's clear he'll come and save me; otherwise he would not have flown by' (παρέπτετο) (1014/5). As prima facie evidence for the use of the *mechane* this is unfortunately contradicted by Mnesilochus' preceding remark (1011) that Euripides, dressed as Perseus, has by 'running out' (ἐκδραμών) given him a sign that he must play the part of Andromeda. Euripides' appearance is only momentary before he retires behind the door to play the part of Echo; when he does return, in the role of Perseus (1099), he tells how on his swift feet he has cut a path through the air.

The obvious means of reconciling all these statements is to assume the use of winged sandals by Perseus/Euripides, but the expected confirmatory evidence of vase paintings of scenes from the *Andromeda* is, in fact, conflicting: although a number do show Perseus in winged sandals, a significant proportion picture him without.[17] The original play, too, poses problems for on the basis of *Thesm.* 1014 it is assumed that Perseus flew on to the stage to rescue Andromeda. Hourmouziades shows that the only existing fragments of Perseus' speech were presumably, in the absence of anapaests, delivered after he landed; he further suggests that the flight was intended to emphasize Perseus' movement *through* the air, and that it is most unlikely that he remained suspended in the air.[18] But if he did not remain suspended he must have unhooked himself, and his harness must have been withdrawn either on stage or off. Hourmouziades continues, probably rightly, that frag. 125 suggests that Perseus is some distance from Andromeda, mistaking her for a statue, and that if Perseus was in the orchestra the combined height of the stage and the *ekkyklema* could give the illusion of distance. He seems therefore to suppose that Perseus landed in the orchestra. However, it is unlikely that the *mechane* jib could have been of a length sufficient to swing him directly into the orchestra, even allowing that this would be unique in extant drama. Furthermore *Thesm.* 1099ff. (*Andromeda* frag. 123N) sounds like an entrance line spoken by Perseus, and as such its strong emphasis on his flight would be somewhat tautologous if he had just flown down before the audience. It suggests, rather, an entrance through the *parodos*, and perhaps a sequence of events in which Perseus appeared on the *mechane* and flew over the scene, perceived Andromeda, then disappeared behind the scene, to return through the *parodos*, (having divested himself of his harness off stage). He would then deliver his entry line with its emphasis on flight to make his identity plain. The *Women at the Thesmophoria* then, probably proceeds as follows. Euripides flies over the stage and disappears, giving Mnesilochus his cue to begin his Andromeda monody. (The difficulty over attributing 1020 to Mnesilochus arises because he injects his personal trouble into the original lament: certainly the lines 1016ff. cannot be appropriated by Euripides/Perseus because, as Webster has shown, they were originally Andromeda's.[19]) Mnesilochus continues until 1055, when Euripides addresses him from off stage identifying himself as Echo (1059), and preparing the audience for the parody of the opening lines of the *Andromeda*. At this point Euripides in order to be audible must be only just off stage, beside the door or, less likely, at a window (windows seem not to have been used in tragedy, and are therefore unlikely in tragic parody). The archer returns through the door at 1082, without noticing Euripides—a detail that would not have been questioned by the audience—and searches in vain for the voice that echoes his words. Then at 1098, Euripides walks into full view as Perseus, and relates how he has flown through the air.

It seems, therefore, probable that the play does contain a short *mechane* scene, in which Euripides appears unexpectedly in flight, over the stage.

Daedalus frag. 188

This fragment is remarkable for its mention of τὸν τροχὸν (discussed above) and its reference to the man working the machine: both suggest parody if we may correctly suppose that it was Aristophanes' normal practice to refer to the machine when parodying a scene. Edmonds has suggested that the actor who speaks these lines is Icarus,[20] but corruption in the second line makes it difficult to discover what is actually happening. Possibly the actor is being hauled up the scene until he is in a position to greet the sun: certainly 'Hail, light of the sun', is a paratragic phrase and may be inserted, as Edmonds suggests, to remind the audience how Icarus flew too close to the sun with the disastrous results for the wax securing his wings. Pasiphae and Daedalus appeared in the *Cretans* of Euripides, and perhaps this was the source of the parody. The scholiast on *Frogs* 849 provides the information that the *Cretans* contained a monody by Inachus notable because it was θρασύς, and possibly here he was flying off at the end. Dating is of little help; Webster places the *Cretans* at ?442/1 B.C. while Geissler gives 420 as the date of the *Daedalus*.[21] Another suggested source, less likely, is Sophocles' play of the same name.

Conclusions

The tragedians used the *mechane* mainly for the production of gods and heroes, frequently, though not exclusively, in flight, and Aristophanes followed their lead when it suited his purpose. Some indication of flight may possibly be found in the use of anapaests by the actor thus portrayed. In parodying the device the comic poet tends to call attention to its working, though these parodies in contrast to those of the *ekkyklema*, consist not simply of the machine but of actual scenes. The exception to these comments is the appearance of Socrates in the *Clouds*, where there is indication neither of flight, parody, nor the machine's technical details. As regards the last a three-line introduction seems to have been sufficient for the machine to be brought into action, but for the sake of an impressive appearance even this could be discarded if the audience's attention could be momentarily diverted. The scenes in which the device is employed are relatively short, a sign probably of the discomfort endured by the actor suspended from the hook, and the problem of how to shed the actor's harness on stage, if he appeared without a mount, must always have been a formidable one. Even so, the continued use of the machine when alternative production methods were possible—in the *Birds*, with the exception of Iris, the gods and birds simply walk on— indicates that the *mechane*'s advantages were thought to outweigh the difficulties of its use.

CHAPTER VI

THE ACTORS

THE THREE-ACTOR RULE

The problem of the number of actors employed in comedy has been discussed extensively without any general agreement being reached. The view, traditional from the time of the scholiasts onwards, of a maximum of three actors, has, during this century, come under constant attack and has been just as constantly defended. A reconsideration of the evidence of the plays may help to shed a little new light.

The protagonist of the attack was Kelley Rees[1], who maintained that Aristotle (*Poetics* 1449a 18), in ascribing three actors to tragedy, was arguing for an aesthetic ideal rather than stating a fact of theatrical production. Rees' lead was followed by A. C. Schlesinger[2] in a series of articles which refuted the arguments based on the presence of silent actors in certain scenes, which had been used to support Aristotle's statement. Schlesinger argued that the theory that no more than three actors could be used, rested on the unconscious assumption that the more conversation in the play the better—that is that any dramatist will make all his characters talk as much as possible. The use of silent actors, and the non-answering of direct questions, formerly taken as proof positive of a rule on actor numbers, were better explained, he claimed, in terms of dramatic and aesthetic effect: thus in the *Oedipus at Colonus* (1099–555) Ismene is silent simply because a speech from her at this point would lack impact. Further, in the same play, limiting the number of actors would necessitate splitting a single role between two actors, which would cause enormous complications.[3] Schlesinger's attack is justified, but similar criticism can be applied to his own arguments which rest on the assumption that the poet could not make a virtue of necessity and that his dramatic technique was so weak that he could not remove an actor from the stage and at the same time make a dramatic point of the exit. This clearly will not pass. The problem, in short, cannot be approached in this way.

First of all we must turn to the ancient evidence, much of which concerns tragedy rather than comedy. Our prime source is Aristotle, who credits Sophocles with the introduction of the third actor, the highest number to which our sources refer.[4] Ancient opinion seems generally to favour the theory of three, though Rees claims this is due to the pervading influence of Aristotle and the application backwards of what was done in the time of the *technitae*, when problems of expense kept numbers to a minimum.[5] On the other hand, if the *technitae* could perform the plays with only three actors, then presumably the original performers could have done likewise, and Demosthenes, taunt of Aeschines for having been *tritagonistes* (Dem. 18, 129, 209, 262, 265) does suggest that this was the lowest grade to which he could sink. All these remarks refer to tragedy. Aristotle disclaims knowledge of the origins of comedy (*Poetics* 1449b 3), but his admission that he does not know who established its complement of actors suggests that he had a specific number in mind. An anonymous writer on comedy credits Cratinus with fixing the number as three,[6] and while, in the face of Aristotle's disclaimer, it would be dangerous to accept this statement uncritically, the number conveniently agrees with that proposed for tragedy, and there is no good reason for thinking that the state would allow comedy more actors than her sister art of tragedy. It was presumably because the Dionysia was not only a religious festival but a dramatic competition that the state laid down the rules and supplied the actors,[7] and we may reasonably suppose that each tragic playwright was limited to the same number. On the other hand, it has been argued that as there was no comic actor's contest at this period, the comic poets could be as free as they wished in choosing their actors: but this is to ignore the fact that the comic poets themselves had a contest, for which some regulations would be necessary. There is no evidence that there was an increase in actor's numbers in tragedy before 449 B.C., when equally there was no actor's competition (and on this argument no restriction on actor numbers), nor does there seem to be any way of distinguishing Lenaean comedies from Dionysian by actor numbers, yet at the former festival a contest of actors was instituted in 442.

Probably, therefore, some control was exercised over the number of actors in comedy, and it seems plausible that tragedy influenced that number. Our tentative conclusion, before going on to consider the plays themselves, must be that comedy follows tragedy's lead.

Some of the problems inherent in using the plays as evidence have already been discussed. The question really centres on whether the poets actually avoid using more than three actors at one time, or whether they introduce as many characters as they desire. We will consider first those scenes that obviously require more than three actors simultaneously, and secondly, those impossible to stage with only three actors because there must be insufficient time for the actor to change costume and mask and return in a new role. The latter leads on to the thorny problem of plot construction and the splitting of roles between actors—a matter of considerable conjecture as, for the most part, the division of roles between actors is purely empirical.

In the first category there is an impressive list of comedy scenes requiring more than three speaking actors on stage,[8] which seems to suggest that we must dismiss the concept of a norm out of hand. The scenes, however, are worth considering in some detail.

One representative example is *Peace* 1240ff. where on stage we have a Trumpet-Maker, a Helmet-Maker, a Spearsman and Trygaeus; a Breastplate-Seller has departed as the Trumpet-Maker entered, and Lamachus' son comes on when these depart. The so-called three actors rule must here apparently be stretched to include five: on the other hand, the number of lines given to each is so few that it can hardly be held to justify the introduction of a fourth and fifth actor solely for these lines. In the section 1224–97 the Breastplate-Seller speaks six lines, the Trumpet-Maker two and a half, the Helmet-Maker and the Spearsman three and a half each, the son of Lamachus ten, and Trygaeus forty-eight—scarcely a shattering of the 'norm'. In the *Birds* 1565ff., Peisthetairus is approached by three gods, Poseidon, Heracles and the Triballian,[9] but the Triballian is required to utter only one and a half lines of broken Greek—as is Pseudartabas in a similar situation in the *Acharnians*. The latter play provides another example of four actors, when Dicaeopolis dismisses the Boeotian (955) who departs carrying the sycophant Nicarchus tied up in a bundle. As he departs through one *parodos* a servant of Lamachus rushes in through the other. Ostensibly, then, there must be a fourth actor to speak five and a half lines, but in fact it seems more likely that the binding of Nicarchus takes place off stage (952 may mark Dicaeopolis' return), which may well be a device to allow a mute or a dummy to be substituted for the actor. Certainly the use of a dummy would make it easier for the Boeotian slave to carry off the body. Example of scenes of this kind can be multiplied: *Wasps* 1416ff. requires four actors, but the Complainant speaks only four and a half lines, most of his argument being presented by Bdelykleon; at 1333 in the same play a drinking companion of Philokleon appears but speaks only three lines. Plathane, in the *Frogs* 549ff., must be played by a fourth actor but speaks a maximum of eight lines and probably less; the presence of the corpse, too, in that play requires a fourth (172ff.) for four lines, the same actor presumably playing the part of Pluto during the contest between Aeschylus and Euripides, where a further five lines are ascribed to him: from 1500–14 he addresses Aeschylus and Dionysus, but the choral ode that intervenes between the end of the *agon* and the reappearance of the actors would have allowed the substitution of a main actor in Pluto's role. All these examples indicate that three main actors, with extras to help out, is a reasonable supposition.

Certain scenes where four actors are present are more difficult to explain. *Clouds* 889ff. is concerned with the arguments between the two *Logoi*, at which Pheidippides is present (886, 990). When the scene concludes Strepsiades, and possibly Socrates too, are immediately on stage, and if the text as it stands is correct there is irrefutable evidence against the use of only three main actors.[10] It is generally agreed, however, that some disturbance of the text is indicated here—Dover, for example, posits a choral ode before the contest begins—and without supporting evidence too much weight ought not to be placed on it. The presence of four actors seems to be demanded by *Women at the Thesmophoria* 280–458, where the Heraldess, Mnesilochus, Woman A and Woman B all have speaking parts; but in this case it seems easier as well as structurally more satisfactory to assume that the part of the Heraldess was played by the chorus leader. Mnesilochus describes the arrival of the chorus of women (280ff.), the Heraldess utters the ritual cry, the chorus sings, the Heraldess bids them address the gods, and the chorus sings once more before the formal debate begins.

In *Lysistrata*, the appearance of Lampito at 81ff. brings the number of actors on stage to four, and here it may be reasonably asked why, if the norm was three, Aristophanes chose to introduce a fourth actor at all. There is no obvious answer, except that he does require some representative from Sparta, but again the actor speaks only eleven and a half lines of broken Greek and cannot be considered as taking a major part in the action. Later, at 439, Lysistrata with her band of women is confronted by an Athenian magistrate, and again more actors may be required. In the next few lines the texts of Wilamowitz, Van Leeuwen, Rogers and the Oxford text all introduce three women to remark on the situation: the Teubner editor, on the other hand, by assigning the lines differently, introduces only a single voice and thus only three actors. An alternative would be to suppose that the speakers are members of the semi-chorus of women, though the parts are so small that there is no real difficulty in supposing that extra actors could have spoken them. The problem recurs at 829ff., when Lysistrata spies Kinesias approaching the Acropolis and talks about him to another woman until Myrrhine recognizes him as her husband. It would be possible to ascribe all these lines to Myrrhine, except for the second half of 836, which would then be spoken by Lysistrata (thus solving the problem), but again a further actor may have been employed. Finally, the scene 1216ff. seems impossible to stage without four actors, though neither manuscripts nor editors offer a really convincing reconstruction of the scene. The *Lysistrata*, then, provides the strongest evidence against the three-actor rule, yet even here a fourth actor's part would be limited to thirty lines at the most and possibly far fewer. The argument is of course open to the objection that with a different distribution of parts the fourth actor might have a considerably larger role; our discussion concerns simply those parts of the play which cannot be produced without four actors. The external evidence discussed earlier however, suggests the three actor hypothesis may have some value and the fact that whenever a scene requires a fourth or fifth actor his part is never of any length lends reasonable support, or at the very least raises the question of why this should be so.

The second category of scenes to be considered is those which require four actors because of insufficient time for the actor to change from one role to another. In the case of Pseudartabas in the *Acharnians*, already mentioned, Dicaeopolis, a Herald, an Ambassador and Pseudartabas are all on stage. The Ambassador departs at 110, Pseudartabas at 122, at 129 Amphitheus is discovered present, and at 134 Theorus appears as Amphitheus departs. All this can be staged by using a substitute actor for Amphitheus at 129, where he is required to speak half a line (if, that is, he can refer to himself as οὑτοσί rather than ὁδί and the words are not rather to be attributed to Dicaeopolis). This arrangement would allow the actor playing first Amphitheus and then the Ambassador to reappear in a third role as Theorus.

A case of role-splitting is to be found in *Women at the Thesmophoria* 929ff., though without any difficulty as regards speaking. Before the Prytanis and his archer enter through the *parodos* (929), Mnesilochus, Euripides and the woman guarding the former are all on stage. Euripides departs at 927 as the Prytanis enters, his part presumably played by a fourth actor. The Scythian archer also requires an extra, but he takes no speaking part in this scene: from 1001 he becomes an important character but the intervening empty stage and choral ode (947–1000) allow one of the main actors to take over his part. The Prytanis speaks only eight lines. The scene in *Women in Assembly* (976ff.) between the Youth and the Hag presents a similar situation. If only three actors were available, one of the Hags must have been played by an extra actor; supposing this were Hag B, the actor playing the Young Girl (1042) would have ample time to change and return as Hag C (1065).

Wealth, too, involves splitting a part where Wealth himself returns from his cure (771). The preceding scene shows Cario and Chremylus' wife; in this scene Chremylus accompanies Wealth while his wife comes out to greet them, and the next scene is introduced by Cario. Some manuscripts preserve indication of a choral performance at 770 and 801, providing an opportunity for a change of role at either end of the scene. With only three actors, the one playing Cario must double in the role of Wealth or Chremylus, but as Cario and Chremylus are present alternately throughout the play it is likely that Cario doubles for Wealth, a substitution made all the easier because, since being cured of blindness, Wealth has changed his character and presumably his mask, and has in any case been absent for 500 lines.

The picture emerging from all this is not clear. Aristophanes seems, on occasion, to have required and used four performers without difficulty, but the parts directly assigned to the fourth remain small. As we have seen, it would be possible to redistribute all the parts to include a fourth actor which would considerably ease the third actor's task, in that (on the three actor hypothesis) he is required to take a variety of different, though usually minor parts: on the other hand these minor roles demand very little characterization and are probably within the capabilities of a single actor, while the external evidence on actor numbers is in favour of a maximum of three. If we suppose an *ad hoc* use of an extra actor as permitted to the comic playwright, then, no doubt, a small part as fourth actor, perhaps unpaid, would have been ideal for any would-be actor to gain experience in the theatre before taking a long and exacting part. Indeed this may account for the licence allowed in comedy in bending what appears in tragedy to have been a fairly strict rule on the number of actors.

The four-actor scenes in comedy discussed above are the exception rather than the rule, the greater part of the action being between a maximum of three. We must, therefore, consider whether any trace of a ruling on three actors can be perceived in the plays. The most numerous and obvious examples are those where one main character leaves the scene and another main character appears after a space of a few lines. The frequency of this occurrence and the often weak excuse for the departure suggests that it is a device for an actor to depart and return in a different role, though in some cases the exit does also have a dramatic effect.

A good example is seen in the *Knights* where the arrival of the Sausage-Seller at 148 brings the number of actors on the stage to three, and on our hypothesis, before Kleon can enter one of them must depart. At 154 one of the slaves goes off to keep an eye on Kleon—yet when the latter rushes on at 235 the slave brings no warning of his approach. It is worth noting that the exits of all slaves playing main parts, this one among them, are motivated, though slaves appeared frequently on the stage as extras, usually mutes, where they could slip on and off without mention. If the poet had use of an unlimited number of actors, it may be legitimately asked why he should go to the trouble of motivating the exit of this particular slave. There is another example, in *Wasps* 135ff. where two slaves are on stage, with Bdelykleon on the roof of the stage building. Before Philokleon can appear, presumably one of the slaves must disappear, and at 138 one duly runs indoors; a moment later Philokleon pops his head out of the chimney. This slave is mentioned no more, though later it becomes necessary to summon others to remove properties from the stage: again it seems tolerably clear that the slave had to disappear because the poet required another main actor. *Birds* 84ff. and *Women at the Thesmophoria* 70ff. both provide situations where, with two characters present on stage, the servant who answers the door must himself go in again before his master can appear; on the other hand in *Acharnians* 395ff., where Dicaeopolis approaches Euripides' door alone, the slave who then appears remains throughout the scene. Examples could be multiplied, but perhaps one of the most significant occurs in the *Frogs*, where during the scene in Hades (460–674) preliminary to the contest between Aeschylus and Euripides, between each of the three episodes a short choral ode is inserted enabling a single actor to undertake the parts of Aeacus, the Serving Maid (this change is covered by the conversation between Dionysus and Xanthias), *Pandokeutria* and finally Aeacus again. Each change of costume behind the scene is paralleled by a similar change of costume on stage, between Dionysus and his slave.

The evidence of the texts points strongly to the conclusion

that, in general, if three actors are on the stage one must depart before another can be introduced, and this is probably the best argument for a three-actor rule. The exceptions are minor and not of sufficient weight to destroy the principle. Supplementary actors were obviously available if the poet required them, but their parts seem to have been kept short, which may explain why such actors never gained an official title but were probably, as Pollux (IV, 110) states, included in the term *parachoregema*.

<h2 style="text-align:center">MUTES AND EXTRAS</h2>

There seems to have been no limit on the number of silent actors who could be introduced, the maximum being set, no doubt, by the munificence of the *Choregos*. Three or less seems, however, to have been normal to judge from the plays, though crowd scenes like the Prytanies at the beginning of the *Acharnians* may have required more: on the other hand a group like the Odomantian army (*Ach.* 156) may have been kept deliberately small for the sake of a joke (or considered a token force). The vast majority of mute roles are slaves, requiring a momentary appearance to bring in or remove a property.

One surprising factor is the relatively frequent appearance of children, both as mutes and in speaking parts. Presumably dithyrambic competitions for boys provided them with the necessary experience for parts like the supplementary chorus in the *Wasps*, that is if this chorus of boys actually sang, rather than mimed the singing of the main chorus. Children also appear in the *Acharnians*, as daughters of the Megarian, where they are simply required to squeak, and in the *Peace* first pleading with Trygaeus not to leave them for heaven, and later (1270ff.) in the parts of the sons of Lamachus and Kleonymus. A boy also appears in a scene in *Wealth* (823), but remains silent. These children are 'extras' or 'supernumeraries' in the proper sense, in that their size would preclude them from playing any but children's roles.

<h2 style="text-align:center">THE CHIEF CHARACTER AS A POINT OF UNITY</h2>

In discussing the use of actors it is interesting to consider how the part played by the main character develops throughout

Aristophanes' comedies, and how this affects the coherence of the plot.

The earliest type of play, well illustrated by the *Acharnians*, simply keeps the main character on stage throughout the action, except during the *parabasis* and choral odes. This is still the case in the *Birds* and the *Frogs* except for a short scene in the latter (738–813) when Aeacus and Xanthias serve as scene-setters for the second half of the play. The *Clouds* follows the same arrangement, except that Strepsiades is perhaps absent during the debate between the *Logoi* (889–1104)—though this may simply be due to the unfinished state of the text. In a slight variation on this pattern, a short introductory prologue may establish the scene before the main character is introduced. Thus in the *Knights*, the Sausage-Seller does not appear until 148, and in the *Peace* Trygaeus is not introduced until 82 though thereafter he is present continuously. The *Wasps* foreshadows a development in technique, having two main characters, Philokleon and Bdelykleon, who balance the action, both being present in speaking roles from 135ff., though Bdelykleon, lying on the roof, has been evident from the beginning of the play. A seemingly similar pattern occurs at the beginning of the *Birds*, with Peisthetairus and Euelpides present together, but the latter departs at 850 and does not return—perhaps a sign of the production difficulties of keeping two main characters on stage if the poet has only three main actors available.

The first play to show any real modification of the pattern is the *Lysistrata* and even here the change is small. Lysistrata is present on stage from the beginning until 864, but from that point on first Myrrhine and Kinesias, and then Kinesias and a Lacedaimonian herald[11] carry the action forward. This latter scene ends with an altercation between the two halves of the chorus, concluding with their reconciliation. An Athenian and a Laconian are then introduced, and together are about to summon Lysistrata when she appears of her own accord at 1107. She remains on stage until 1188, when all three go in and a short ode is sung. The subsequent action (1216ff.) is obscure, but if the Oxford text is correct in its distribution of parts, Lysistrata does not reappear until 1271 but remains on stage thereafter until the end of the play. She has been absent for some 250 lines, and it is precisely at this point that the structure of the play is weakest and the distribution of parts a problem.

The *Women at the Thesmophoria* and the *Frogs* show Aristophanes reverting to his original scheme; but *Women in Assembly*, with its use of two main characters who appear alternately, represents a distinct break. Praxagora is present from the beginning until 284 when she leaves the stage to her husband, not reappearing until 504. At 727 both depart, and though at the end of the play Blepyrus momentarily returns and is led off to the feast, the intervening portion completely ignores these two characters and introduces new ones. Unfortunately, here again the structure of the play is weakened and the identification of characters made uncertain once the cohesive element of the main players is removed, with the result that the play's central portion is difficult to follow. *Wealth* seems to be Aristophanes' answer to the problem, where he again employs two main characters but alternately throughout the play creating a curious see-saw pattern, which does, however, have the merit of permitting the introduction of a variety of new characters from scene to scene, two actors being constantly available. The two main characters, Cario and Chremylus appear together in the first scene, but thereafter they are never together again, only alternately. This immediately results in complete clarity in the play's construction and a continuing centre of focus for the action. Thus does Aristophanes add variety to his plot construction and within the confines of a probable three-actor rule attempts to maintain fluidity of movement in his play.

APPENDIX

THE DIVISION OF ROLES BETWEEN ACTORS

The following tables of the division of roles between the actors in the plays do not purport to be definitive, but merely a guide to what may have been the arrangements. Other schemes can be found in *PCF* pp. 149ff. and in Russo at the conclusion of each chapter. Most editions of the plays also set out schemes.

Acharnians
Actor I: Dicaeopolis.
Actor II: Herald (43–173), Daughter of Dicaeopolis (245–83),

Euripides (407–79), Lamachus (572–622), Megarian (729–835), Boeotian (860–954), Farmer (1018–36), *Paranymphos* 1048–57), Lamachus (1072–141, 1190–226).

Actor III: Amphitheos (45–55), Ambassador (65–110), Theorus (134–66), Amphitheos (175–203), Kephisophon (395–479), Sycophant (818–27), Nicarchus (910–28), Servant of Lamachus (959–70), Herald (1000–3), Messenger A (1071–7), Messenger B (1085–94), Servant of Lamachus (1174–89).

Extras with speaking parts: Pseudartabas (100–24), Amphitheos (129), Megarian's Daughters (729–835).

Mutes: Prytanies (40–173), Archers (54ff.), Ambassador (64ff.), Eunuchs (100–24), Odomantians (155–73), Dicaeopolis' wife? (245), Xanthias (259–83), Pipers (860–6), Slaves (887), Nicarchus (952–4), Ismenias (954), Slaves? (1004ff.), Bride (1057–68), Slaves (1095ff.), Girls (1200–34).

Knights

Actor I: Sausage-Seller (150–1401).

Actor II: Slave B (Nikias?) (1–154), Paphlagon (Kleon) (235–1252).

Actor III: Slave A (Demosthenes?) (1–497), Demus (728–1408).

Mutes: Slave (1385), Treaties? (1389).

Clouds

Actor I: Strepsiades (1–888) (1107–509), Right Logic (889–1104).

Actor II: Pheidippides (1–125), Disciple of Socrates (133–220), Pheidippides (816–1200), Amynias (1259–99), Pheidippides (1325–475), Disciple of Socrates? (1492ff.).

Actor III: Servant of Strepsiades (18, 56–8), Socrates (218–887, 1105–69), Pasias (1214–55), Socrates? (1492ff.), Wrong Logic (889–1104).

Extras with speaking parts: Witness (1246), Chaerephon (1492ff.).

Mutes: Students (184ff.), Astronomy & Geometry (201ff.), Xanthias (1485).

The state of the text, whether due to revision or corruption, makes the apportioning of the parts in the scene with the Logics and in the final scene difficult.

Wasps

Actor I: Bdelykleon.

Actor II: Slave A (Sosias) (1–138), Philokleon (144–1515).

Actor III: Slave B (Xanthias) (1–1008, 1292–325), *Artopolis* (1388–412), Xanthias (1474–515).

Extras with speaking parts: Fellow Drinker (1332–4), Complainant (1417–41).

Mutes: Three Attendants (433), Slaves (529), Dog Labes (899), Cur (901), Puppies (976), Grater (963), Flute-Girl (1333ff.), Three Dancers (1500ff.).

The part ascribed to Sosias in the *O.C.T.* is, in this scheme, attributed at some points to Xanthias but as both probably wore the same mask it is doubtful whether the audience would have been able to distinguish them.

Peace

Actor I: Trygaeus.

Actor II: Slave B (1–49), Hermes (180–233), *Kydoimos* (255–88), Hermes (362–726), Slave (824–1126), *Drepanourgos* (1197–206), Breastplate-Seller (1224–39), Son of Lamachus (1270–91).

Actor III: Slave A (1–113), *Polemos* (236–88), Hierocles (1052–119), Crest-Maker (1210–20), Helmet-Maker (1250–64).

Extras with speaking parts: Children of Trygaeus (114ff.), Trumpet-Maker (1240–9), Spearsman (1250–69), Child of Kleonymus? (1298–302).

Mutes: *Opora, Theoria* (528ff.).

Birds

Actor I: Peisthetairus.

Actor II: Euelpides (1–846), Priest (863–88), Oracle-Monger (959–90), *Episkopos* (1021–31), Messenger A (1122–63), Iris (1202–59), *Patraloias* (1337–71), Sycophant (1410–66), Prometheus (1494–551), Poseidon (1565–692).

Actor III: Servant of Hoopoe (60–84), Hoopoe (92–675), Poet (904–53), Meton (992–1019), Statute-Seller (1035–54), Messenger B (1170–85), Herald (1271–307), Kinesias (1372–409), Heracles (1574–692), Messenger (1706–19).

Extra actor with speaking part: Triballian (1565–693).

Mutes: Four Birds (267ff.), Two Servants (435), Two Servants (656), Slave (850), Flute-Player/Crow (861), Slave (1311).

Lysistrata

Actor I: Lysistrata (1–864, 1112–87, 1271–320).

Actor II: Kalonike (6–253), Magistrate (387–610), Woman A (727–34), Woman C (742–59), Kinesias (845–1013), Athenian Ambassador (1086–188), Athenian? (1216–95).

Actor III: Myrrhine (69–253), Woman A (439–603), Woman B (735–9, 760–2), Myrrhine (837–951), Spartan Herald (980–1013), Spartan Ambassador (1076–188), Athenian? (1216ff.).

Extra actors with speaking parts: Lampito (81–244), Woman (830–6).

Mutes: Slave (199), Archers (387ff.), Child (879), Slave (908), *Diallage*? (1114).

The difficulties of the scene 1215ff. make it impossible to assign the parts at this point.

Women at the Thesmophoria

Actor I: Mnesilochus.

Actor II: Euripides (1–279), Woman A (380–764), Euripides (871–1209) in various roles.

Actor III: Agathon's Servant (39–70), Agathon (101–265), Woman B (443–58), Kleisthenes (574–654), Woman C (760–935), Scythian Archer (1001–225).

Extra actor with speaking part: Prytanis (929–44).

Mutes: Slave (238), Thratta (279), Mania (727), Scythian Archer (929–46), Dancing Girl (1172ff.).

Frogs

Actor I: Dionysus.

Actor II: Xanthias (1–813), Aeschylus (830–1523).

Actor III: Heracles (38–164), Charon (180–270), Aeacus (464–78), Maid (503–21), *Pandokeutria* (549–78), Aeacus (605–813), Euripides (830–1481), Pluto (1500–33).

Extra actors with speaking parts: Corpse (173–80), Plathane (551–78), Pluto (830–1481).

Mutes: Corpse-Bearers (173–180), Three Servants of Aeacus (608), Muse of Euripides (1306).

Women in Assembly

Actor I: Praxagora (1–284), Man (327–56), Praxagora (504–727), Heraldess (834–52), Hag A (877–1044), Maid (1112–43).

Actor II: Woman A (30–284), Blepyrus (311–727), Man B (746–876), Young Girl (884–1042), Hag C (1065–97), Blepyrus (1129–83).

Actor III: Woman B (35–284), Chremes (372–476, 564–729, 730–871), Youth (938–1111).

Extras with speaking parts: Woman C (54–284)—3 speaking lines, Hag B (1049–95).

Mute: Slave (738).

Wealth

Actor I: Cario (1–321, 627–770, 802–958, 1097–170), Poverty (415–609), Wealth (771–99), Hag (959–1094, 1197–203).

Actor II: Chremylus (1–626, 771–801, 959–1096, 1172–209), Just Man (823–954), Hermes (1099–168).

Actor III: Wealth (1–251), Blepsidemus (335–623), Chremylus' Wife (641–769, 788–801), Sycophant (850–950), Young Man (1042–93), Priest (1171–96).

Mutes: Boy (823ff.), Friends (782).

CHAPTER VII

THE CHORUS

THE DEVELOPMENT OF THE CHORUS[1]

The last two surviving plays of Aristophanes illustrate a decline in his use of the chorus as an integral part of the play. In *Women in Assembly* the play still takes its name from the chorus, and they still sing songs of interest, but already the practice has begun of introducing choral interludes not written specifically for the play, and in *Wealth* we have only a simple *parodos* and a section of dochmiacs to greet Wealth's return of sight. The evidence of New Comedy on this is clear: the chorus has disappeared from the action and is retained only for breaks, often simply playing the part of revellers—a reversion to the probable origin of the comic chorus in the *komos*. [2]

The reasons for this sudden decline—sudden in the sense that the *Frogs*, with the *Birds*, is the most metrically complex of all the plays yet closest in date to *Women in Assembly*—are debatable, though in some respects parallel to the similar decline in tragedy. Plainly the scholiasts recognized a break in the comic tradition at the end of the Peloponnesian War and in accordance with it divided Middle Comedy from Old, and though the chorus itself continued, even if depleted, it had lost its integral part in the play.[3] This break in tradition is chiefly attributed to a change in the audience's attitude towards the state and politics, the result, no doubt, of war-weariness and disillusionment, which caused the playwrights to turn to more social and economic themes and thence to more realistic social settings, culminating in the comedies of Menander.[4] Just as in tragedy the chorus, unsuited as a body to taking genuine part in the action, constituted a stumbling block to poets reaching out to realism, so in comedy its death-knell was sounded by the move away from fantasy. Also, as Webster points out,[5] many of Aristophanes' most exciting lyric effects are achieved in parodying Euripides, and his death and the consequent loss of this challenge may be partly responsible for the metric poverty of the new plays. But this decline of the chorus is in a sense merely the final round of a conflict which begins with Aristophanes' attempt to make more dramatic the triadic form which, it is assumed, provided the basic elements of comedy: *parodos, agon, parabasis.*[6]

Of this triad the *parabasis*, probably the conclusion of the original *komos*, was the least realistic element Aristophanes had to contend with, since here the chorus threw off whatever identity it had assumed and addressed the audience on matters having little to do with the plot but much with politics and politicians. In the first five of Aristophanes' plays the anapaests introducing this section concern a defence of the poet against the criticisms, or supposed criticisms, of his audience, and as such are completely divorced from the action. However, in the subsequent parts of the *parabasis*, notably *epirrhema* and *antepirrhema*, the chorus generally returns to its stage character, at least in part. Not until the *Birds* and the plays following it is there any real attempt to incorporate the *parabasis* within the structure by making the chorus speak in character throughout. In *Lysistrata* the chorus consists of two groups, the old men and the women, who are in conflict throughout the first half of the play. Their differences are finally composed at 1014ff. and the *parabasis*, though unusual in form—a series of threats uttered by both sides—is included within the action and dramatic logic preserved. Similarly the women of *Women at the Thesmophoria* are still speaking in character while they deliver a shortened form of the *parabasis*; but in the *Frogs*, the last play with a full complement of choral odes, the chorus of Mystae, while paying lip-service to their character at the beginning of the *parabasis*, mostly revert to the older type with their political advice and satire of obnoxious politicians. It was this *parabasis* (so we are told) which led to the play's being produced a second time. The two latest plays show no trace of a *parabasis*, which presumably indicates that the poet found it no longer necessary or even acceptable in the type of play he was concerned to write. The second *parabasis*, found in *Knights, Clouds, Wasps, Peace,* and *Birds*, undergoes a similar change. In the first three, the subject of the song is entirely independent of the plot, but in *Peace* the farmers who form the chorus sing of the joys of farming and country life, while in *Birds*, apart from a short address to the judges a similar dramatic consistency is evident. It seems clear that the poet is striving to unify the second *parabasis* with the rest of the play, yet, though partially successful in his attempt, after *Birds* he drops the second *parabasis* completely and never returns to it.

We noted above that the *parabasis* originally marked the completion of the action, and the *Acharnians*, *Wasps*, and *Peace* appear to take this form, their main business being completed before the *parabasis* and the remainder of the play consisting of loosely connected incidents, illustrating the results of the decision reached before the *parabasis*. In this, too, development is found in the later plays. The second half of *Birds* is more closely bonded to the first, but the basic earlier pattern is repeated. Subsequent plays, however, and the earlier *Knights* and *Clouds*, show the poet trying to make his work an entity by abandoning the conclusion that precedes the *parabasis*. In this attempt too the *parabasis* was doomed: originally its delivery was one of the most important functions of the chorus, marking the completion of the play's main theme, but with the expansion of that theme to cover the whole of the drama its place in the drama disappeared and it is hardly surprising that in *Women in Assembly* and *Wealth* no trace remains. The decline of the *parabasis* reflects the decline of the chorus.

The reduction of the chorus' participation in the action is particularly significant in the light of the survival of the word XOPOY in manuscripts of the last two plays of Aristophanes.[7] It is tempting to connect the apparent abandoning of separate choral odes with Aristotle's statement (*Poetics* 1456a 29) that Agathon and, following him, later poets wrote choral songs not pertinent to any particular play but mere interludes (*embolima*) readily transferable from play to play. Several fragments of late tragedy tend to confirm this statement.[8] Flickinger assumes from this that Agathon wrote no odes for his plays at all, but the assumption is unnecessary and partly, at least, controverted by Aristophanes' parody of Agathon's odes in *Women at the Thesmophoria* 101ff. Whether the aim of this parody was to demonstrate the small weight attached to Agathon's verses or to demonstrate metrical and musical liberty is uncertain, but it proves that at this stage of his life he was writing odes which were presumably well-enough known to be parodied. The ode itself is a rather individual type of lyric dialogue between a female character and a chorus, and not therefore one that could be readily transferred from play to play—a practice which Aristophanes might have been expected to comment on if it were new and strange. It seems best to assume that *embolima* were not in use as early as this, and that if Aristotle is correct they were a development of Agathon's later years.[9] Their introduction clearly implies that the chorus is losing any influential part in the action and becoming merely a 'divertissement', a trend evident in *Women in Assembly* and *Wealth*, where choral influence is minor, confined to support of the main character without any decisive influence on the plot.

The earlier plays show the chorus in a far more forceful light, usually in opposition to one or more of the main characters. The plot of the *Acharnians* turns on the opposition between the chorus and Dicaeopolis until the former are won over; in the *Wasps*, the chorus support Philokleon against Bdelykleon, and it is they who are first persuaded by the latter's arguments and urge Philokleon to join in believing him; similarly the Birds oppose Peisthetairus and Euelpides until won over, while the *Women at the Thesmophoria* stands close to the *Acharnians*, with the chorus of women engaged in a vendetta with Euripides and hence Mnesilochus, only resolved at the end of the play when Euripides makes his peace with them and rescues his kinsman. In all these the chorus are actively concerned in promoting or hindering the plot and have a strong interest in the outcome; they display a similar interest in the *Lysistrata*, where the fortunes of the two semi-choruses both reflect and emphasize the fortunes of the actors until agreement is reached (1014ff.); in the *Knights*, where their support of the Sausage-Seller is counterbalanced by their active dislike of Kleon, and in the *Peace* where they are opposed to war. The later plays, however, are clear illustrations of how, when the chorus has no opposition to contend with, they simply become supporters of the main character. In the *Women in Assembly* the chorus enter as supporters of Praxagora, listen to her speech, follow her obediently to the Assembly, and later return with her. At this point XOPOY appears in the manuscripts, but it is plain that the chorus can have no influence on what follows, and are cyphers following Praxagora's lead, present merely to echo her views. Midway we have the *Frogs* with its two choruses: the Frogs themselves lean to the earlier type, indulging in a battle with Dionysus, but the Mystae, while they sing some beautiful lyrics, seem to be introduced mainly to set the scene as the Underworld, without having any vital connexion with the drama. *Wealth*, in so far as we can judge, follows *Women in Assembly*, with the chorus as no more than friends and supporters of Chremylus. These two plays would suggest that plural titles in Middle Comedy (of which there are a number) need not imply any important role for the chorus in the play.

The relatively tiny part played by the chorus in iambic dialogue with the actors on the other hand, seems to increase, especially in one scene in *Wealth* where Cario leads in the chorus (257ff.) and carries on a dialogue with them in iambic trimeters. In much the same way the Wasps converse with their sons (*Wasps* 230ff.) and the semi-chorus of men and women abuse each other in the *Lysistrata* (467ff.). In these two examples, however, the dialogue takes place within the chorus; *Wealth* is unique in sending an actor to summon the chorus and then introducing a long conversation between that character and the *coryphaeus*—presumably the individual rather than the whole group. Conversation between actor and chorus is, of course, usual, often as a device for an actor to tell his story, but the length of this passage makes it exceptional. Other incidental conversation between chorus and actors is, as I have indicated, of a very limited nature, consisting normally of encouragement to a character about to face some test, and cannot be considered to have any real bearing on the status of the chorus within the play.

SIZE AND ARRANGEMENT OF THE CHORUS

The ancient authorities are, for once, unanimous in maintaining that a comic chorus consisted of twenty-four members,[10] though it seems that later, at the Delphic Soteria the number declined

to as few as seven. Confirmation of the former number is found
in a scene in the *Birds* where the chorus of Birds are introduced
singly,[11] and, if the four birds who appear before the actual
chorus are excluded, the number corresponds exactly with the
scholiast's calculations. The scholiast on *Knights* 589 adds the
information that when the chorus was composed of men and
women, the man outnumbered the women by thirteen to
eleven, while if women and boys or slaves, the women outnumbered the rest by the same margin. It has been suggested
that this strange piece of information can be made to tally with
the scene in the *Birds* if the bird names with masculine and
feminine endings are taken as representing the sex of the actual
birds.[12] If so, the point would have been lost on the audience,
for choruses in comedy evidently did not wear the phallus (as
Blake assumes that they did). Against the hypothesis of unequal
numbers the strongest argument is the *Lysistrata* with its two
semi-choruses. The women douse the men with their buckets of
water, and later remove a gnat from the men's eyes, and such
activities surely presuppose equal numbers on either side rather
than two men too many. Perhaps unequal division would have
been possible in the case of what appears to have been a mixed
chorus, namely the Mystae in the *Frogs*,[13] but there is no cogent
reason for conjecturing it.

The chorus normally entered in almost military formation,
its members drawn up in a rectangle, six in length, four in
depth, with the lines of best dancers nearest the audience.[14]
This was the standard entrance, but the variations were many:
the chorus in Aristophanes sometimes rush in—the Acharnians
burst into the orchestra in their search for Dicaeopolis, so do
the Knights—sometimes enter in no particular order apparently,
as in *Women in Assembly*. The Birds too are seen to crowd into the
parodos (295/6) but are then introduced singly. An exception is
the *Clouds*, where their performance begins behind the *skene*
before they march in, while, if the scholiast is to be believed, the
Frogs never appear at all.

The flute-player would lead the chorus into the orchestra and
then take his stand by the *Thymele* in the centre of the dancing
area. Quite what happened when two semi-choruses entered
separately, as in the *Lysistrata*, or when the chorus rushed in, is

not clear. A single flute-player was the normal provision, and works of art never depict more, nor do the grammarians—or the cost involved—suggest the likelihood of extra players. The *Birds*, however, creates a special problem[15] where the flute-player is required to perform in imitation of the nightingale during the summoning of the birds by the Hoopoe, before the chorus appears (*Birds* 209ff., 227ff.).[16] The summons finished, the Hoopoe watches the Birds' arrival. First come the four special birds mentioned above, whose function is not clear but who are distinct from the twenty-four seen crowding the *parodos*. It has been suggested by Blake that they were musicians, perhaps harpists, to supplement the flute-player, but we may question why four should be necessary, and at what cost: an alternative suggestion that they were speciality dancers[17] would be strange if true, since the already unusual procedure for the introduction of the birds and the oddity of their costumes hardly requires further titivation. The chorus of Birds is subsequently introduced one by one, but with no mention of the flute-player. His presence may have been taken for granted by the audience and would not therefore require comment by the poet, especially if he wore his normal costume rather than a bird's, but it may be that he was already present. The four extra birds remain a mystery.

During the action of the play the chorus stood with its back to the audience facing the actors,[18] and thus in a position to announce the arrival of actors from one of the *parodoi* or through the central door. Before the *parabasis*, however, they turned to face the audience, and it is interesting to note how often a short introduction, sometimes delivered by the *coryphaeus*, precedes the *parabasis*, presumably to allow the chorus to take up its position.[19] It seems to have been usual at this point for the chorus to split into two halves, and during the epirrhematic parts of that piece to turn to face the audience. Partial removal of their clothing or discarding of equipment further suggests that lively dancing may well have accompanied this section of the play.

Though the chorus could employ song, recitative and speech, it is not certain that all of them necessarily joined in all the different forms. When they took part in dialogue the *coryphaeus* presumably spoke the lines, but the amount of solo speaking he undertook cannot be accurately gauged—certainly much of his time must have been taken up in organizing the chorus, leading the dancing and in all probability giving the flute-player his cues for beginning the musical accompaniment. Haigh[20] maintains that all the anapaestic tetrameters were spoken by him, including the speech at the beginning of the *parabasis* and also speeches like the one inserted in the middle of the *parodos* in the *Frogs*; he similarly claims for the two *coryphaei* the conducting of the conversations between the semi-choruses of men and women in the *Lysistrata*. Certainty is impossible without further evidence, and his conclusions, while possible, must remain hypothetical.

As the entrance of the chorus could be managed in a variety of ways, so also their *exodos*:[21] sometimes the choreuts march out, as in the *Acharnians* and *Clouds*, often preceded by an actor; sometimes a more vigorous ending is achieved by a danced finale, as in *Wasps*, *Lysistrata*, and *Women in Assembly*—the two latter calling for special dancers as well. Only in *Ass.* 310 is there a hiatus in the chorus' part, when they leave the orchestra to return later (478) ostensibly from the Assembly.[22]

The nature of the dances used to bring the play to its end, and indeed of all the dances employed in the plays, and their relationship to the metre of the verse remains unsolved. Perhaps the best-known dance associated with comedy was the *kordax*. It had a reputation for obscenity, and consequently Aristophanes renounced its use in *Clouds* 540, but the scholiast there is quick to point out (with what evidence is not known) that this did not prevent him from using it elsewhere. The dance at the end of the *Wasps* (1482–537) has been suggested as an example, and its description conforms well with a vase at Corneto in Italy said to illustrate the *kordax*.[23] An interesting round dance is found in *Thesm.* 953ff., where the characteristically rectangular formation which distinguishes tragedy and comedy from the circular dithyramb seems to be discarded. Attempts have been made, notably by Miss Lawler, to identify other dances and the sort of steps involved, but the dimness of our vision of the actual dances still clouds our knowledge of Aristophanes' chorus.[24] The question of dancing during the action, as opposed to during the odes, is raised by the scholiast in R on *Frogs* 897, who mentions ἡ πρὸς τὰς ῥήσεις ὑπόρχησις and supported by a scholiast's remarks on the quarrel scene between Strepsiades and Pheidippides (*Clouds* 1353), that the chorus danced in imitation of the quarrel. The comments may, however, be merely a guess to explain the phrase πρὸς χόρον λέγειν. Dancing during the action would certainly have distracted the audience, but the possibility cannot be ruled out. Vigorous dancing required freedom of movement and there are a number of consequent references to the removal of clothing or putting down of equipment before the dance begins.[25] Most frequently this implies the removal of the *himation*, as in *Ach.* 627, though here, unlike the *Wasps*, there is no indication of what happens to the garments: in the *Wasps* the boys who accompany the chorus run off with the clothes and thus clear the orchestra.[26]

SUBSIDIARY CHORUSES AND SPECIAL DANCERS

Responsibility for providing extra choruses seems to have rested on the *choregos*. The supply was therefore dependent upon his generosity, and as far as he was concerned a few speciality dancers were probably cheaper to provide.[27] Nevertheless the *Wasps* boasts a second chorus of boys, who escort their fathers to the law courts carrying lanterns. Their presence gives the chorus an excuse for conversation and an opportunity to display their poverty, but at 408 the boys are ordered off to fetch Kleon, and never reappear; their part is small and apparently calls for little spectacular effect of either dress or dancing. The chorus of Frogs is a somewhat special case. It is possible that they never actually appear and that their lines are sung by the normal chorus, or that if they do appear the normal chorus double their part and change their costumes in the forty lines separating their departure as Frogs from their arrival as Mystae. In the *Lysistrata*, an extra chorus of Lacedaemonians who come from the party that Lysistrata has been holding may be present during the final scene, though as Webster[28] points out the two semichoruses of the ordinary chorus, rearranged so that men and women alternate, could have carried this out satisfactorily; while Lysistrata's final comment to the Laconian to sing is, despite the manuscript tradition, obviously singular. The text is confusing and certainty impossible.

Special dancers and singers are usually introduced towards the end of the play, presumably to add variety and leave a vivid impression in the minds of the judges and audience. The only exception to this is the four birds who precede the chorus in the *Birds*. In *Peace* 1270ff. the sons of Kleonymus and Lamachus are introduced in the final scene to sing for Trygaeus, but the results are so distasteful to him that he brusquely dismisses them. In *Wasps* 1500ff. two dancers are again introduced, this time as the sons of Karkinus, and as the actors depart the chorus draws aside to allow the two to dance in the orchestra before following them out dancing.[29] A female dancing-girl performs in the final scene of the *Women at the Thesmophoria* to distract the attention of the Scythian Archer who is guarding Mnesilochus; in the *Women in Assembly* the *meirakes* in the last scene may well be extras, though Roos has persuasively argued that they are members of the chorus.[30] Whatever the correct interpretation, special dancers are once more used to enliven the last scenes of the play. Their use at this point may also be an indication of their relevance to the plot, since they could be easily written out without damaging the plot if the *choregos* refused to pay for them.[31]

During the final quarter of the fifth century B.C. the influence of the chorus on the play's success must have been considerable, and it is unfortunate that our appreciation of its part is so limited, deprived as we are of almost all knowledge of the music and dancing, the pattern and gesture that accompanied the performance. The importance that Aristophanes attached to the chorus' part is apparent from his refusal in his earlier years to be κωμῳδοδιδάσκαλος (*Knights* 516).

CHAPTER VIII

COSTUME IN OLD COMEDY

The ancient descriptions of comic dress, based largely on Pollux IV, 115ff., are mainly of late authorship and of doubtful application to Old Comedy: it is the texts of the plays, the vases and terracottas that are the best guide to what was worn, though always with the proviso that the artist is not a photographer and tends to interpret what he sees on the stage. The terracottas, perhaps, are less prone to this fault, seeming to portray characters as they actually appeared.

The most controversial subject in the field has been the actors wearing of padding and the phallus. The commonly held view, that the phallus was normal in comedy, which is borne out by the monuments, was attacked by Beare and others on the strength of the passage in *Clouds* 537ff. where Aristophanes claims to have banished it from his play.[1] Beare argued that the references to the phallus in the plays could refer to the actor's own body, but as Webster has pointed out the actor's 'skin' was a pair of close-fitting tights—the wrinkles at the joints visible on vases and terracottas are ample evidence of this—which by themselves were ambiguous and it was the wearing of the phallus that distinguished the actor's sex. The phallus is also, of course, the symbol of Dionysus. As women the actors probably wore white tights and padded breasts. On this assumption we should not share Beare's surprise that when Mnesilochus is stripped of his feminine disguise his phallus comes to light (*Thesm.* 643ff.), nor that when Praxagora and her women dress as men they do not wear the phallus, for this would distinguish them as actual men rather than women dressed as men. As regards the visibility of the phallus, mention of it does not necessarily mean that it is visible but some scenes seem to require it, as for example *Wasps* 1343, where it is assumed that Philokleon offers his phallus to the flute-girl as he climbs on to the stage, and *Lysistrata* 987ff.

with its double talk on Spartan letter sticks. For much of the time, however, it probably remained hidden beneath the cloak.

The main weight of Beare's argument, however, rests on the passage from the *Clouds* 537ff. which he accepts at its face value as a refusal to lower the tone of the comedy by introducing actors wearing the phallus. Webster, on the other hand, following Korte and Wilamowitz, argued that the line's emphasis was on καθειμένον and that Aristophanes was claiming his actors appeared with their phalli tied up—both positions are illustrated on an oenochoe in Leningrad (*PV* Ph 6)—and that the hanging phallus was the symbol of a sexually dissipated life. But the question must be raised how far Aristophanes can here be trusted in his statements. Later in this passage he claims to have eliminated a number of items from the play, but editors have been quick to point out that the text belies this claim. Conceivably the contradiction arose through two editions of the *Clouds*, our present one being an incomplete revision of the first (certainly the remarks about the phallus and the other criticisms belong to the second edition), but as the text stands the play opens with Strepsiades bemoaning his lot and ends with Xanthias running on to burn down the Reflectory, practices which Aristophanes expressly claims to condemn and to highmindedly dismiss from his plays (543). The editors have naturally sought to absolve him from a charge of inconsistency, with little success. The inconsistency is patent, but, be it noted, introduction of the actor with the flaming torch and so on is kept to the end of the play, and by then Aristophanes has already planted the suggestion in his judge's minds that such is only the practice of his inferior adversaries. It is quite possible then, that in claiming to have excluded the phallus, Aristophanes is concerned only to score a point off his fellow competitors, and would have been highly surprised to see the present-day results of his claim. On the other hand it would have been difficult for him to make the claim if the phallus had been very much in evidence up to this point in the play, but the text seems to indicate that it had not. There are no references to the phallus before the *parabasis*, and though later two do occur (653, 734) even here it is not necessary to assume that the phallus was visible. Possibly, then, during the first half of the play the phalli were covered and even tied up as well, so that Aristophanes could plausibly claim that he had excised this element from his comedy. The play, however, was a failure, and it may be that the cause of this was his attempt to remove some of the grosser elements and substitute wit instead. Certainly in the *Frogs*, where a similar attempt is made, the poet seems to prepare the way for the omission of vulgar buffoonery in the second half by the actions of the first, and by his remarks at 1109ff. where he compliments the audience on their sophistication by speaking encouragingly of their aptitude for the finer points of poetic style. The failure of the *Clouds* may well have taught Aristophanes what it was profitable to omit and what it was not. We do not have to believe him, however, in any general sense when he claims to have left out the phallus; the remaining plays strongly suggest its use, and without it a number of scenes become inexplicable, while the evidence of vases and terracottas provides ample support for its use.

References to the wearing of padding tend by contrast to be obscure. The description of Dionysus as γάστρων (*Frogs* 200) is probably a hit at his padded stomach, and a remark from the *Clouds* (1238) that Pasias would hold six *choes* is no doubt to be interpreted in the same way. A fragment of Euboulus (30K) tells of Dolon who was so fat he could hardly tie his shoe-laces and Antiphanes (frag. 19K) mentions a man whom his neighbours called 'Wine-skin'. The terracottas provide corroborative evidence for the texts depicting huge swelling stomachs on both male and female figures. Through the later monuments can be traced a gradual movement towards decency in actor dress which culminates in the disappearance of both padding and phallus, possibly due to the moral legislation passed by Demetrius of Phalerum in 317 B.C. Certainly the change to decency is complete in the scenes of New Comedy, though Diphilus in his play that was an ancestor of Plautus' *The Rope* seems to have transmitted a reference to the phallus (*Rope* 429). As there is no trace of the movement towards decency in the monuments contemporaneous with Aristophanes, we must assume that it gained its impetus during the time of Middle Comedy or later.

We are given a highly complex and detailed description of the remainder of the actor's costume by Pollux, but his designations are too stylized for Old Comedy where costume seems to have followed the fashions of the day; once again the plays and the monuments must furnish the evidence. Indeed two parallel scenes in Aristophanes, *Thesm.* 249ff. in which Mnesilochus dresses as a woman, and *Ass.* 73ff. where Praxagora dresses as a man, provide probably the most important evidence for Greek dress in general in the fifth century, and certainly the most detailed evidence for the theatrical costume worn over the tights.

The *chitōn* was an undergarment worn by both men and women though the feminine garment is frequently described by the diminutive *chitōnion*. In fact the male *chitōn* was generally shorter than its feminine counterpart, as is evident from *Ass.* 268 where the women have to tuck up their *chitōnes* to appear as men, but the terracottas show that the male *chitōn* could also be long, particularly in the case of well-to-do elderly gentlemen. The female version was usually made of flax, if this is the correct interpretation of *Lys.* 150, and was often diaphanous (*Lys.* 48, 150) while *Frogs* 1067 describes the man's garment as woollen. It normally had two arm holes (cf. the *exōmis*) (*Knights* 882 cf. Plato Com. 229K) and was the usual male dress for the house, as shown by Dicaeopolis' demand for his *himation* when invited out to dinner (*Ach.* 1139).[2] A variation on the *chitōn* but worn off the shoulder since it had only a single arm hole was the *exōmis*, primarily a short working tunic with a girdle round the waist, and well illustrated in a bronze of a slave carrying dishes (*MOMC* AB1). The semi-chorus of men in the *Lysistrata* wear this (662), but remove it to allow themselves greater freedom of movement. The authors of the *Greek Lexicon* quote Aristophanes frag. 8 for its use by women, but there is neither reason to suppose that this fragment does refer to a woman nor any other supporting evidence for the statement.

The normal outer garment was the *himation*, again common to both sexes, and in a variety of colours (*Wealth* 530). It consisted of a single rectangular piece of woollen cloth draped round the body with the end thrown over the right shoulder, hence the disdainful remark directed at the Triballian (*Birds*

1567) for wearing it over his left shoulder. It may have been fairly expensive, but the price of twenty drachmae quoted by the Young Man to the Hag (*Wealth* 982) is probably inflated.[3] *Ass.* 535ff. suggests a difference between the male and female *himation*; presumably the male garment was thicker for Blepyrus' wife takes her husband's and leaves her own as a blanket for him, claiming in excuse that it was cold and she is frail, while in *Thesm.* 250 Agathon is asked to provide an *himation* when Mnesilochus dresses as a woman, even though the latter has just taken off his own (214).[4] Descended from the *himation* were a series of cloaks, mainly worn by men. The *tribōn*, a poor man's cloak, coarse and small and usually worn without a *chitōn*, was much favoured by philosophers, hence the pun in *Clouds* 870. Doubtless Socrates and his pupils were so attired, and Cario, the poor slave of Chremylus, claims to have seen through the holes in his in the temple of Asclepias (*Wealth* 714).[5] The well-dressed counterpart was the woollen *chlaina* (*Birds* 493, *Lys.* 586) primarily a winter garment if the plays are to be believed (*Birds* 1090, *Ass.* 416) worn loose over the *chitōn* and specifically masculine (*Thesm.* 142).[6] It is coupled in the texts (*Wasps* 738) with three other cloaks, the *sisura* made of goat's hair, which could be used as a blanket (*Lys.* 933), the *kaunakes* and the *sagma*, thick and of Persian origin (*Wasps* 1137), the *sagma*, of soft wool woven in Ecbatana (*Wasps* 1142) being large and luxurious.[7] Another type, the *chlamys*, was worn by soldiers and horsemen and is specifically mentioned as the dress of the Spartan Herald (*Lys.* 987).[8]

A particularly fine and fashionable form of the *himation*, used primarily on festive occasions (*Birds* 1693, frag. 491 cf. Men. *Dysk.* 257, frag. 303 Körte), was the *chlanis* made of wool and often striped. It was probably large, as frag. 54 reports someone as making three cloaks from a single *chlanis*, though Edmonds maintains that the reference is to skimping on material, as the poet is claiming a rival has made three plays out of one of his plots. In the same luxury bracket is the *xustis*, a garment of some antiquity falling out of fashion at the end of the fifth century and mainly in ceremonial use. It is ascribed to Megacles in the *Clouds* 70.[9] At the other end of the scale we have the countryman dressed in skins. In *Birds* 933 a slave wears the *spolas* or jerkin

over his *chitōn*: to wear it *without* the *chitōn* was apparently a
mark of barbarity and one assigned to Straton living among the
Scythians (*Birds* 944). The *diphthera* too is clearly a countryman's dress, probably no more than a hide or sheepskin drawn
round his shoulders. The terracottas afford no clear example of
these costumes, but a number illustrate a *chitōn* with dots on the
surface, which may be an attempt to indicate the texture of
leather.[10]

Many of these garments, as has been noted, were common to
both men and women though generally with some difference in
style. There were, however, a number which were the sole
preserve of women. The *krokōtos*, a saffron-coloured undergarment, was the equivalent of the *chitōn*, worn beneath the
himation and in evidence on the majority of terracottas that
represent women, though the colour no longer remains. As
might be expected it is the first garment that Mnesilochus puts
on when he is dressing as a woman (*Thesm.* 253), and that
Praxagora leaves off when dressing as a man (*Ass.* 332). Dionysus wears the same garment beneath his lion skin (*Frogs* 46ff.)
and it was his normal outfit: nevertheless Aristophanes chooses
to exploit its feminine connexions by having Heracles guffaw
with laughter at the sight of Dionysus in lion skin and 'petticoat'
at his door.

The *peplos*, like the *xustis*, had by the end of the fifth century
B.C. dropped out of fashion and is not mentioned in the plays as
an article of dress; its place was taken by the linen tunic. One
form of this, the *orthostadion*, was ungirdled, its pleats hanging
straight down to the floor, and is referred to as Cimmerian, a
term seemingly explained by Lysistrata's reference to diaphanous *chitōnes* (*Lys.* 45, 48). As the tunic was not as warm as the
peplos a variety of wraps were worn over it, one of which, the
engkuklon, is donned by Mnesilochus as he goes to the assembly
of women.[11] It is in fact the equivalent of the male *himation*,
though not so warm (*Ass.* 536). A number of minor items of
attire are mentioned: the *strophion*, a girdle or headband, is worn
by Mnesilochus in the latter form along with the *kekruphalos*, or
hair net (*Thesm.* 257): Lysistrata has a veil or *kalumma* (*Lys.*
530) which she ties on the *Proboulos*.[12]

Such is the variety of costume that would be seen on the

stage, though doubtless there were other variations on the main items. Little attention is given in the plays to headgear, but the terracottas have many examples of the *pilos* or conical felt hat that was especially popular with travellers, and the wide-brimmed hat, the *petasos*, favoured alike by young men-about-town and countrymen. Though it is not mentioned by Aristophanes, his characters must doubtless be imagined wearing it. He is more explicit over footwear. The older men of Athens seem to have favoured the *embas*, or felt shoe. Philo-kleon wears them (*Wasps* 103, 275, 447) so does Strepsiades (*Clouds* 719, 858), but the youth of the day considered them old-fashioned and so Bdelykleon forces his father, after his decision to change his way of life, to take them off and substitute the fashionable Laconian shoes (*Wasps* 1158). The latter were of red felt and seemingly restricted to men, hence Mnesilochus' remark that if Agathon had them they would be among the things that would prove his masculinity (*Thesm.* 142).[13] Praxagora and her friends take their husband's 'Laconians' when they go to the Assembly, and Blepyrus is left his wife's 'little Persian slippers'. For stronger shoes there was a variety of sandals. The Young Man in the *Wealth* claims to have paid eight drachmae for a pair, but this may be somewhat exaggera-ted, while the Oracle Monger (*Birds* 973) on the strength of his oracle claims a new *himation* and a pair of *pedila*. Sandals were presumably the normal footwear of labourers and travellers.

In tragedy the normal footwear was the *cothurnos*, a high boot with a thin sole. Because of its association with that art Dionysus wears it in the *Frogs* (47, 557), and perhaps other tragic charac-ters in comedy did too. The same boot was the normal footwear for women, as the semi-chorus of women in the *Lysistrata* demon-strates, and it is this unfortunate association again that provokes Heracles' laughter when Dionysus knocks at his door.

The everyday characters who appear in the play must, then, be imagined as dressed in the garments described above. How-ever, there are a large number who do not conform to that category, such as characters connected with tragedy, the gods and so on. Presumably characters connected with tragedy wore the normal tragic actor's dress, the long-sleeved *chitōn* and flowing *himation*—the dignified dress that Aeschylus is credited with introducing (*Frogs* 1061ff.), and Euripides on occasion with abandoning to introduce his heroes in rags.[14] Euripides himself probably appeared in Aristophanes in tragic dress, hence the Scythian Archer's mistaking him for a woman (*Thesm.* 1194) since tragic *himation* and contemporary female fashion were similar. Certainly the audience must have been able to see the point of the mistake.

As regards the gods, it seems unlikely that either their dress or their masks differed from those of men, yet it is also true that frequently the audience is expected to identify a certain god without any direct reference. The number of gods whom Aristophanes thus introduces seems limited, but among them is Hermes. In the *Peace* 180ff. Hermes appears on stage, informs Trygaeus of the whereabouts of Zeus, and departs (233) without divulging his name. He reappears at 361 just as Trygaeus and the chorus are about to rescue Peace, and is addressed by the former in a manner which implies that the audience has already recognized him. The obvious assumption is that the characteristic garb Hermes displays on vases[15] with winged boots, *petasos* slung around his neck and *caduceus* in hand, was paralleled in the theatre and hence instantly recognizable. Poseidon is similarly treated. In the *Birds* 1565 he enters with Heracles and the Triballian. Heracles is identified at 1574; the audience has already been prepared for the arrival of the Triballian, whom it is doubtful whether they could have identified without some aid, but Poseidon is not named until 1638. However, the joke at 1614 where he swears by himself requires his identification before this point, and as his best known attribute is the trident it is possible that he carries this with him to provide the audience with the information it requires.

Heracles stands rather outside this category because he alone of the gods or demi-gods appears to have a special mask, as well as his characteristic lion-skin dress and club which would make identification easy. So in *Frogs* 38ff., where he answers Dionysus' knock he must have been recognizable though he is never actually named. When Dionysus appears dressed as Heracles (*Frogs* 22), however, he has to name himself to avoid confusing the audience in precisely the way he later confuses all the inhabitants of the Underworld (605ff.). The same play poses

the problem of identifying Pluto. I have already argued[16] that
he must have been present throughout the contest between the
poets, thus enabling the audience to recognize him when he
speaks. His identification from the beginning of the scene (given
the hint in 784) probably depended on the presence of a throne,
and possibly also his carrying a sceptre and wearing a crown, as
illustrated on an oenochoe in Leningrad (*PV* Ph 6).

Finally there is the arrival of Iris in the *Birds*. At 1170 a
messenger informs the audience that a god has flown over the
city walls, and at 1175 Peisthetairus reports that the god is a
male. At 1197 the audience gathers that a winged god is
coming, whereupon Iris appears and is asked who she is, a boat
or a hat. In reply she names herself. Editors seem agreed that
the reference to boat or hat is a pun on her long flowing head-
dress, but was this part of the normal insignia or merely introduced for the joke? On vases Iris normally has wings and wears
a cap but there is no trace of a head-dress[17] and it is probably
better not to see any trace of a recognizable insignia.

One further group, the special choruses and the flute-player,
remains to be discussed. The chorus as a whole, it seems from
vases and sculptural evidence, did not wear the phallus
(*MOMC* AS 3, AS 4, *PV* Ph 9), but this excepted, their dress as
a human chorus seems to have been identical with that of the
actors. Aristophanes criticizes the dress in which the older poets
had introduced their choruses (frag. 253, cf. Pherecrates frag.
185K) but this may be nothing more than a convenient way of
scoring off his opponents since it appears to have no factual
basis. In the case of the Bird, Wasp and Frog choruses, available
evidence is slight. Two Attic black-figure vases, one showing
dancers dressed as birds, wearing bird-like costumes with wings
and what appears to be feathers sewn on their *chitōnes*, the other
depicting men dressed as cocks wearing cock masks and long
himatia, give some indication of how the bird chorus may have
looked,[18] though in Aristophanes' play each member of the
chorus is identified as a different bird and is therefore presumably distinguished in some way. The text implies that the
most important feature in their description is the crest and
therefore the mask (*Birds* 291), and possibly the rest of their
clothing was not individually differentiated, though the second

Hoopoe is described as moulting and having his feathers plucked out (284). The costume of the Wasps largely depends on the reading to be followed in *Wasps* 408. The manuscripts read λαβόντες, a reading accepted by McDowell in his recent edition of the play, which implies the Wasps take off their *himatia* and hand them to their accompanying chorus of boys, and the scholiast's note makes it clear that this was the text he read. Brunck was the first to introduce βαλόντες, which appears above the line in MS. B, and he has been followed by the majority of scholars, his interpretation of the passage being that the boys are to throw off their *himatia* and run off to Kleon for help. The original reading, however, gets rid of the awkwardness of the chorus having to re-drape their garments when they have finished: they simply give them to the boys who run off with them, just as in the *Peace* the chorus get rid of the ropes before singing the *parabasis*. Probably the Wasps were dressed in yellow striped *himatia*, wore special masks and had stings attached to their tights. The Frogs, if they actually appeared, were no doubt dressed in the 'frog green' that the poet attributes to Manes (*Knights* 523), probably the normal tights dyed green. A chorus of Knights appears on a black-figure vase in Berlin,[19] where they ride on the shoulders of men disguised as horses, a position which they could hardly have maintained throughout the play. Possibly *Knights* 595ff. is to be taken as an indication that some of the chorus are dressed as horses but the rest of the play makes it more plausible to suppose that the chorus merely walked on, wearing a similar helmet and corslet to those on the vase.

The flute-player's dress is not mentioned in comedy, but the vases indicate his costume as the long elaborately patterned *chitōn* with sleeves, such as might be expected for a person of standing and wealth. Occasionally, however, vases show the flute-player in the same costume as the chorus, and if the nightingale in the *Birds* was played by the flute-player then in this instance he presumably adopted a bird costume.[20]

The foregoing account makes it plain that the normal dress of the comic actor was that of everyday life, with the exception that padding was worn beneath the tights that formed the actor's 'skin', and that to these was stitched a phallus which

might or might not be displayed. The costume varied little
whether worn by gods, citizens or slaves, though the first group
could sometimes be distinguished by the insignia which they
carried.

CHAPTER IX

THE MASKS

The theatrical conditions of the fifth century B.C.—the open-air setting, the size of the theatre, the distance between actors and audience—meant that exaggeration of the actor's characteristics was necessary to give the audience some clearer appreciation of the part he was to play. Thus the mask that exaggerated facial expression was a necessary adjunct to the performance, whatever the origins of its use might have been, even though the relatively small amount of detail that the mask could portray must have been invisible to the farthest rows of the audience.

No actual mask of the fifth century has survived; the use of linen, or occasionally cork or wood for their manufacture, makes this hardly surprising, but their does exist a great body of material illustrating the form and the use of masks, through which various stages in their development can be traced. Old Comedy is unfortunately poorly documented, and the evidence for it consists mainly of monuments from early Middle Comedy supplemented to some extent by deduction from later periods. These subsequent periods are, by contrast, rich in evidence, and therefore useful in permitting trends in the masks to be identified and their development traced back to earlier comedy. We have, fortunately, a check on the monuments in Pollux' description of masks (IV, 133ff.), which seems to be based on an Alexandrian scholar of the third century B.C. and may be traced back to the work on masks of Aristophanes of Byzantium.[1] Similar data is provided by the pseudo-Aristotelian *Physiognomonika*, which attempts to relate various features of masks to natural characteristics. These reference works, taken with the monuments, give a composite picture of mask types in Middle and New Comedy and allow for reasonable conjecture concerning availability of masks for the earlier works of Aristophanes.

In compiling a list of those masks which might have been available to the poet we have four different sources, all deriving ultimately from Pollux, who, referring directly to Old Comedy, states that masks were made to the likeness of the person concerned, that is that portrait masks were worn.[2] The fact that in Aristophanes' plays many well-known politicians are portrayed and satirized would suggest that this statement is correct even if only a guess by Pollux, but Dover rightly warns of the difficulties inherent in the production of portrait masks.[3] They require in their subject distinctive features that can be exaggerated or suggested in some way that produces instant recognition by the audience—features that Aristophanes' targets cannot always have possessed. Kleon's portrayal in the *Knights* is a case in point. Aristophanes claims that the mask-maker was so frightened of Kleon that he refused to make a portrait mask: Dover argues that this is simply an excuse for giving the politician a hideous mask (and one that would have been even worse if the mask-maker could have stood the sight) possibly because Kleon's face was not sufficiently distinctive to be easily portrayed in a mask. Whatever the explanation, Aristophanes seems to imply that the audience would expect some attempt at a portrait mask. Aelian's story[4] that Socrates stood up during the performance of the *Clouds* so that foreigners in the audience might know who he was, may again be evidence for a portrait mask. Politicians, however, like Kleon in the *Knights*, did not always appear in their own character; Pericles was portrayed as Zeus by Cratinus in the *Thracian Women* (frag. 71 K) and in *Nemesis* (frag. 111 K) and as Dionysus in *Dionysalexandros*, though in each case it is possible that a portrait mask was used together with attributes of Zeus or Dionysus. As the political climate became too dangerous for satire, and as the more 'romantic' plays of New Comedy became popular, it is to be expected that such portrait masks would disappear, although some may have survived into later comedy in the form of standard masks.

Secondly, a number of early monuments provide examples of masks that must have been in use in Aristophanes' lifetime. The Lyme Park relief (*MOMC* AS 1), possibly the funerary monument of Aristophanes himself, depicts a poet with a papyrus roll in one hand gazing at the mask of a slave held in the other, above which is the mask of an old man. The monument is dated to 380 B.C., and must therefore refer to Old Comedy.[5] Earlier than this are a small number of Attic vases that date from 420 onwards, and a larger number of Apulian ones of later date which seem nevertheless to have strong ties with the fifth-century Athenian theatre.[6] From the period 400–375 come the first of the Athenian terracottas which became so popular and which provide so much later information on masks and costumes. These early statuettes stand midway between Old and Middle Comedy, and thus reflect the older styles of masks.

Thirdly, the wealth of evidence for the masks of New Comedy makes it possible to compare those illustrated on vases and terracottas with the descriptions of Pollux, and to distinguish in his lists those which receive only poor representation in the monuments.[7] It can then be argued (though caution is needed) that these are relics of masks used in earlier comedy, possibly included by Pollux because revivals of earlier plays required them. This provides a further body of masks to be assigned tentatively to an earlier date, and more firmly assigned if their antecedents can be traced through the monuments. Certain mask types included by Pollux can be dated within reasonable limits: the *hetaira* masks, though possibly used by Pherekrates who is said to have introduced the *hetaira* to comedy, are unlikely to have been much in evidence before Middle Comedy, when such women begin to appear frequently in the comedies; the parasite's mask too would be a later addition, though traces of such a character may be found in Aristophanes' plays.[8] The beardless masks of New Comedy may well be traced back to the beardless mask of effeminates such as Kleisthenes and Agathon, though it was largely the influence of Alexander that brought about the fashion for shaving and so the main impulse for the beardless mask.[9]

Pollux concludes his list of tragic masks with an account of special masks for extraordinary characters and for such personifications as the Muses, the Seasons etc., all of which he claims were also available for comedy. If he is correct this provides another set of special masks for such characters as *Opora* and *Theoria* in the *Peace*, and Poverty in the *Wealth*, who is described in the play as a cross between a tragic fury and a land-lady, which suggests something different from the normal 'landlady' type of mask. The Clouds on the other hand, seem not to have been specially masked, being described as women with long noses, despite the fact that they would seem to qualify as 'special' under Pollux' criteria. It may be that he is either making unjustified deductions from the texts or spreading his net too wide when he talks of special masks, though possibly he has specific plays in mind. Certainly characters such as Pseudar-tabas and the Megarian's daughters who are dressed as pigs, might be expected to wear special masks. None of the gods, however, appear in the special mask lists, and the evidence of vases and terracottas confirms that when the gods appeared on stage they wore ordinary masks and were indistinguishable from the mortals in the play. Heracles alone has a mask to himself, well illustrated both on Attic terracottas and vases and on South Italian vases.

These are the four sources for masks that can be fairly securely traced back to Old Comedy; but immediately any attempt is made to assign them to the plays a variety of problems arises. First, there is the shortage of masks if each character in a play like the *Acharnians* with its multitude of minor parts is to be assigned a different mask. Such a distribution is by no means necessary, however, since there seems no valid reason why different characters in a single play should not wear the same mask, as long as they are introduced and their identity made obvious from the beginning—the distance between actors and audience, in any case, would make dress a far better guide to change of character than mask. Some support for this hypo-thesis may be found in one of the two New York sets of terra-cottas taken from a single grave in Athens (*MOMC* AT 8–14). Three of the figures in this set wear the same mask, and though it has been suggested that they represent the same character at different moments in the plot, it is more likely that they are different characters but using the same mask. Similarly *PV* Ph 14 depicts two cooks attacked by geese, both of whom (the cooks) wear the same mask.[10] In some plays, too, the parts seem so arranged that similar roles fall to the same actor enabling him to retain a single mask, though others admittedly demand characters played by one actor which show no similarity. It has been suggested that the theory is reasonable provided that two characters wearing the same mask are not present on stage together. This is doubtless true if the two are to be kept completely separate in the minds of the audience and exhibit their own personalities throughout, but not necessarily so if they are, for example, slaves and there is no real reason for distinguishing one from another. This reasoning could apply to the two slaves who introduce the *Peace*,[11] and it may be precisely because the two are indistinguishable that we have a problem as to which slave departs and which remains present throughout the play. It is a problem for the textual critic, which for the audience may never have occurred, faced as they were with two actors who require only to be distinguished as slaves without any personal characteristics. Two people wearing the same mask on stage together may, then, be a possibility.

The second problem is the descriptions of the masks which occasionally occur in the texts. Are these intended as description to supplement the mask, or to call momentary attention to some feature of it? No clear answer can be given, but the idea of simple description would seem a little superfluous. Either of the other two explanations might equally well be right, and all that it is possible to do is to discover a mask that approximates to the description given and allocate it to the character. The descriptions are for the most part very general, concerning long or short noses etc. and can therefore fairly easily be employed. What is more conjectural is whether it is permissible to apply the results of an inquiry into the mask of a character in one play to a similar character in another—whether Aristophanes really had a standard mask for a herald, or whether he changed the masks about according to whim at any particular time. If the latter, then the problem of allocation of masks is unreal since it becomes impossible to discover the original masks. However, the seemingly small number of masks (Pollux mentions only twenty-six) and the degree of conformity that seems later to have been introduced suggest that the treatment of minor parts by the poets of Old Comedy may have influenced later comic writers. The main characters in the plays are normally too well defined to make mask allocation a problem for them: the difficulty is with the minor yet frequently recurring characters, such as poets, priests, heralds etc. and it is likely that any move towards standardization of mask would have shown itself first among these.

A further problem is the status of mutes, and whether they wore masks. No mutes appear in the lists of *dramatis personae* (i.e. of the masks to be employed in the play) in the manuscripts of Menander and it is interesting that both on the Dioscourides mosaic and its parallel scene from Mytilene of the *Synaristosae* of Menander[12] the slave girl who appears seems not to be masked, yet we know from the *Cistellaria*, Plautus' adaptation of the Greek original, that the girl is required to remove the table. Probably, then, slaves who appeared in the role of stage hands did not wear a mask. The evidence for Aristophanes is unfortunately less clear, for mutes do appear in his lists of *dramatis personae*, as for example in the *Peace*, *Opora*, *Theoria* and Peace herself. However, these lists are a later addition to the text, probably no earlier than Alexandrian,[13] and do not necessarily reflect the actual conditions of Old Comedy. Conversely, Pollux' remarks discussed above, make it possible that *Opora* and *Theoria* were given masks, so it is difficult to distinguish between a mute who should receive a mask and one who should not, though slaves performing as stage hands might be excluded from the list.

The lack of any examples of children's masks is puzzling, since children appear frequently in the plays. The Anthesteria vases depict children with masks, but they are performing the parts of adult actors and naturally wear adult masks (cf. *PV* Ph 5). It is impossible therefore to assign masks to children who appear in the plays.

The problems of the allocation of masks are, as we see, complex, and any attempt to provide a solution such as the one below must be hypothetical in the extreme, depending largely on a subjective assessment of the characters. I have made an attempt to include the poet's description of each character, where this was impossible giving a personal assessment, and, after allocating the mask, to discover a confirmatory parallel in the monuments. The exercise may perhaps be of some use in demonstrating what a comedy of Aristophanes may originally have looked like on the stage.

APPENDIX

ALLOCATION OF THE MASKS

The masks are denoted by the letters ascribed to them in A. D. Trendall, *Phlyax Vases* (Ph) *BICS* sup. 19, (1967) and T. B. L. Webster *Monuments Illustrating Old and Middle Comedy*, *BICS* sup. 23, (1969).

pm = portrait mask, sm = special mask (as per Pollux IV, 141ff.).

ACHARNIANS

Character	Description	Mask	Parallels
Actor I			
Dicaeopolis	Countryman 202ff.	L	AT 20 countryman
Actor II			
Herald 43ff.[1]		N	AT 49 cf. Messenger 1071
Dicaeopolis' daughter 245ff.		S	
Euripides 407ff.		pm	
Lamachus 572ff.		pm	
Megarian 729ff.		K/ZA	Cf. Boeotian, ZA Ph 84
Boeotian 86off.	Rustic	K	AT 23 pipers
Farmer 1018ff.	Rustic	K	AT 57 rustic
Paranymphos 1048ff.	Young and good	H	AT 17 cf. BT 1
Actor III			
Amphitheos 45ff.[2]	Sober man	H	AT 17
Ambassador 64ff.	Strange dress 64 reflected in mask? *alazōn* 109	D	BT 1, Ph 4 for rakish element
Theorus 134ff.	*alazōn* 135	D	As above

Character	Description	Mask	Parallels
Cephisiphon 395ff.	For name schol. R.	pm/N	AT 35, N slave mask
Sycophant 818ff.[3]	Meddlesome	C	Lycomedian mask cf. *Wealth* 913
Nicarchus 910ff.	Meddlesome	C	
Servant of Lamachus 959ff.[4]		N	
Herald 1000ff.		N	
Messenger A 1071	τὰς ὀφρῦς ἀνεσπακὼς 1069	N	AT 49
Messenger B 1085		N	AT 49
Servant 1174ff.		N	

Extras

Character	Description	Mask	Parallels
Pseudartabas 100	King's Eye, ναύφαρκτον βλέπεις 95	sm	
Megarian's daughters 729ff.	Dressed as pigs	sm	

Mutes

Character	Description	Mask	Parallels
Prytanies 40ff.		E	
Archers 54ff.	Foreigners	ZA	Ph 84
Eunuchs 100ff.	One like Cleisthenes with a beard, one like Straton 120 cf. *Knights* 1374	N QQ	Beard should look artificial
Odomantians 100ff.	Foreigners	ZA	Ph. 84
Dicaeopolis' wife 245		TT	AT 77
Boeotian pipers 860ff.		K	AT 23
Brideswoman 1056		U	
Hetairae 1199ff.		X	
Slaves		B	AB 1 Kitchen slave

Character	Description	Mask	Parallels
Chorus			
Acharnians 204ff.	στιπτοὶ γέροντες πρίνινοι 180, ἀγροῖκοι 371	A	AS 3

[1]N is ascribed on analogy with the mask that seems to fit the messenger in 1071.

[2]Amphitheus is clearly the 'good man' in the scene: those who obstruct him are counted as rakes on the evidence of the Ambassador's description of their journey.

[3]In *Wealth* 913 the sycophant is accused of πολυπραγμόνειν, which suggests the mask Pollux describes as the Lycomedian (meddlesome mask) of New Comedy. C is possibly its ancestor.

[4]Messenger A (1071) demands mask N, and for the convenience of the actor playing the slave parts this has been kept throughout.

KNIGHTS

Character	Description	Mask	Parallels
Actor I			
Sausage-Seller 150ff.	Uneducated 189, *alazōn* 903	N	AT 35 Pedlar, AT 61
Actor II			
Slave B 1ff.[1] Paphlagon 235ff.	Nikias? *panourgos* 250, *alazōn* 269, mask 230ff. cf. *Wasps* 1031ff.	B(pm) sm	AB 1
Actor III			
Slave A 1ff. Demus 728ff.	Demosthenes? 1) ἄγροικος ὀργὴν κυαμοτρὼξ ἀκράχολος, Δῆμος πυκνίτης, δύσκολον γερόντιον ὑπόκωφον. 41ff.	B(pm) PP	AB 1 Old tettix mask

Character	Description	Mask	Parallels
	2) Rejuvenated, noble aspirations 1329ff.	H	AT 17
Extras			
Slave 1386ff.		K	AT 12
Treaties 1389		sm/V	AT 9, Ph 79
Chorus			
Knights 247ff.	καλοί τε κἀγαθοί, 227	sm/H	B/f vase Berlin *BHT*² fig. 126

[1]The actual identification of the slaves as Nikias and Demosthenes is highly unlikely, see K. J. Dover '*Equites* 11–20', *CR* NS 9 (1959), 196, 'Portrait Masks' in *Komoidotragemata*, 16ff.

CLOUDS

Character	Description	Mask	Parallels
Actor I			
Strepsiades 1ff.	ἄγροικος 47, 138 πρεσβύτης 476	L	AT 20
Dikos Logos 889ff.[1]		H	
Actor II			
Pheidippides 1ff.[2]	Rake ἐπὶ τοῦ προσώπου τ' ἐστὶν 'Αττικὸν βλέπος 1176	D	BT 1, Ph 4
Disciple of Socrates	*alazōn* 102, ὠχρὸς 1112	D	See *Ach.* Ambassador
Amynias 1259ff.	Just man	H	AT 17
Actor III			
Servant of Strepsiades 56ff.		K	AT 12, AT 57
Socrates 218ff.	See disciple	pm/ES	See Dover *Komoidotrag.*

Character	Description	Mask	Parallels
Adikos Logos 889ff.	θρασὺς 890, ἀναίσχυντος 909	D	
Pasias 1214ff.	Just man	H	AT 17
Extras			
Witness 1246ff.		H	
Chaerephon?		pm	
Geometry/ Astronomy		sm	
Chorus			
Clouds 275ff.	αὗται δὲ ῥῖνας ἔχουσιν 344	RR	Long-nosed women

¹If the scholiast is right that the *Logoi* appeared in wicker cages like fighting cocks, then possibly special cock masks were worn (*BHT*² fig. 123, 124). If they wear normal masks they are presumably opposed as H (the honest man) and D (the rake). This implies Pheidippides and *Adikos Logos* on the scene together both wearing the same mask, but as no conversation passes between them this need not be a difficulty, and it has the advantage that Pheidippides is later easily identified with the *Adikos Logos* by the audience, so that those who oppose him, Pasias and Amynias are Just Men and wear mask H. The contest of the *Logoi* would be thereby demonstrated in the further workings of the plot.

²Pheidippides may wear a different mask after 1170ff., where great emphasis is laid on his identification before he appears. As much play is made with the paleness of the students, it is best to assume he reappears in a whitened version of the original mask. The disciples of Socrates are credited with the same mask because the actor then need only change dress, not mask, and because Pheidippides becomes one of the pupils.

WASPS

Character	Description	Mask	Parallels
Actor I			
Bdelykleon 1ff.	Good man, young	H	
Actor II			
Sosias 1ff.	Slave—no further identification	N	AT 60 Kitchen slave

Character	Description	Mask	Parallels
Philokleon 144ff.	δριμύτατος 278, στρυφνὸν καὶ πρίνινον ἦθος, 877	A	Cf. description of chorus in *Ach.*
Actor III			
Xanthias 1ff.	Slave 1297	N	ST 17 see 1292ff., Ph 28
Artopolis 1388ff.[1]		U	Cf. chorus in *Lys.* who are 'seed of agora' 457
Extras			
Drinker 1332		E	
Complainant 1417		E	
Mutes			
Slaves 433	Phrygians	PP	Foreign cook (Athenaeus)
Dog Labes 899	*panourgos* 932	sm	
Grater 963		sm	
Two curs 976		sm	
Flute-Girl 1335	χρυσομηλολόνθιον	X	GV 1
Dancers 1500ff.	Boys	?	No evidence
Chorus			
Wasps 230ff.	ὀξύθυμος 406, 1105, ὀξυκάρδιος 430	A	No evidence for Wasps, but these are men who behave like Wasps
Boys 230ff.		?	

[1]See T. B. L. Webster, 'The Masks of Greek Tragedy', *BRL* 32 (1949), 118ff.

PEACE

Character	Description	Mask	Parallels
Actor I			
Trygaeus 82ff.	Countryman 570	L	AT 20
Actor II			
Slave B 1ff.		B	AB 1
Hermes 180ff.[1]		N	Ph 95
Kydoimos 255ff.	Slave 254	K	
Drepanourgos 1197	Happy man	N	AT 35 pedlar
Thorakopoles 1224	Angry man	P	IT 9
Son of Lamachus 1270		?	
Actor III			
Slave A 1ff.		B	AB 1
Polemos 236ff.	ὁ δεινός 241	sm/Z	Cf. CT 8 (3rd century)
Hierocles 1052	*alazōn* 1045, πολλὰ πράττων 1058	C	Lycomedian mask
Lophopoios 1210	Angry man	P	IT 9
Kranapoios 1250	Angry man	P	IT 9
Extras			
Trygaeus' daughters 114ff.	Distressed	?	
Trumpet-Maker 1240ff.	Angry man	P	IT 9
Spearsman 1255ff.	Angry man	P	IT 9
Son of Kleonymus? 1298ff.		?	
Mutes			
Opora 523ff.		sm	Pol. IV, 143

Character	Description	Mask	Parallels
Theoria 523ff.	οἷον δ᾽ ἔχεις τὸ πρόσωπον οἷον δὲ πνεῖς, ὡς ἡδὺ κατὰ τῆς καρδίας 524	sm	
Chorus Farmers 301ff.	γεωργοὶ etc. 296	A	AS 3 Cf. *Ach.* chorus.

[1]Plato 188K suggests that Hermes had no fixed mask (see *BRL* 32 (1949), 116).

BIRDS

Character	Description	Mask	Parallels
Actor I Peisthetairus 1ff.	'plucked Blackbird' 805	E	Short-nosed mask
Actor II Euelpides 1ff.	'caricature of a goose' 806	G	Long-nosed mask cf. CT 1, Ph 17 traveller
Priest 863ff.	Troublesome	C	Lycomedian
Oracle-Monger 959ff.	Interfering	C	
Episkopos 1021ff.	Troublesome	C	
Messenger A 1122ff.		N	Cf. messenger A in *Ach.*
Iris 1202ff.	Looks like a ship	V	No example elsewhere
Patraloias 1337ff.	νεανισκὸς sent to join army 1362	Z	CT 8 soldier
Sycophant 1410ff.	Meddlesome	C	Cf. *Wealth* 850ff.
Prometheus 1494ff.	Good man	L	

Character	Description	Mask	Parallels
Poseidon 1565ff.	Distinguished from Peisthetairus i.e. long-nosed	G	A god on Ph 6 etc.
Actor III			
Servant of Hoopoe 60ff.		Bird	
Hoopoe 92ff.		Bird	
Poet 904ff.	Long hair 911, needy	AA	Carefully distinguished from slave
Meton 992ff.	Town-planner	pm/N	
Statute-Seller 1035ff.		N	
Messenger B 1170		N	
Herald 1271ff.		N	
Kinesias 1372ff.		pm	
Heracles 1574ff.		J	AT 10 etc.
Messenger 1706ff.		N	
Extras			
Triballus 1565ff.	Barbarian	PP/ZA	Foreign slave mask
Mutes			
Four Birds	See 270, 274, 278, 287	Bird	
Slaves 656, 850		B	If any mask
Flute-player 861	Crow	Bird	
Chorus			
Birds 295ff.	Named individually	Bird	

LYSISTRATA

Character	Description	Mask	Parallels
Actor I			
Lysistrata 1ff.	τοξοποιεῖν τὰς ὀφρῦς 8, σκυθρωπὸς 707	T	
Actor II			
Kalonike 1ff.	Probably of similar age to Lysistrata 7	TT	Wife mask of Middle Comedy
Proboulos 386ff.		C	Lycomedian
Woman A 727ff.[1]		T	
Woman C 742ff.		T	
Kinesias 845ff.		L	
Athenian Ambassador 1086ff.		L	
Actor III			
Myrrhine 69ff.	Younger than Lysistrata?	S	
Woman A 439ff.		TT	
Woman B 735ff.		T	
Spartan Herald 980[2]		N	AT 49
Spartan Ambassador 1076ff.		N	
Athenian 1216ff.		A	See chorus of old men
Extras			
Lampito 78ff.	Spartan	R	
Mutes			
Archers 387ff.	Scythians	ZA	Ph 84

Character	Description	Mask	Parallels
Reconciliation 1114ff.		sm	Pol. IV, 141ff.
Slave 199, 908		B	If any mask
Child 879ff.		?	
Chorus			
Old Men	τυφογέροντας ἄνδρας 336	A	AS 3
Old Women	γρᾶες 635	U	Older than Lysistrata

¹If Women A and C wear the same mask some of the textual difficulty over their identification is overcome, for then to the audience they are indistinguishable.

²Presumably Spartans wear Attic masks and indicate their origins by dress and speech.

FROGS

Character	Description	Mask	Parallels
Actor I			
Dionysus 1ff.	Effeminate	Z	Usually portrayed as clean-shaven Ph 20 cf. Ph 13
Actor II			
Xanthias 1ff.		B	Ph 139
Aeschylus 830ff.	δεινὸν ἐπισκύνιον ξυνάγων 823	pm	
Actor III			
Heracles 38ff.		J	AT 10 etc.
Charon 180ff.	Old man 139	G	
Aeacus 464ff.	Slave 750	P	IT 9 Angry slave
Maid 503ff.		U	Ancestor of Pollux' 'little housekeeper'?
Pandokeutria 549	Vicious	RR	Wolfish woman Ph 23

Character	Description	Mask	Parallels
Euripides 830ff.	φρενοτέκτονος ἀνδρὸς 820	pm	
Extras			
Corpse 173ff.		sm	
Plathane 551ff.	Vicious	RR	
Pluto 830ff.	Must be recognizable; unnamed	G	
Mutes			
Slaves 608		B	Ph 84, if any mask
Muse of Euripides 1306		T	AT 82 with castanets
Chorus			
Frogs 209ff.		Frog	No examples
Mystics 316ff.	Men and women	A & T	AS 3 etc.

WOMEN AT THE THESMOPHORIA

Character	Description	Mask	Parallels
Actor I			
Mnesilochus 1ff.	ἄγροικος, γέρων 63, κηδεστής Εὐριπίδου	L	AT 20—pm unlikely
Actor II			
Euripides 1ff.	πολιός εἰμι καὶ πώγων' ἔχω 190	pm	
Woman A 380ff.	τάλαινα 385	T	Not distinguished from chorus
Euripides 871ff.[1]	As Menelaus	pm	Ph 20?
	As Echo	pm	
	As Perseus	pm	Ph 1, see *MTS* AV 34
Actor III			
Servant of Agathon 39ff.		P	

Character	Description	Mask	Parallels
Agathon 95ff.	ὡς γυνὴ 143, Κυρήνη 98	pm/QQ	Beardless mask
Woman B 443ff.	Widow	T	
Kleisthenes 574ff.	γυναῖκες ξυγγενεῖς τοὐμοῦ τρόπου 574	pm	
Woman C 76off.		T	
Archer 1001ff.	Scythian	ZA	Foreign slave cf. Ph 84
Extras			
Prytanis 929ff.		AA	
Mutes			
Slaves 238		B	AB 1
Dancing Girl 1172		X	
Chorus			
Women 290ff.		T	Ph 7
Heraldess 290ff.		T	Probably chorus leader

[1]Euripides probably wears a portrait mask throughout. There is a small problem at 116off. where the chorus recognize him immediately as Euripides yet a moment later the Scythian mistakes him for an old woman. It would be sufficient if Euripides drew his cloak over his head, cf. AT 15, 16 etc., and thus hid his beard.

WOMEN IN ASSEMBLY

Character	Description	Mask	Parallels
Actor I			
Praxagora 1ff.		TT	Wife of Middle Comedy
Man 327ff.		E	
Heraldess 834ff.		T	Cf. heraldess in *Thesm.*

Character	Description	Mask	Parallels
Hag A 877ff.	ἀνάσιμος 940	U	AT 83
Maid 1112ff.		U	
Actor II			
Woman A 30ff.		T	See chorus
Blepyrus 311ff.	γέρων 323	A	KT 5, note stick
			cf. 546
Man B 746ff.	Mocker of laws	D	Ph 10 etc.
Young Girl	χρυσοδαιδάλτον	V	
884ff.	973		
Hag C 1065ff.	πότερον πίθηκος	Y	AT 29
	ἀνάπλεως ψιμυθίου		
	1072		
Actor III			
Woman B 35ff.		T	See chorus
Chremes 372ff.	Obedient to laws	G	Ph 6
Youth 938ff.		D, O?	BT 1, GV 9
			worried lover
Extras			
Woman C 54ff.		T	
Hag B 1049ff.	ἔμπουσα 1056,	RR	Long-nosed, as
	ἐκείνου τὸ		Clouds
	κακὸν ἐξωλέστερον		
	1053		
Mutes			
Slave 738		B	If any mask
Chorus			
Women 285ff.		T	Ph 7

WEALTH

Character	Description	Mask	Parallels
Actor I			
Cario 1ff.	Domestic slave	B	AB 1
	1097		

Character	Description	Mask	Parallels
Poverty 415ff.	βλέπει γέ τοι μανικόν τι καὶ τραγῳδικόν 424 πανδοκεύτριαν ἢ λεκιθόπωλιν 426	sm	Pollux IV, 141ff.
Wealth 771ff.	Joyful	E	Ph 6
Hag 959ff.	Painted with white lead 1064, γραὸς	Y	AT 29
Actor II			
Chremylus 1ff.	Reasonable man 245	L	
Just man 823ff.[1]	Happy	L	
Hermes 1099ff.		QC	See *Peace*
Actor III			
Wealth 1ff.	Blind πρεσβύτην ῥυπῶντα κυφὸν ἄθλιον ῥυσὸν μαδῶντα νωδόν 265	sm	Cf. *Oedipus the King.* Perhaps a variant of E
Blepsidemus 335	Meddlesome	C	Lycomedian
Wife 641		TT	AT 77
Sycophant 850ff.	πολυπραγμονεῖν	C	Lycomedian
Youth 1042ff.	εὐπρόσωπον 976	O	
Priest 1171ff.		C	
Mutes			
Friends 782ff.		K	
Boy 823ff.		?	
Chorus			
Farmers 257ff.	ἀσθενεῖς γέροντας 258	K	AT 57

[1] If the Just Man were young, H would almost certainly be correct for him. As he brings his son it must be assumed that he is older. It is convenient then to allocate L to him, as this allows Actor II to use the same mask continuously.

THE STAGING OF THE PLAYS

Acharnians

As the play opens, Dicaeopolis enters the orchestra by one of the *parodoi* and approaches the stage. He muses with himself for the first twenty lines as he waits for the Assembly to convene, expressing his determination to force the citizens to discuss the negotiation of peace with Sparta. In the course of his mutterings, he establishes the scene as the Pnyx (20). At 29 he sits down wearily and describes the entry through the *parodoi* of the Prytanies (40) who are scrambling for the front row of seats just as he had earlier forecast. The problem now arises of the relative position of Dicaeopolis and the Prytanies: if the latter face the audience then all who address the Assembly, such as Theorus, Pseudartabas etc. will necessarily have their backs to the audience. However, the Prytanies are of less visual value than the ambassadors, their chief purpose being to identify with the audience, whose representative they are (cf. 27)—so it would seem appropriate if they took their place round the perimeter of the orchestra with their backs to the audience, and the edge of the orchestra might then represent the 'consecrated line' (44). As for Dicaeopolis, he must be part of the scene yet distant from it so that he can make asides to the audience and also deal with Amphitheus after his expulsion from the Assembly. A position for him on the steps leading to the stage therefore seems reasonable.

With the Prytanies Amphitheus enters, but when he suggests that he be sent to Sparta to negotiate a peace, he is immediately ejected from the Assembly by the Archers (55) and departs through the orchestra. He is present again at 129, when Dicaeopolis conceives his grand scheme for a private peace with Sparta and requires him as a messenger, but his momentary appearance here is taken by an extra. Possibly the change-over of actors takes place in the *parodos* and Amphitheus remains at the end of the *parodos* during the action subsequent to his forcible ejection from the Assembly, in which various dignitaries arrive through the opposite *parodos*. One of these, Pseudartabas, departs at 125 for his free meal in the *Prytaneion* and probably climbs on to the stage to make his exit through the door. He is followed into the theatre, after the short scene in which Dicaeopolis summons Amphitheus and sends him off to Sparta, by Theorus and a band of scrawny mercenaries who address the Assembly. Dicaeopolis feels a drop of ill-omened rain and the Herald declares the Assembly dissolved (173), the various participants hurrying out through the orchestra, as Amphitheus runs in with the treaties and describes his flight from the anti-Spartan Acharnians. Dicaeopolis accepts the thirty-year treaty, indicates that the next scene will be set at the Rural Dionysia (202) and goes in through the door, while Amphitheus flies through the *parodos*.

His departure is followed by the immediate arrival of the chorus of Acharnians who rush in through the opposite *parodos* searching for Amphitheus, determined to stone him. Dicaeopolis is heard shouting inside the house, and the chorus draw to one side to await his arrival. He appears at 241 and proceeds to arrange a procession (lines 242/3/4 must each be followed by a pause) with a basket-bearer at the head, followed by Xanthias with the phallus pole preceding Dicaeopolis' daughter, Dicaeopolis bringing up the rear. The procession seems to have led down into the orchestra if, as seems likely, 257/8 is intended as a joke at the audience's expense but the point when it moves off is difficult to judge. Line 257 might be suggested as the moment, but perhaps more likely is 262, where there is a change of metre: if so, then 257 must be taken in a more cautionary sense. The procession winds round the orchestra, and is already returning to the stage when the Acharnians attack and hurl their stones (280ff.). The participants in the procession run off, perhaps through the *parodos*, leaving Dicaeopolis alone, probably still holding the sacrificial pot (284), though his remark about it may be directed to those who are running off. He appears to reach the comparative safety of the steps to the stage, for at 328 he is able to depart indoors and return with a scuttle of charcoal (330 indicates that he goes indoors to fetch this), in order to make the Acharnians, charcoal-burners themselves, comply with his request for a hearing on why he has made peace. The audience may well have echoed the angry mutterings of the chorus during this section, and the production of a hostage in the form of a brazier could have provided light relief in what may have been a dangerous moment for the play. The chorus are forced to drop their missiles (341/2) and Dicaeopolis puts down his sword—perhaps the sacrificial knife (the entry indoors would have enabled him to dispose of the pot if he still held it). He promises to convince the chorus that neither side in the war is wholly wrong and offers to speak with his head on a chopping block, but whether in fact he returns to the house to fetch one or rather points to the altar on the stage seems uncertain; the latter would make for easier staging.

Before Dicaeopolis can speak, however, he finds it necessary to deck himself out in rags to excite the pity of the Acharnians. The obvious source for the rags is Euripides and it is to his house that our hero now goes: presumably he approaches the door once more, knocks, and summons the slave (395) who informs him that Euripides cannot see him. Nevertheless he persists and Euripides, lying on a couch with his feet up and surrounded by piles of tragic clothing, is rolled out on the *ekkyklema*. Dicaeopolis requests the loan of various items of clothing, including the rags worn by Telephus. Whether these were rags, as 435ff. suggests, and not ordinary tragic costume that became 'rags' because they were so described, is uncertain, but the latter would free Dicaeopolis of having to remove his 'rags' at some point later in the action, for then his dress would cease to be 'ragged' as soon as it ceased to be called such. Dicaeopolis' requests eventually become too much for Euripides, and he orders his house to be closed in words with a tragic ring; the *ekkyklema* slides back and Dicaeopolis turns to address the chorus once more. His speech is addressed to the spectators as much as the chorus (497), on the cause of war and the apportioning of blame for it. It results in the chorus dividing in two, presumably physically as well as ideologically, half agreeing with Dicaeopolis, the others, after a short scuffle, summoning to their aid the general Lamachus, an aristocrat to whom war is an obvious benefit. The soldier rushes in through the *parodos* in full battle array and confronts Dicaeopolis, and the struggle between the two semi-choruses is now echoed in the battle of words between these two. Lamachus eventually departs (662) through the orchestra while three lines later Dicaeopolis goes in through the door having announced that his market will be open to Spartans, Megarians and Boeotians.

Though no new arguments have been offered to convince them, both semi-choruses now agree that Dicaeopolis is in the right, and they combine to deliver a *parabasis* which urges the audience to accept the poet's conclusion that the woes of the city spring directly from the war. At the conclusion of this passage Dicaeopolis appears through the door, and at once establishes the scene as his market place, perhaps indicating the edge of the stage as its boundaries. A Megarian enters the orchestra leading his two starving daughters, whom he persuades to climb into sacks to be sold as pigs; he then approaches the stage (749). Dicaeopolis, interested in the pigs, feeds them (802), and having decided to buy them goes inside (815). Immediately a sycophant appears in the orchestra and tries to denounce the Megarian, but the reappearance of Dicaeopolis puts paid to his scheme and he is driven off by the 'market clerks'—usually interpreted as leather thongs wielded by Dicaeopolis. The Megarian leaves (835) by the *parodos* opposite the one by which the sycophant rushed out.

The chorus sing of Dicaeopolis' good fortune in a short ode that ends with the appearance of a Boeotian and his slave, escorted on their way through the orchestra by a crowd of Theban pipers. The pipers are immediately driven off by Dicaeopolis (864) who seems to be still present on stage. The Boeotian ascends the stage and displays his wares to the Athenian, who quickly summons his slave to bring out brazier and bellows to prepare a meal of Boeotian eels (887ff.). The difficulty is to find suitable payment for the Boeotian, but the sycophant (a breed unique to Athens) opportunely reappears in the orchestra; Dicaeopolis siezes him and takes him inside ostensibly to tie him up (928), but probably to allow for the substitution of a dummy. Dicaeopolis returns, gives the load to a slave, and the Boeotian cheerfully goes on his way out of the *parodos* (954). At the same moment the slave of Lamachus runs on through the opposite *parodos* to ask Dicaeopolis to sell him eels for his master, but being unsuccessful he leaves by the same way, while Dicaeopolis goes in through the door taking with him all the properties on the stage (970), except perhaps the brazier which is required for the next scene.

The choral ode that follows concerns the joys of reconciliation and peace. At its conclusion a herald runs into the orchestra, announces the Feast of the Jugs and a drinking contest and hurries out again at the other side. Immediately the scene bursts into life, as Dicaeopolis enters through the door and urges his slaves to bring out spits and start cooking a meal over the fire (1003ff.). During these preparations, which must take place at one side of the stage, various people enter to beg a portion of the peace: first a farmer enters (1018) through one of the *parodoi* and pleads with Dicaeopolis for a drop, but to no avail, and he departs the way he came (1036). Next comes a bridegroom in search of peace. His brideswoman, by her whispered comments to Dicaeopolis, is more successful; she obtains the ointment and the two depart happily (1068). The chorus now announce the arrival of a messenger with chilling news for Lamachus—the demand that he make ready for a campaign against the Boeotians. Lamachus rushes out through the door at 1072. A second messenger arrives through the *parodos* with news for Dicaeopolis—an invitation to a feast. The two men stand on opposite sides of the stage ordering their slaves to provide various pieces of equipment suitable for their enterprises, while the slaves bustle backwards and forwards through a single door (1097ff.). It is noticeable that much of what Dicaeopolis calls for is supplied from the cooking equipment formerly brought out (cf. 1104, 1110, 1119 etc.) thus enabling the stage to be cleared when the two parties set off in opposite directions through the *parodoi*. At some point of the proceedings the brazier must be removed.

At the conclusion of the following choral ode another messenger arrives calling on Lamachus' slaves to prepare for the arrival of their wounded master (thereby establishing the scene as Lamachus' house). The war hero limps in through the *parodos* at 1190 supported by his slaves as Dicaeopolis totters in at the other side (1198) supported by two girls. Lamachus is helped on to the stage, reaches his door, and then decides to be taken to the doctor, and so the two parties depart through opposite *parodoi*. The consequences of war and wine having been so graphically illustrated, the chorus dances out in joy behind the wine-filled Dicaeopolis.

Knights

The play opens with two slaves entering through the central door who, in their first words establish the scene (1–5), explaining the owner of the house is their master. They are both seeking a plan of escape but neither has any idea what form it should take, so each encourages the other to speak first, not with any great success. They eventually seize on desertion (26) as the best way out of the impasse, and explain the relevance of what has been happening. It seems that a slave, newly imported into the household, has made their life unbearable. The slave is Paphlagon (representing the demagogue Kleon) and by lying, stealing, and taking credit for the achievements of others he has managed to worm his way into the favours of his master Demus (the Athenian people). It is possible but unlikely that the two original slaves, here termed A and B, represent Nikias and Demosthenes, Athenian generals of the day. Slave A is now sent into the house for some wine, while his fellow-conspirator lies down (98) perhaps propped up against the stage altar. The wine is brought and Paphlagon reported asleep, so Slave A is again sent in for an oracle (109), with which he returns. He hands it to Slave B, who proceeds to drink the wine and exclaim at the contents of the oracle which, happily, forecasts Paphlagon's downfall. A Sausage-Seller appears by chance in the orchestra at 146, on his way to sell his wares and carrying a table for the purpose under his arm (152). He is hailed by the slaves as their saviour (and that of the state) since he possesses all the necessary qualifications—ignorance and impudence. He ascends to the stage and climbs on to his table (169). Meanwhile Slave A has gone in through the door, ostensibly to keep watch for Paphlagon (154), and Slave B is left to explain to the Sausage-Seller that he is to be the leader of Demus. At some point during the following scene he must descend from his table, but there seems no obvious indication of the moment. The exposition is interrupted by the entrance of Paphlagon himself, who hurls himself through the door on to the stage, causing the Sausage-Seller to bolt for the orchestra, while Slave B attempts to restrain him (240) and summons the chorus of Knights as reinforcements. Paphlagon and the Sausage-Seller are hemmed in by the chorus in the orchestra and they fight, the chorus supporting the latter and even, according to the scholiast, striking Paphlagon (273). It seems, however, that the two actors manage to reach the comparative safety of the stage, as the following section (278ff.) consists of a battle of insults and abuse between Paphlagon and the Sausage-Seller in which the former boasts of his prowess in winning his own desires from the Athenians and is accused by the Sausage-Seller of dishonesty. Slave B apparently stays on stage during the remainder of this scene, perhaps in the background, being required to comment on the scene occasionally. The wordy battle between the two chief characters becomes a battle of fists once more at 451, the chorus encouraging the Sausage-Seller to strike Paphlagon with his sausages, which presumably are still in evidence on the table. At 475 Paphlagon threatens to go to the Council, but to prevent the audience being deceived into thinking that the next scene will represent the *Boulē*, the final words of the scene make it clear that the Sausage-Seller is to return to the present place (497). The two then depart through the *parodos* for the Council chamber (691 makes it clear that they do not go through the door). It seems clear that Slave B also disappears at this point: perhaps he follows the contestants.

The chorus send them on their way, emphasizing that Agorakritus (the Sausage-Seller) is to return when he has won (501), and deliver the *parabasis*, which explains Aristophanes' reasons for not producing his earlier plays himself and then celebrates the exploits of the war. At 611 they introduce the return of Agorakritus via the *parodos*, and hail him as conqueror. He relates, presumably from the stage, the happenings in the Council (624ff.), doubtless accompanying his story with much comic business—the use of imitative speeches must imply something of the kind—until Paphlagon enters, again through the *parodos*. The two proceed to insult one another once more and then advance to the door (724) and summon Demus, whose entrance has been prepared for at 714. He comes out of the house and confronts the two who are scheming for his affection, but before a decision can be reached on who loves Demus best, Paphlagon demands an Assembly and insists it takes place on the Pnyx.

While the chorus sing a few lines (756–62) the scene changes to the Pnyx, indicated by the rolling out of the *ekkyklema*. It perhaps carries some rocks on its front edges, and a seat for Demus towards the front where he can sit in judgement. Its use provides the easiest transition from one setting to the next. Paphlagon begins by praying to Athene (763), but it seems unlikely her statue was on stage, for if it were a more personal form of address to her might have been expected. The two contestants then fall to mudslinging again, the chorus occasionally interrupting until 870. At 872 Agorakritus provides Demus with a pair of shoes and a *chitōn*, and it seems probable that he takes off his own to give to him, as Paphlagon certainly does when he attempts unsuccessfully to wrap Demus in his own cloak (891). The Sausage-Seller counters this offer by giving Demus ointment (906) and a hare's tail (909), these items having been presumably concealed about his person during the preceding scenes. The struggle continues until at 947 Demus demands his ring back from Paphlagon, who suggests that the two contestants fetch their oracles. The chorus send them off (970) and the two seem to rush through the door together—even though the house has been identified as Demus'—as they do again later for their gifts (1110). The chorus continues to attack Paphlagon until the two return with piles of oracles at 997. At 1110 they again depart, this time for gifts, returning at 1151 carrying them in hampers. At 1164 Paphlagon presents Demus with a stool and Agorakritus counters with a table (1165)—perhaps the one he brought on at the beginning. They each try to outdo the other until the Sausage-Seller offers Demus a hare's tail that is Paphlagon's (thereby paralleling Kleon's act in claiming the credit for the victory at Pylos). Demus is then persuaded to look in the hampers (1214), and finding Paphlagon's half-full he concludes that he has kept back the gifts for himself, and therefore demands he return his crown

(1227), declaring Agorakritus the victor. Paphlagon begs to be 'rolled back in' (1249), which suggests that the *ekkyklema* has been used throughout this scene and is now withdrawn, and with it all the impedimenta of the scene. Demus and Agorakritus remain until 1263 when they go back in through the door.

The now empty stage provides the chorus the opportunity to sing a second *parabasis*, at the conclusion of which the Sausage-Seller enters, followed by a slave carrying a stool, probably through the door. He describes the rejuvenation of Demus by boiling, and the sound of the Acropolis gates opening is then heard, indicating Demus' entrance through the central door (1331). Demus, young, enthusiastic, and cured of his earlier political blindness dismisses Paphlagon, summons the Sausage-Seller to dinner and thus ends the play. It seems probable that a number of lines have disappeared from the play's conclusion.

Clouds

The play begins as the *ekkyklema* comes forward carrying two beds, one containing Strepsiades, the other his son Pheidippides. The former, worried by his impending bankruptcy and unable to sleep, sits up and soliloquizes on the length of the night and the trouble his son has got him into with his horses. The scene is set at night, as the references to darkness and sleep indicate (2, 12, 16) and the order to the slave to provide a light confirms (18). The slave enters through the door with a light and a ledger, and Strepsiades busily looks through the book and calculates his debts. He may rise from his bed at 33, thus disturbing Pheidippides, though possibly he just turns and twists on the bed. The light goes out at 55, incidentally emphasizing his poverty. By 78 at least he has risen, for he shakes Pheidippides awake and asks if he loves him. His son affirms his love, swearing by the clay statue of Poseidon, God of Horses, that stands by the bed (83), and agrees to obey him. He follows his father off the *ekkyklema* which is immediately withdrawn (89). They walk to the edge of the stage, or perhaps into the orchestra where Strepsiades points back to the door and identifies it as the *Phrontistērion* or Reflectory of Socrates (95) and suggests that his son enrol there to learn the Worse of the two Logics so that he need never pay his creditors. Pheidippides, however, refuses to co-operate and departs for the house of his uncle Megacles, probably through the orchestra but possibly through the door (125).

Undeterred, Strepsiades decides that the only answer is to learn the techniques of argument himself and so advances to Socrates' door and knocks (132). A pupil comes out, shutting the door behind him (see 181) and speaks with him, describing the exploits of Socrates in discovering how far a flea can jump etc. Strepsiades, duly impressed, asks that the door be flung open and the school displayed. That the setting has by now changed from the opening scene is made obvious by Strepsiades' plea to be excused his country ways now that he is in town (138). The door opens (184), and the *ekkyklema* comes forward once more carrying several pupils of the Reflectory, all bent double seeking out the secrets of the earth, while their bottoms learn astronomy. At 200 they all rush back indoors and two strange figures, Geometry and Astronomy, are left visible, together with a map of the world (206) in which Strepsiades takes great interest, until he suddenly notices a man hanging in a basket (on the *mechane*) and on enquiry discovers it is Socrates (218). He questions him on why he is hanging up, and then asks him to descend while he explains his own purpose in coming. Socrates descends (238) and bids Strepsiades sit on the holy σκίμποδα (254). It seems possible that the property used for this is Strepsiades' bed from the earlier scene, which has reappeared on the *ekkyklema*. (At some point Geometry and Astronomy must have disappeared, perhaps as Socrates arrived.) Socrates take off his chaplet and hands it to Strepsiades (255), then summons the chorus of the Clouds (269ff.). They are heard singing outside the orchestra (275–90, 299–313), and, according to the scholiast, thunder is heard at 294. The chorus do not enter until 326, when they appear as women (341): the explanation of their appearance is offered by Socrates in the following lines. The scene continues until 497, where Strepsiades is ordered to remove his cloak, and at 509, with some trepidation, he goes in through the door followed by Socrates as the *ekkyklema* is withdrawn and the stage cleared.

The chorus send Strepsiades on his way with words of encouragement, then turn to the audience and sing the *para-*

basis in which they extol the merits of Aristophanes' plays over those of his rivals. Socrates reappears through the door at 627, vexed with Strepsiades' stupidity. He summons his pupil to bring out his bed (633), which he does, throwing it down on the stage (634) and lying on it, continually tossing about while he is supposed to be thinking. Socrates walks a short way off (705ff.), returning at 723 to question him, but the foolishness of his answers so exasperates him that he drives Strepsiades from his house (790). Strepsiades retreats to the orchestra and talks with the chorus, who recommend him to bring his son to Socrates instead. He agrees, and, bidding the philosopher wait for him, departs through one of the *parodoi* probably carrying his bed with him (though possibly a slave may take it indoors). Socrates goes in and the chorus sing a short ode.

At 814 Strepsiades and his son reappear through the *parodos*, but the father goes in through the door at 843 and returns carrying a cock and hen, the significance of which he explains to Pheidippides with a display of his new-found knowledge. These properties are mentioned no more and so must be got rid of; perhaps Strepsiades places them for the moment in his *kolpos*. The two approach the door (860), now once more the house of Socrates. Strepsiades is without cloak or shoes, having left them in the philosopher's house. Socrates is called forth (866), accepts Pheidippides as his pupil and proceeds to describe to him the debate about to take place between the *Dikos* and *Adikos Logos* (the Better and Worse Logics), at which he himself will not be present. He then departs into the house, Strepsiades making his exit through the *parodos*; (the text at this point is corrupt).

The *Logoi* now enter on the *ekkyklema*, possibly in wicker cages from which they are freed either at 940 or 952ff. The presence of Pheidippides throughout the ensuing scene is confirmed by 929. The debate over the old and new styles of education continues until 1104, when the *Logoi* suddenly depart and Strepsiades and Socrates return. It seems probable that a choral ode has been lost at this point. Socrates now accepts Pheidippides for further training and takes him indoors, while Strepsiades departs through the orchestra as the chorus utter grim prognostications.

The return of Strepsiades carrying a pot of meal is marked at 1131: he approaches Socrates' door and knocks, to be greeted by the philosopher, who in the following lines makes careful preparation for the entry of Pheidippides, which suggests that perhaps the audience may have difficulty in recognizing him. The play's frequent allusions to the paleness of the disciples may suggest that Pheidippides is now wearing a whitened mask (120, 1112). As Pheidippides comes on through the door, Socrates departs indoors. Father and son remain on stage, or perhaps walk round the orchestra while Pheidippides displays his newly acquired skills in disputation. By 1212 they are about to enter through the door when one of Strepsiades' creditors comes into the orchestra, discussing his woes with a witness. He approaches the father and son and demands payment, but his arguments are easily countered by the two. (It seems at 1248 that a 'kneeding board' is visible on the stage.) As he departs defeated through one *parodos*, a second creditor enters through the other bewailing his fate. He too is utterly baffled by the sophistic argument with which he is confronted and is driven off by Strepsiades with a whip (1302). Father and son seem to enter the house at this point, while the chorus sing of the dangers of Strepsiades' action in having his son educated in evil.

Suddenly Strepsiades rushes screaming out of the house, hotly pursued by Pheidippides who soundly beats him (1321ff.). A scene follows imitative of that between the *Logoi* (1330ff.), in which Pheidippides justifies the beating of his father and persuades him of the correctness of his action. Strepsiades sees the error of his ways, blames the Clouds for encouraging him to have his son thus trained, and then invites him to join in an attack on Socrates, but Pheidippides refuses and goes indoors at 1475—the reference to the pot here may be to the one in which Strepsiades brought the meal to Socrates (1146). Strepsiades determines to put an end to Socrates' teaching and summons his slave Xanthias, who hurries out of the door carrying ladder, torch and pick. They set the ladder against the house, climb onto the roof and attack it. The heads of Socrates and various of his disciples are seen poking out of the windows in horror (1493ff.), and eventually all the disciples rush out through the door and, hotly pursued by Strepsiades, who has descended from the roof, run out of the orchestra followed by the chorus (1510).

Wasps

At the opening of the play the scene is bare except perhaps for a statue by the side of the door (875, although the reference there may be to the stage altar). Bdelykleon may be visible on the roof asleep. Two slaves enter through the door, and perhaps stand yawning for some time before speaking. They indicate that it is night (2) and may take gulps of wine from a flask, as Rogers suggests. The two begin to describe the dramatic situation (54ff.), explaining that Bdelykleon (Kleon-hater), asleep on the roof (67), is keeping his father Philokleon (Kleon-lover) prisoner in the house (70) in an attempt to cure him of his addiction to jury service. It seems probable that by 135 the two slaves are lying by the door to all appearance asleep. Suddenly Bdelykleon stands up on the roof and rouses them (136), calling one of them to run and join him on the roof to prevent Philokleon from escaping. One of the slaves rushes in, either through the door or via one of the *parodoi*, and a moment later Philokleon's head appears through the roof, where he pretends to be smoke. Meanwhile the slave by the door pushes against it vigorously to prevent any escape that way. (The slave who has gone inside is not seen again.) Bdelykleon claps down the cover on the smoke hole and puts a log on it (147) whereupon his father attempts another unsuccessful escape through the door (152). Bdelykleon decides to descend from the roof, and disappears from view to re-enter through the *parodos* a few moments later, but Philokleon is already trying to escape through the window (156). He threatens to nibble through the net which covers the upper part of the house, but is told he has no teeth to enable him to do so (165)—this conversation is presumably conducted from a window since it must be audible. Philokleon now changes his tactics and decides he must go to market to sell the donkey; but again his plan is defeated as Bdelykleon himself goes indoors, leads out the animal and discovers Philokleon clinging to its belly. He is pushed back in, calling for help, and the slave is ordered to barricade the door (200ff.) but before he can do so Philokleon is trying to escape under the tiling of the roof, like a sparrow. Bdelykleon calls for a net, though this may only be a continuation of the sparrow metaphor rather than a reference to a stage property. All Philokleon's exits are seemingly barred, and the slave therefore suggests that he and Bdelykleon settle down to sleep, but his master reminds him that the other dikasts will soon be here to call for Philokleon (217ff.). Nevertheless it seems likely that Bdelykleon and the slave do sit down before the house and nod off to sleep (364 suggests they are both armed with spits) leaving the chorus of old jurymen, dressed like Wasps, free to manoeuvre undisturbed when they enter at 230 attended by boys with lamps.

Rogers and Van Leeuwen, presumably misled by 336/7, seem to misunderstand the text at this point in sending Bdelykleon back to the roof. There is no indication of this in the play, rather proof that he does *not* go. Van Leeuwen in particular is driven to explaining that the expression 'before the doors' (362) can be used to include Bdelykleon on the roof—a highly unlikely piece of Greek. Bdelykleon in fact takes the place of the first slave who ran indoors earlier, and this sufficiently explains the references to 'the two before the doors' (362) and to Bdelykleon 'sleeping before you' (337). Similarly it explains Bdelykleon's command in the singular to the slave to wake up (395), and saves supposing a hurried departure from the roof by Bdelykleon when the Wasps prepare to attack (416ff.).

The chorus talk with the boys who are lighting their way, and wonder why Philokleon is not there to join them (273). He eventually appears at the window (316) and together they plan a means of escape. He nibbles through the net over the window (368), fastens a rope round himself and is beginning to let himself down when Bdelykleon awakes, arouses the slave and orders him to climb on the window and belabour Philokleon with the wreath. The Wasps, determined to rescue their friend, toss their *himatia* to the boys (408), who run off with them, and pushing out their stings (420) buzz threateningly in the orchestra (415), planning their attack. Bdelykleon summons reinforcements of slaves (433), who surround Philokleon, while he himself and the first slave go in (452) to return with sticks and apparatus to smoke out the Wasps. The Wasps are quickly

routed and the battle won. Bdelykleon now promises to persuade Philokleon of his foolishness (513ff.), taking the Wasps
as judges of the debate. The old man asks for a sword with
which to kill himself if he is over-persuaded (cf. 713). Philokleon is granted first chance at speaking but before he can begin
Bdelykleon asks for his writing case and makes notes in it
throughout the debate. The old man maintains there is no
greater delight than being a juror in that all the litigants flatter
and cajole him, he can bend the laws as he wishes and yet still
he draws his pay for it. Bdelykleon shows signs of restlessness
(642) towards the end of this speech but is given his chance to
reply at 644. He exposes the paucity of the juryman's pay compared with the income of the state or the bribes the demagogues
receive. The chorus are quickly persuaded that Bdelykleon is
right (725ff.) but the old man proves more stubborn until
Bdelykleon suggests that he carry out his judging at home
whenever there is any matter which requires it. Philokleon is
delighted, and at 798 Bdelykleon goes into the house, returning
with a variety of objects to be employed as the constituents of
the law court. It seems that seats are available (825, 905) in the
following scene, and perhaps Bdelykleon, or his slaves, bring
these on too. A fire is brought and a pot of gruel set beside it
(811), a cock (815), a statue of Lykos etc. At 836 the slave comes
on leading the two dogs who are to be prosecutor and accused
(Kyon, so named for Kleon, and Labes, after Laches, an
Athenian general in Sicily), then other properties are brought
(see J. C. B. Lowe, *Hermes* 95 (1967), 53ff.). The trial begins and
continues until 990, the slave prosecuting on behalf of Kyon,
and Bdelykleon defending. The scene appears to be imitative
of Athenian law court procedure and was presumably reflected
in the acting. At 990 Bdelykleon leads his father to the voting
urn and tricks him into acquitting Labes (apparently he votes
with his eyes closed). Philokleon faints on being told that he has,
for the first time, voted for acquittal. At 1008 all the actors go
in through the door, the slaves presumably removing the
properties.

While the stage is empty the chorus sing the *parabasis* complaining of the audience's inability to appreciate the *Clouds* produced the previous year. Father and son reappear at 1122 and

Bdelykleon attempts to prepare his father for his new life by persuading him to accept fashionable dress and manners, forcing him to put on a woollen robe (1150) and Laconian shoes (1159ff.). They then practise 'subsiding into couches' but this may merely indicate some comic business on the stage perhaps using the chairs from the previous scene. Next they turn to the accomplishments of the elegant diner, where Philokleon excels himself in capping verses that Bdelykleon suggests and at 1264 they set off for dinner, through the orchestra. A second *parabasis* follows.

A slave runs into the orchestra (1292) and relates the outrages Philokleon has committed at the banquet. As he departs through one *parodos* (1325), he announces the arrival of Philokleon through the other. The old man supporting on his arm a flute-girl (stolen from the party) and followed by a band of angry citizens, enters the orchestra and climbs onto the stage offering his phallus to the girl to help her to ascend. A baking-girl carrying a tray rushes in through the orchestra (1388) demanding payment for her bread, but she gets no satisfaction, and another complainant and his witness appear and are similarly treated (1417). Eventually Bdelykleon, who presumably entered among the band of angry citizens, manages to carry his father into the house (1449), the flute-girl perhaps accompanying them, and the remainder of the revellers disperse from the orchestra.

A choral ode in praise of Bdelykleon's behaviour follows, brought to a conclusion by the arrival of a slave from the house (1474), who prepares the audience for the dancing contest that is to follow. The door is opened and Philokleon appears dancing, challenging anybody who will take him on. At 1501 a dancer appears in the orchestra followed by two others (1504, 1508). The chorus draw back (1516) to allow them room to perform, and at 1537 all exeunt, actors leading chorus in the dance.

Peace

Two slaves enter through the door as the play begins, one carrying a kneading-tray in which he is making cakes of dung to feed an enormous beetle, which is out of sight behind the scenes. Slave A keeps popping in and out of the door with these

dung cakes, but eventually his companion can bear the smell
no longer (17) so the other takes the tray and removes it from
the stage (see D. M. McDowell, *CR* N.S. 15 (1965), 17). At 30
Slave B peeps in through the door to see if the beetle has
finished his meal, and so the scene continues until 43 when the
two slaves cease tantalizing the audience and expound the plot.
Slave A makes an excuse to depart indoors at 49 and is seen no
more. The other slave continues the story explaining that his
master has been seeking to persuade Zeus to make peace, and,
after various unsuccessful attempts, has now acquired a giant
dung beetle on which he hopes to fly to heaven. An interruption
from his master (Trygaeus) from behind the scene (62) helps
reinforce this argument and produces an air of expectation in
the theatre as the audience awaits the arrival of the hero. The
slave looks indoors again (78) and describes the take-off of
Trygaeus on his mount, which now appears over the roof of the
skene on the *mechane*, and comes to rest suspended above the
stage while Trygaeus explains his project to the audience (105).
The slave tries to dissuade him from going to heaven, but being
unsuccessful he summons Trygaeus' daughters (111), who plead
with him, but again to no avail, as he flies off at 149. The
daughters return indoors. The use of anapaests by Trygaeus
(154ff.) suggests that he is now moved up and down on the
mechane to simulate flight, perhaps in a rather jerky manner if
his remark to the *mechanopoios* (174) is any indication.

He is brought to land at 178, and identifies the door as the
house of Zeus, just as Hermes appears through it. He threatens
Trygaeus, who may retreat a little, the action perhaps distracting the audience long enough for the beetle to be swung off.
Trygaeus introduces himself and offers Hermes a piece of meat,
which mollifies him, and he explains that Peace, for whom
Trygaeus has come, has been placed in a cave by War and that
the cave is 'down below' (223/4). He also points out the stones
lying about it, possibly piles of stones by the side of the doorway.
Hermes is interrupted, however, by a noise from within which
he takes to be War coming out, and he therefore rushes in (233)
while Trygaeus hides by the doorway. War appears (236)
carrying in his hands a huge mortar (238), and altogether he
seems to be larger than life: ὁ κατὰ τοῖν σκελοῖν might even

imply that he appears on stilts. He summons out his slave *Kydoimos* at 255 and sends him off, first to Athens and then to Sparta for a pestle—probably he runs out and back through the *parodoi*—but without success, and both go back in again at 288 with *Kydoimos* clearing the stage of properties. Trygaeus, who has made comments aside throughout this scene, now returns to the centre of the stage and summons the chorus to appear with picks, bars and ropes.

The chorus enter (301) and insist on dancing for joy at the prospect of rescuing Peace (325). At 361 Trygaeus is about to see how the stones can be moved when he is interrupted by the return of Hermes (362), who is bribed into acquiescence by Trygaeus' gift of a gold cup (424): this must be the cup with which Hermes pours a libation at 435. Trygaeus meanwhile orders the chorus to remove the stones, and some of them climb on to the stage, the remainder taking part in the prayer to the gods which is offered probably at the stage altar. During this episode the door must be opened, if it was not left open on Hermes' return, and while the chorus are on stage they must attach ropes to the *ekkyklema*. The hauling scene begins at 459, but to start with the chorus have little effect and ask Hermes and Trygaeus to join them (469). The latter protests indignantly that he has been helping, and perhaps he was standing on the stage imitating the labours of the chorus. Various people are ejected from the chorus before the next attempt (473ff.), but it is uncertain whether they are actually removed from their ranks or are simply catalogued as people hostile to peace and thus considered to hinder the chorus in their exertions, the expulsions being merely symbolic. Another concerted effort by the chorus (486ff.) moves the *ekkyklema* a little, and the final effort, undertaken by the farmers alone, succeeds (508ff.); the *ekkyklema* comes forward carrying a bust of Peace and her two maids *Opora* and *Theoria*, to be welcomed by Trygaeus and the chorus who sing the joys of peace. Hermes explains that Peace left the land because of the actions of the politicians and the intransigence of Athens and Sparta (603ff.) and discloses that she will not speak to the audience (658), but will only whisper in his ear. At the end of the scene Hermes bids Trygaeus take *Opora* back with him as his wife and give *Theoria* to the *Boulē*

(713). Trygaeus agrees and turns round for his beetle, but is informed that to return to earth all that is necessary is for him to walk past the statue of the goddess through the door (726), which he and the two maids do, while the *ekkyklema* carrying Peace and Hermes is withdrawn (728).

The chorus, having handed over their ropes and tackle to the attendants, deliver a *parabasis* in praise of Aristophanes' comic verve and boldness in attacking Kleon and others. Trygaeus and the two girls return at 819 through the *parodos*, thus marking the change of scene, and are greeted by the slave who appears through the door at 824. During the ensuing exchange Trygaeus mounts the stage and gives *Opora* to the slave, to be taken in and prepared for the wedding (842), the slave and the girl departing at 855 and the slave returning at 868. Trygaeus now turns to the audience (871) for somebody to whom he can entrust *Theoria*—meanwhile the slave is making indecent approaches to her (879)—but decides to present her to the *Boulē* himself and, descending to the orchestra, goes to the seats where the *Boulē* sit and hands her over to a Prytanis (906).

The sacrifice to Peace follows. At 937 the slave leaves to fetch a lamb from inside, while Trygaeus indicates that he will fetch an altar and then points to the one by the door (942), exemplifying the intervening remarks of the chorus. He also finds a basket containing chaplets, grain and a sacrificial knife and a fire (948), perhaps introduced by the slave at 824, who now returns with the lamb. The ceremonial starts at 956 with the slave walking round the altar sprinkling holy water and grain, but is stopped at 1018 with the excuse that Peace does not favour blood sacrifices. The slave takes the sheep in—and thus saves the *choregos* expense (1020). Trygaeus puts more wood on the fire (1026), then enters the door for a table with which he returns at 1039 accompanied by a slave presumably bringing some meat as a substitute for the original sacrifice, and together they prepare to cook the meat.

The smell of the cooking brings in Hierocles the soothsayer through the orchestra (1044), he climbs on to the stage (1052) and tries to obtain a share of the meal, but is driven off with blows by Trygaeus (1119) and flees through the orchestra. The other two return into the house, leaving the properties on the stage for use during the following scene which begins at 1191 after a choral ode. The scene is now the wedding feast. The slave is ordered to wipe the table, introduced earlier (1039), then a variety of people enter through the *parodos*. A Sickle-Maker is the first to congratulate Trygaeus and is invited indoors to the wedding feast with his friend the Casket-Maker (1207). The next three, the Crest-Maker (1210), the Breastplate-Seller (1224) and the Trumpet-Maker (1240), who claim their businesses are ruined, are all dismissed and disappear again through the orchestra; similarly dealt with are the Helmet-Maker and the Spearsman who enter about 1250 and depart at 1264. Immediately two boy singers appear through the door, but they only succeed in annoying Trygaeus. The first is dismissed and departs through the orchestra (1294), the second goes indoors (1302). At 1316 slaves are sent off to fetch the bride, and on her arrival a procession is formed which winds its way out of the orchestra accompanied by songs of joy from the chorus following at the rear.

Birds

The central doorway may be surrounded by scenery panels offering some representation of a rocky background for the play. At the beginning two men, accompanied by their slaves, enter through the orchestra: they carry birds (a jackdaw and a raven) and equipment for a sacrifice—basket, pot, myrtles (43), spits (359). They walk to the stage, climb on to it and at 56 knock at the door with a stone. The door opens and a Plover-page appears: he displays a large beak and his appearance so frightens the men that they fall over each other in their haste to get away (cf. 86), and it seems probable that the two slaves bolt out of the orchestra. The two men recover their composure sufficiently to persuade the Plover-page to call his master the Hoopoe, and he goes in. At 92 the door is opened and the *ekkyklema* comes forward a short distance, carrying a bush that effectively covers the doorway. The Hoopoe steps off it, wearing a costume that lacks either feathers or wings. A long scene follows in which one of the men, Peisthetairus, bemoans the difficulties of life in Athens (the lawsuits and other abuses) and asks the Hoopoe to direct them to a better land. This he is unable to do: Peisthetairus thereupon propounds a plan to found a kingdom of the Birds—a utopia that will survive economically by passing the smoke of sacrifice from men to the gods. The Hoopoe agrees to the plan and suggests he inform the other birds. To do this he has to go into the copse: he steps on to the *ekkyklema* as it comes forward to its full extent and perhaps changes place with a professional singer. His wife, the Nightingale, joins him in song—that is, the flute-player accompanies him, whether off stage or from the *ekkyklema* is not clear. At 262 the Hoopoe stops, and steps off the *ekkyklema* as it is withdrawn. Four strange birds enter the orchestra, and perhaps dance across it and out before the main body of the chorus enter behind the flute-player, all being identified individually (297ff.). They are shocked and angered by the presence of humans in their midst and threaten to tear them to pieces (337), and marshal their forces accordingly (343). Fortunately the two men have their equipment for the sacrifice and use it to protect themselves. The reference in 357 to the impossibility of an owl attacking the pot is obscure. By 364 the Birds are ready for battle, and whirl threateningly in the orchestra; but the Hoopoe intervenes, and by 381 their anger is slackening sufficiently for the two men to feel they can put down the pot, while still keeping hold of the spit. At 435 the two bird slaves are summoned and take the sacrificial equipment inside the house; about this time also the slaves of Peisthetairus and Euelpides must return, for at 463 they are sent in for a wreath and water for Peisthetairus to wash his hands before he expounds his plan for the foundation of the city to the chorus (550ff.). It is a straightforward piece of economic bargaining: he threatens economic embargo on the gods (no more love affairs etc. on earth) and on men (the birds will eat their seed and pick out the eyes of their animals) unless they support the birds. Not unnaturally the Birds are enthusiastic about the scheme and the Hoopoe invites the two men into his nest (642) and asks their names, while the two in return, enquire how they are to obtain wings. (Apparently the Birds know of a root which causes wings to grow.) Finally the two slaves carry the baggage into the house, while the chorus ask that the Nightingale be left for them. The Hoopoe calls her out of the nest, and she goes into the orchestra and joins the chorus. She is perhaps only a mute pretending to play the flute. The actors leave the stage and the chorus sing the *parabasis* (676ff.).

The *parabasis*, which presents the Bird's version of creation, comes to an end as Peisthetairus and Euelpides return to the stage accompanied by a slave (801). They have both been equipped with wings, and they proceed to mock one another about them. Together they choose a name for the city (*Nephelococcygia*—Cloudcuckooland), and Euelpides is then despatched to help with building the walls (837ff.), and departs through a *parodos* while Peisthetairus preparing a sacrifice, summons a slave to carry round basket and laver. During the remainder of the scene this state-sacrifice is continually interrupted. The first disturbance is caused by a priest (851) who enters the orchestra accompanied by a crow/flute-player (who remains silent). He calls the Basket-Bearer to him (864) but is despatched at 894 (895ff. despite the O.C.T. must be assigned to the chorus). A poet enters singing at 904, and is presented by the slave with jerkin, *chitōn* (933) and tunic (946), thus leaving the slave 'naked'. Exit the poet at 951. The slave once more takes the laver (958) and walks round, only to be interrupted by an officious Oracle-Monger (959) with his roll of made-to-measure oracles. He is beaten off (990), as is Meton a land agent who next appears with measuring rods (992). A commissioner with a party of fellow commissioners then receives the same treatment, and they too flee through the orchestra followed shortly after by a Statute-Seller who enters at 1035. These last two so try the patience of Peisthetairus that he orders the slave to collect the sacrificial implements together and they go inside to complete the sacrifice there (1057).

A second *parabasis* follows before Peisthetairus comes out of the house (1118), and introduces a messenger from the newly-built wall that surrounds the state. He hurries in out of breath (1122), ascends the stage, describes the building of the walls and hurries off again (1163). As he departs, another messenger runs in (1170) with the news that a god has flown over the walls. The action now becomes rapid and the chorus excited (1189). At 1197 the sound of the *mechane* is heard, and Iris appears flying over the stage (1199). She lands, and an argument with

Peisthetairus ensues during which she attempts to fly off again (1244) but is prevented by him. However, at 1260 she is dismissed with a clap of the hands and flies away.

The arrival of a herald from earth with a golden crown for Peisthetairus introduces the next scene (1271). He describes the multitude of men who are coming (1305), Birdland having become very fashionable, and is ordered to go into the house and send out Manes with baskets of wings for them. The slave eventually appears at 1325 and, after constantly complaining of his slowness, Peisthetairus boxes his ears at 1336. The first person to arrive is a young would-be patricide (1337), who receives wings and a cockspur and is sent off to fight (1369). As he departs through one *parodos*, Kinesias, a dithyrambic poet, enters through the other and is also given wings; he is followed by a sycophant (1410) whose remarks are cleverly turned against him by Peisthetairus, who then whips him out of the orchestra and himself goes in through the door, clearing the stage as he goes (1469).

The chorus sing a short ode attacking Kleonymus and Orestes, when at 1494 a strange figure wrapped in an *himation* and carrying a sunshade enters the orchestra. He approaches Peisthetairus who has re-entered through the door and unwraps himself (1503) so that Peisthetairus recognizes him as Prometheus bundled up to prevent Zeus recognizing him. He explains that Olympus has been brought to its knees, that peace feelers from the gods are likely to be forthcoming and that Peisthetairus should demand Zeus' wife Sovereignty. He departs (1552) carrying a stool and holding the sunshade over his head.

A further choral ode is followed by the entry up the *parodos* of the peace deputation, Poseidon, Heracles and the Triballian god (1565). They remain in conversation in the orchestra until Peisthetairus appears with his slaves to prepare a meal (1579), at which point they ascend to the stage. Peisthetairus at first takes little notice of them, but eventually persuades them to accept his terms and they depart together through the *parodos* to fetch his future bride (1693). It seems probable that throughout this scene much play is made with Heracles' attempts to get a meal.

The passage of time is indicated by a choral ode. At 1706 a

messenger enters through the orchestra and announces the return of Peisthetairus with his bride, and they enter at 1718. The chorus becomes excited (1720) as he leads her on to the stage where they dance (1761) before departing in a marriage procession down the *parodos*.

Lysistrata

Lysistrata appears through the *parodos* (1) and, looking round impatiently, begins to speak. Her neighbour Kalonike appears at 6 through the door, and tries to reassure her that the women will come to hear her plan to save Greece. Eventually a crowd of women enter through the *parodoi* at either side of the orchestra (65, 66) and climb on to the stage where one of them, Myrrhine, an Athenian, speaks. The Spartan Lampito enters at 77 accompanied by a number of friends (85) and she too ascends the stage. Lysistrata asks the women if they want peace, and when they unanimously accept she explains the mechanism for achieving it—a sex strike against their husbands. The result is an immediate volte-face as they all turn away and prepare to depart through the orchestra (125). Lampito alone remains firm, and the remainder are persuaded. The idea of seizing the Acropolis is introduced (176), and all decide to take an oath of allegiance to one another agreeing to make themselves as desirable as possible for their husbands, but to deny themselves to them. A wine-jar and a cup are brought from inside by a Scythianess (199), who seems to have been present for some time, and the oath is sworn (211ff.) and the wine-cup passed round the circle (238). Meanwhile a noise is heard inside that heralds the capture of the Acropolis by the older women and all the women, except Lampito, enter through the door into what has now become the Acropolis. Lampito is despatched to Sparta, through the *parodos* (242).

A semi-chorus of old men now slowly enter (254) carrying olive logs and a pot containing fire (297), which they put down (307). They light their vine torches and stand ready to smoke out the women from their stronghold. A parallel chorus of women appear at 319 carrying jugs of water which they set down, before coming face to face with the men and proceeding to insult them. The battle of words exasperates the men, who attempt to set fire to the women's hair with their torches but are themselves doused with water instead. The ensuing affray is only stopped by the arrival through the orchestra of a Magistrate accompanied by three archers (387), who ascend the stage. The archers are about to force the gates with crowbars so that the Magistrate can get at the treasury, when the doors are opened and Lysistrata and a band of women come out (430). One archer is ordered to arrest Lysistrata, but the other women threaten him and beat off the attack of the other archers. The Scythians are driven off stage and take to their heels. The Magistrate has remained on the stage; he too is insulted by Lysistrata, who places a veil over his head (533), presumably taking off her own, and provides him with a basket of wool (535). To the magistrate's indignant question she replies that feminine control of the Treasury will quickly bring the war to a close. She offers him political advice for the city (574–86), and then, having decked him out as a corpse and put a wreath on his head she dismisses him and he departs, complaining bitterly of his treatment as he runs through the orchestra. Lysistrata and her women meanwhile go back into the Acropolis.

The two semi-choruses now strip for action (637, 662, 686), and proceed to trade angry abuse, but before they come to blows again they are interrupted by the return of Lysistrata (706) complaining that the women are trying to escape. There then appear through the door a number of women (728, 735, 742, 758) one after the other, all of whom with a variety of excuses are trying to escape through the orchestra, but they are restrained by Lysistrata and sent back inside. Two remain present, however, while Lysistrata reads them an oracle (770ff.) foretelling their success in winning peace if 'the birds band together' and at 780 they all depart indoors once more.

A short choral ode intervenes, with some comic business between the two semi-choruses (792ff., 821ff.), followed by the appearance of Lysistrata and another woman on the roof. She points to the presence of a man in the orchestra and summons the other women to identify him. Myrrhine appears and recognizes him as her husband Kinesias, and leaves Lysistrata alone on the roof to deal with him (842). He approaches the door accompanied by a slave and carrying a baby and begs to see his wife. Lysistrata disappears, and a few moments later Myrrhine appears on the roof (870). She is persuaded to descend and comes out through the door (889), taking the baby in her arms while Kinesias attempts to embrace her. The slave is quickly dispatched with the baby (908) and Myrrhine begins to remove her garments but continually runs off through the door to fetch her husband a bed (920), mattress (925), pillow (929), rug (937), ointment (939), and finally more ointment. Kinesias lies down on the bed expectantly while Myrrhine is running in and out. Finally she removes her shoes (950), and then runs away through the door. The chorus of men sympathizes with Kinesias.

A Spartan herald enters (980) and addresses Kinesias describing the woes of men in Sparta. Kinesias suggests the Spartans send peace delegates immediately while he encourages the Council to select their Athenian counterparts and on this optimistic note the two depart through opposite *parodoi*, Kinesias probably taking the bedding with him.

The forthcoming peace is exemplified in the uniting of the two semi-choruses during the ensuing ode, with the women wrapping the men in cloaks and removing a fly from their respective eyes (1021, 1026). They announce the arrival of the Spartan envoys (1072), who come slowly into the orchestra, while at 1082 the Athenian envoys enter from the other side and Lysistrata enters through the door (1107) to lecture them on the folly of internal war in Greece. She sends Reconciliation (1114) to lead the two groups on to the stage, and having persuaded them to settle their differences she takes them into the Acropolis for a feast (1187). The chorus sing a short, mocking ode.

The following scene is confused (1216ff.) and the manuscript attributions are of little help. It may be that a special chorus of Athenians enter the orchestra and its leader approaches the door and attempts to get into the banquet or perhaps it is simply some reveller who approaches. Whatever the explanation of the beginning of the scene, it continues with a semi-chorus of Athenians coming out through the stage door followed or accompanied by a Lacedaemonian semi-chorus, who start speaking at 1242 and then enter the orchestra to dance, while one of them sings. The Athenians follow them and sing (though it is possible that these Athenians may be the original chorus). Meanwhile Lysistrata has come out again (1273), and finally it seems that everyone dances out of the orchestra with the chorus presumably joining in.

Women at the Thesmophoria

Euripides and his relative (who may be called Mnesilochus, but is never named in the play) enter through the *parodos* at the opening of the play in the course of a long and, for Mnesilochus, exhausting walk. Eventually Euripides points to the door (26) and identifies it as Agathon's house (29). A servant comes through the door (37) carrying myrtle branches and a fire and prays to the gods for silence while the Muses sing inside his master's house. The two keep out of sight by the stage and watch, though Mnesilochus keeps interrupting the tragic outbursts of the slave. The two eventually show themselves (59), climb on to the stage and ask to see Agathon. At 70 the slave goes indoors again and the two wait for Agathon's appearance, while Euripides explains to Mnesilochus that the women of Athens, about to gather at their annual festival, the *Thesmophoria*, are plotting how to deal with Euripides who, they feel, has defamed them in his plays. The explanation is concluded as Agathon appears at 95 rolled forward on the *ekkyklema*. He is dressed as a woman (since he is composing a female part) and carries a lyre on which to practise his newly written odes (he has no chorus with him). Having sung his ode he is approached by Euripides and the situation explained to him, but he refuses to risk his life by going in disguise to the *Thesmophoria* to speak in Euripides' defence. Mnesilochus then agrees to undertake the mission and sits down on the edge of the *ekkyklema* and is shaved. Finding the experience painful he attempts to flee off the stage, but is prevailed upon to return (230) and the shaving is completed. He then rises to be singed, which makes him dance about in pain. The dressing scene follows in which Mnesilochus is decked out in a saffron robe kindly provided by Agathon—he probably takes off his own. Agathon is rolled back (265), while Mnesilochus forces Euripides to swear to help him if he gets into trouble. Then the *ekkyklema* is rolled forward once more (278) carrying statues of Demeter and Persephone (whose festival it is) and perhaps a small altar, as well as a number of seats. Euripides departs at once, while Mnesilochus pretends to dismiss his slave and then describes the entry of the chorus with their torches into the orchestra. The actors also enter at the same time and climb onto the stage. Mnesilochus probably takes his seat on the altar.

The Heraldess (the chorus leader) introduces the opening prayers and the invocations, which continue until 371 when she calls the meeting to order to discuss the punishment of Euripides. The first woman rises to speak, puts on the chaplet (380) and lists Euripides' faults. She proposes they poison him. The chorus praise her (433) and also praise the second woman who makes a more personal attack on Euripides. Her speech finished she departs, probably through the *parodos*, and Mnesilochus stands up (466) to reply to the indictment on the somewhat unpromising grounds that Euripides has exposed only a few of the women's faults. The amazement of the chorus (520) and the angry threats of the other women are about to boil over into a fighting match with him (566) when the arrival, through the orchestra, of the effeminate Kleisthenes is announced (571). He has come to warn the women of the presence of a man in their assembly. They decide to search for him (598) and ask Kleisthenes for help. Mnesilochus attempts to evade the search, but is stripped (636) and discovered. Kleisthenes runs off (654) to find a Prytanis, while the women keep guard on the spy.

The chorus meanwhile sing an ode (655ff.) and search the orchestra for any more men. Mnesilochus then seizes the 'baby' of one of the women (cf. 608), runs to the stage altar with it and sits down (692) threatening to sacrifice the child. The chorus suggest piling wood round the altar to smoke him off (726), and two of the women run out through a *parodos* to find some, returning with it at 739. Mnesilochus has by this time unwrapped the 'baby' which turns out to be simply a flask of wine (733), and this he drinks down, taking care that none of the 'blood' spills into the cup the women are holding underneath. A priestess enters (about 760, see 758), and is left to guard Mnesilochus while the other woman runs off to fetch a Prytanis. Mnesilochus soliloquizes; then, remembering the *Palamedes* of Euripides, tries to summon the poet by carving a message for help on the votive tablets hung round the shrine of the goddess. He remains seated on the altar, guarded, while the chorus sing the *parabasis* (785ff.).

At its conclusion Mnesilochus decides to assume the name part in Euripides' *Helen* in order to attract his rescuer, and at 871 Euripides enters pretending to be Menelaus. Mnesilochus throws himself into Euripides' arms (912), but before the latter can rescue him a Prytanis and his archer enter through the *parodos* (923), whereupon Euripides beats a hasty retreat through the one opposite. The Prytanis bids the archer take Mnesilochus inside and tie him to a plank, while the captive pleads in vain to be permitted to remove his dress. At 946 the *ekkyklema* is withdrawn inside carrying the archer, Mnesilochus and perhaps also the guard, while the Prytanis exits through the orchestra.

A choral ode follows in praise of Dionysus, until at 1001 the *ekkyklema* again comes forward carrying the archer and Mnesilochus—the latter tied to a plank. At 1007 the archer goes in through the door for a mat to sit on, and Euripides suddenly appears overhead for a moment on the *mechane* (1011). Mnesilochus breaks into a monody from the *Andromeda*, while Euripides takes up a position by the door from which he plays the part of Echo. The archer returns at 1082 and is teased by Echo, until Euripides comes on to the scene as Perseus (1098). He tries to rescue Mnesilochus/Andromeda from his bonds, but is unable to deceive the Scythian and so departs (1133).

Again a choral ode intervenes which comes to a conclusion with the return of Euripides through the orchestra (1160). He makes his peace with the chorus (1170), promising that they will never need to complain of him again, then calls in a dancing girl, who dances before the Scythian and then sits on his knee. The Scythian kisses her (1190) but before he can repeat the action she runs off through the *parodos* with him in chase. Euripides immediately frees Mnesilochus and they run out through the opposite *parodos*. The Scythian returns baffled (1210), and eventually, misdirected by the chorus, runs off the wrong way searching for the prisoner. The chorus sing a formal ending to the play (1231).

Frogs

Dionysus enters the orchestra accompanied by his slave
Xanthias who is riding on a donkey and carrying a vast amount
of luggage slung from a yoke around his shoulders. Dionysus is
dressed in Heracles' normal costume of lion skin and club over
his own more effeminate dress, but is identified at 22. The two
advance slowly to the foot of the stage where Dionysus orders
Xanthias to dismount (35), as they have reached Heracles'
house. Dionysus climbs on to the stage and knocks; in answer
Heracles appears and bursts out laughing on seeing Dionysus'
costume. The latter explains his purpose in coming (60ff.) which
is to visit the Underworld and return with the recently dead
Euripides. Heracles thereupon describes the various landmarks
on the way to the Underworld and the people and animals to be
met, thus enabling the audience to recognize the various
characters as they appear. He then goes inside once more (164),
and the other two descend into the orchestra where they prepare to set off again, Xanthias complaining of the weight of the
luggage. A corpse is brought into the orchestra carried by four
bearers. Dionysus hails it and asks it to carry the bags down to
the Underworld, but it refuses at the price offered and departs
down the *parodos*. Immediately the ferryman Charon is discovered present, his boat represented by the *ekkyklema*. He
refuses to carry the slave Xanthias over Acheron and tells him
to walk round the lake and meet his master at the Stone of
Dryness (194). Xanthias departs through the *parodos* leading the
donkey with him (196). Meanwhile Dionysus embarks, initiat-
ing a little comic business by sitting *on* the oar (198), and
eventually begins to row. The Frogs, whose entrance is prepared at 207, enter (209) and a singing battle between them and
Dionysus ensues which continues until the *ekkyklema* is withdrawn to the door and the Frogs retire defeated. Dionysus steps
from the boat (270), pays his fare and Charon disappears
indoors.

Xanthias is waiting at the end of the *parodos* and runs to join
Dionysus when called (272), and they set off again into the
orchestra, peering about them (278). At 286 Xanthias thinks he
sees the Empusa and Dionysus rushes to hide behind him, only
to run out again when the animal changes into a shapely girl

(291). However, when Xanthias identifies the beast for him he runs to his priest in the audience for protection (297). The two are moving cautiously forward once more when the sound of a flute is heard behind the scenes, and the singing of the chorus of Initiates. The Chorus enter at 324, singing as they appear through the *parodos*. The two conceal themselves by the side of the stage while the Initiates sing in praise of Dionysus, Demeter and Persephone; then Dionysus enquires of them the way (435) and is directed to the door (440). Xanthias picks up the baggage, the two climb the stage, and Dionysus knocks (464). Immediately Aeacus the door-keeper rushes out, seizes Dionysus (taking him for Heracles), abuses him, and departs back in search of reinforcements (478). Dionysus, panic-stricken, persuades Xanthias to play the part of Heracles and the two change costume. A maid now appears through the door, tells of the delights awaiting Heracles, invites Xanthias inside and departs herself (520). Xanthias is about to enter when he is restrained by Dionysus, and the two change costume again (528). Then a baking-girl enters shouting for her friend Plathane, and the two soundly abuse Dionysus who immediately changes costume with Xanthias once more. A noise is heard behind the scenes (603) and Aeacus reappears with his guards, three further slaves being summoned at 608 as Xanthias shows signs of resisting arrest. The two are seized, but Xanthias magnaminously offers to allow Aeacus to torture his 'slave' Dionysus (615) to prove that he (Xanthias) never stole anything from Pluto; he agrees, however, to be whipped alternately with Dionysus, (when the latter protests this travesty of justice), to discover which of the two is really the god, the assumption being that the god will feel no pain. Aeacus therefore proceeds with the treatment, but as both howl he is unable to distinguish between them and eventually takes them indoors to allow Pluto to do so. They enter through the door (673) taking the baggage with them, while the chorus sing the *parabasis*.

A slave, (possibly Aeacus again) and Xanthias reappear at the conclusion of the *parabasis* (738) and explain that Euripides is challenging Aeschylus for the Chair of Tragedy at Pluto's table and that a poetic contest has been arranged between the two with Dionysus as judge. At 812 an excuse is made to get the slaves off the stage, and the chorus introduces the contest. The *ekkyklema* comes forward (830) carrying Euripides, Aeschylus, Dionysus and Pluto and probably chairs for the contestants. At 871 incense and a fire are brought on, while the contestants pray and the contest at last gets underway with Euripides accusing Aeschylus of tricking his audience with silent characters, unintelligible bombast and the like, while Aeschylus, in the same vein, critizes Euripides for his realism, his sophistic scepticism etc. They parody each other's lyric passages and at 1305 the Muse of Euripides appears on the scene dressed as a *hetaira* playing castanets—the only fit accompaniment for Euripides' verse. Next, large scales are brought on (1378ff.) so that the verse of the contestants may be weighed, but it is the pan of Aeschylus that sinks every time. He is eventually declared the winner as well as the one who will return to Athens, thanks to Dionysus' appreciation of his political advice. The whole company go in as the *ekkyklema* is withdrawn (1481).

A short choral ode indicates the passing of time, then Pluto leads out Dionysus and Aeschylus (1500) and gives the latter a sword (1504) and a rope (1506) intended for certain Athenian politicians. The chorus accompany them out of the orchestra (1533).

Women in Assembly

The play begins before dawn with Praxagora, dressed in her husband's clothes, entering through one of the *parodoi* and walking through the orchestra where she addresses herself to her lamp. Another person enters (27) by the opposite *parodos*, and Praxagora retires towards the scene-building while she ascertains who this new arrival may be (29). On identifying her as a friend she approaches the door, describing it as that of her neighbour's house, and is about to scratch on it when it opens and the woman comes out. More women, all carrying torches (41) now enter through the *parodos*—these probably form part of the chorus. They carry with them their husbands' clothes and beards with which to disguise themselves (60). The purpose of the gathering, it is explained, is a take-over of the Assembly by the women, and in preparation for it they prepare to practise their parts (120) and to don their disguises. For this scene the actors probably sit down along the edge of the stage (cf. 144) with the chorus either simply standing in the orchestra or sitting round its edge, as it was suggested the Prytanies did in the *Acharnians*. Woman A rises to speak, is given the chaplet (131), and perhaps moves forward to the altar in the orchestra to announce her plans. However, she is quickly ordered to sit down again (144) after a number of slips of the tongue that immediately her as a woman. Woman B takes her place, but her blunders are equally evident and she too yields place and returns to her seat in favour of Praxagora (169). She rehearses a speech proposing that the government of the city be turned over to the women, and encouraged by her words, the women all arrange their dress so that they look like men (270), and the actors depart through the *parodos*, leaving behind the semi-chorus (284) (if the women who entered earlier form this body). Either the whole chorus then enter, or, at least, another semi-chorus to supplement that already present—there seems no way of distinguishing. They sing a short ode and also depart for the Assembly (310), leaving the stage empty.

Blepyrus, Praxagora's husband immediately enters through the door (311) dressed in his wife's clothing, and looking for her and also for somewhere to ease himself (320ff.). At 327 a neighbour appears at the window of the house (this removes the necessity of having him appear in female dress) and talks with him for a moment before disappearing at 356 with the intention of visiting the Assembly if he can find his cloak. Blepyrus continues his attempt to ease himself to be interrupted this time by Chremes, entering through the orchestra (372) from the Assembly. He reports the presence of a great crowd of 'pale-faced fellows' at the Assembly who forced through a bill to hand the city over to the women folk. He departs by the opposite *parodos* (477) while Blepyrus goes in again through the door.

The chorus re-enter (478), indicating that they have returned to their starting point (489), and draw near to the *paraskenia* while they remove their beards. Praxagora also returns (504), enters the house with her clothes (513) and appears on stage again (517) just before Blepyrus can similarly appear through the door (520). He enquires about her absence but accepts her explanation that she was helping a woman in labour and informs her of the Assembly's decision to hand over the running of the state to the women. She appears surprised and delighted. At 564 text and sense indicate that another man is present in the scene who must have entered at some point during it, perhaps with Blepyrus. His identity is uncertain, but it has been plausibly suggested that he is Chremes who was present earlier. Praxagora now propounds her communistic plans (583ff.); everything is to be held in common including gold, wives, husbands etc. and before a man can make love to an attractive woman he must first satisfy the plain ones. Probably all this is delivered from the stage and it is not until 711 that she goes off through the *parodos* to the Agora to receive her people's goods.

At this point the manuscripts contain the word XOPOY, indicating a choral performance. At 730 Chremes(?) reappears carrying out his goods, probably assisted by one of his slaves (cf. 833). He is interrupted by the arrival of a second man (Man B) who, having entered by the *parodos*, climbs on to the stage (752) and ridicules him for obeying the new law. Their debate is disturbed by the entrance of a female herald, who hastens in through a *parodos*, delivers her message and makes her exit through the opposite side (852). Man B is ready to depart immediately but Chremes(?) sets off for the public store, his slaves carrying his goods. Man B stands for a moment in thought, then leaves through the opposite *parodos* (876).

Again the manuscripts indicate a choral performance, before a Hag and a Young Girl appear leaning out of the windows of the house (877). They sing alternately to the flute (893ff.) while they await the arrival of the Youth who is to be the first victim of the new law. He enters the orchestra at 934 bearing a torch (979). The two disappear from the windows (936/7), but the Hag reappears momentarily at 942 to keep an eye on the Youth. He knocks violently at the door (975) as the girl leaves the window to let him in, but it is the Hag who opens the door. A struggle ensues on the doorstep as the Hag tries to drag him in, while the Girl reappears at the window (1037) and insults the Hag until she is scared off. Before the Youth can run to the Girl however, a second Hag rushes in through the orchestra and begins to drag him off, but the arrival of yet a third Hag interrupts her and a tug-of-war ensues between the two until they drag the Youth towards the door (1092) and all three disappear through it (1111).

It seems probable that a choral ode is missing at this point, though the manuscripts contain no indication of the fact. At 1112, however, a maid enters through a *parodos*, searching for her mistress's husband, presumably Blepyrus. The chorus advise her to wait for a moment, and Blepyrus appears (1130) and follows her off to a meal. The chorus and audience are all invited to dinner (1144ff.) and the final scene is enlivened by special dancers. All dance out of the orchestra, the chorus bringing up the rear.

Wealth

A blind old man groping his way across the orchestra followed by Chremylus and his slave Cario, the latter bearing a wreath (21) and carrying a slice of meat (228), is the introduction to this play. After complaints from Cario about the uselessness of their wanderings the two approach the old man as he reaches the stage (58), and he explains to them, under threat, that he is the god of Wealth (78) made blind because of the jealousy of Zeus who dislikes Wealth's association with the wise and just. Together the two persuade him to overcome his fear of Zeus by pointing out to him that he (Wealth) is in fact the most powerful of the gods (129ff.) in that money is the basis of Zeus' rule, apart from being what men prize most. Finally Cario is sent off (229) to fetch Chremylus' companions from the fields, and he departs through the *parodos* having first given his piece of meat to Chremylus. The latter invites Wealth into his house, and the two enter (252) as Cario returns with the chorus of Old Men, who lean on their sticks (272). They sing various joyful odes with Cario leading them, until at 321 he enters the house to obtain bread and meat.

The manuscripts here read XOPOY. At 322 Chremylus appears through the door and addresses the chorus, but is interrupted by the arrival in the orchestra of his neighbour, Blepsidemus (332). The latter suspects that his friend's sudden acquisition of wealth is due to criminal activities but when the situation is explained to him he too becomes anxious to help in the restoration of Wealth's sight so that he can distinguish the good citizen from the bad. They are about to fetch him when a wild woman, dressed like a Fury, bursts into the orchestra. They both run for their lives, probably making for the *parodos*, but she stops them (417) and identifies herself as Poverty (437). The *agon* commences at 489, consisting of an argument between Poverty and Chremylus on whether Poverty or Wealth is the more useful to mankind. Poverty argues well, citing progress and industry as the results of her presence, and indeed is proving victorious, but Chremylus refuses to be persuaded by her (600ff.) and orders her to depart, which she does (618) through the *parodos*. Chremylus calls Cario to make ready to take Wealth to the temple of Asclepias (624) but there is no indication whether this action is to be imagined as taking place behind the scenes or whether the characters appear on stage and lead off through the orchestra. The latter is perhaps to be preferred.

Again the manuscripts indicate a choral performance while the stage is empty, and before the next scene opens a night is considered to have passed. Cario joyfully enters the orchestra (627) bearing the message of Wealth's being cured, and climbing on to the stage (638) he narrates the tale of the temple ritual to Chremylus' wife who appears through the door (641). She returns inside (769) to fetch gifts with which to welcome Wealth on his return, while Cario leaves through the *parodos* on his way to meet the party as they come. There follows a short choral ode marked in the manuscript; at 771 Wealth and Chremylus appear in the orchestra surrounded by a large swarm of people whom the latter drives off (782). The two climb on to the stage (787) as the wife comes out, but Wealth refuses to accept the usual gifts outside, and all therefore go indoors (801).

Again a missing ode is indicated. Cario returns through the door (802) and narrates the benefits bestowed by Wealth. As he concludes, a man and his small son (843), carrying a tattered cloak and a pair of shoes, enter the orchestra (823) and talk with him. They are on their way to dedicate the clothing to the god, but before they can do so a sycophant and his witness enter (850) and bemoan their fate at having been put out of a job. Cario and the Just Man seize the sycophant, wrap him in the cloak and hanging the shoes from his forehead send him off (943). He and his witness exeunt at 950 uttering threats. The other three now vacate the stage by going into the house (958).

Another choral performance is indicated at this point. Then an Old Woman enters (959) through the orchestra, climbs on to the stage (964) and addresses Chremylus who enters through the door. She explains how the Youth who formerly courted her has now left her (975ff.), but at 1038 he enters carrying a torch, and climbs on to the stage (before 1052) and attempts to burn her with his torch. The two men tease her and then all enter the house (1096), the youth and the old woman first, followed by Chremylus.

The break is covered by an unrecorded choral ode, after which Hermes enters quietly, approaches the door, knocks, and hides by the side of it. Cario, carrying some guts, opens the door, looks round, and seeing nobody, is about to shut it again when Hermes stops him (1099). He is starving because no-one sacrifices to the god of Luck now that Wealth has recovered his sight, and so he is driven to beg for a position in the household. He is eventually admitted as a slave and handed the guts (1170).

The empty stage would seem to require a choric performance though none is indicated in the text. Then enters a priest (1171) searching for Chremylus, who answers him and comes out through the door. The priest of Zeus (1175) complains of the paucity of sacrifices now that Wealth is no longer blind and he too is welcomed to the household.

The play concludes with a procession. Slaves appear from indoors carrying torches (1194) followed by Wealth (1196); the Old Woman is also on stage (1197) and they all lead into the orchestra and off (1209), the chorus following at the rear.

NOTES

1. For Thespis see *Marm. Par.* on a year about 534. The *Fasti* begin *c.* 501 see *IG* II², 2318. For the introduction of tragedy to the Lenaea see *IG* II², 2325.

2. Sophocles competed a few times, see *PCF* p. 41. Agathon was victorious there in 416 (Plato *Symp.* 173a; Ath. 217a, b).

3. *POxy* xxxv, no. 2737 seems to suggest that performance at the City Dionysia may have had higher prestige than performance at the Lenaea.

4. 'Staging' 493ff.

5. See *PCF* pp. 25–9, also R. E. Wycherley, 'Lenaion', *Hesperia* 34 (1965), 72ff.

6. See Diog. Laert. V, 26.

7. See *IG* XI, 105–34, Sifakis pp. 19ff.

8. *PCF* p. 58. For the general background cf. Aesch. *in Ctes.* 43, Dem. *Meid.* 74, *Ach.* 502ff.

9. *Birds* 786ff.

10. Webster, 'Staging' and 'Le Théâtre Grec et son Décor', *L'Antiquité Classique* 32 (1963), 562.

11. J. T. Allen, *The Greek Theatre of the Fifth Century, California Publications in Classical Philology* 7 (1919–24), p. 79 conjectures six to eight hours for a day's performance. *PCTh* p. 123 reckons that twelve hours of daylight would allow two hours for scene changes.

12. T. B. L. Webster, 'The Order of Tragedies at the Great Dionysia', *Hermathena* 100 (1965), 21ff.

13. Aristid, *On Rhetoric* vol. ii p. 2 (Dindf.).

14. Hourmouziades p. 4.

15. Schol. Ar. *Wealth* 953, Plut. *Phok.* 30.

16. *PCF* p. 66.

17. *Ath. Mitt.* 20 (1895), C. Anti, *Teatri Graeci Arcaici*, Padova (1947), Russo, ch. 1.

18. See *Clouds* 326, *Birds* 296, *Peace* 731, *Birds* 794, *Peace* 872, *Clouds* 292, *Birds* 1743–52, the last two referring to a thunder and lightning machine.

19. K. J. Dover, *Lustrum* II (1957), 57.

20. The number of such references is likely to be affected by the political climate in the city at any given time, especially if, as has been suggested, there was a law forbidding political attacks. Schol. Ar. *Birds* 1297, which is largely the basis for this suggestion, is probably due to a misunderstanding

of certain vague remarks concerning the change from Old to Middle Comedy.

21. It may be the nature of the play that accounts for the large number of political references but it is possible that the abandoning of tribute throughout the empire and the substitution of a five per cent tax on imports and exports about this time meant the number of allies present in Athens was reduced and that Ar. treated the Dionysia of 414 B.C. as a purely domestic festival. The dating of the tax measure is obscure cf. Thuc. VIII, 28 (see Gomme, Andrews and Dover ad loc.) *ATL* II, 78, III, 91, 148, 358, 363, *CAH* V chron. table II.

CHAPTER II

1. For a fuller treatment see eg. E. Fiechter, *Das Dionysus-Theater in Athen. I*, Stuttgart (1935), *PCTh* pp. 15ff. and plan 3.

2. 'Staging', 493ff. cf. *PCTh* p. 21. For the latest discussion of this and the stage as a whole see C. Anti and L. Polacco, *Nuove Ricerche sui Teatri Greci Arcaici*, Padova (1969), who again demand a door through 'H'.

3. A stone found in the outer wall of the auditorium may originally have been used to designate these seats, see *PCTh* p. 20, and cf. Poll. IV, 122.

4. Arist. *E.N.* 1123a 23 seems to be the first example of its use, cf. Plu. 805d, Poll. IV, 108, schol. Ar. *Knights* 149.

5. For example the frequent address to the audience for comic effect, *Frogs* 297, 783, *Clouds* 1201, *Wasps* 74ff.

6. S. Srebrny, 'Quaestiunculae Comicae', *Eos* 43 (1948), 48, who, however, makes no attempt to connect the 'resting places' with it.

7. Ed. *Frogs* (1930), ad loc.

8. The term is applied to the theatre in *IG* XI, 163, A38.

9. See Tucker op. cit., Van Leeuwen, *Frogs* (1896), ad loc.

10. *PV* Ph 1; *BHT* fig. 202.

11. See T. B. L. Webster, 'South Italian Vases and Attic Drama', *CQ*. 42 (1948), 15ff. also *PV*. Ph 58 and *MOMC* p. 3 for the interesting Phrynis-Pyronides vase. *PCF* p. 211 now accepts *PV* Ph 1 as evidence for comedy.

12. Pp. 63ff. See also his references.

13. Arnott p. 29 cf. *PCTh* p. 58.

14. Cf. similarly Eur. *H.F.* 108ff., *Ion* 739 of about the same date.

15. Pp. 29ff. He may be correct in contending (p. 33) that *Knights* 169 is proof, where the χαὶ implies the Sausage-Seller has already climbed on to the stage. On the problem of the terms, see also D. Gray, 'Houses in the Odyssey: Up and Down', *CQ*. NS 5 (1955), 1ff.

16. See pp. 67ff.

17. Arnott suggests (p. 40) that Dicaeopolis' remark at *Ach.* 719 may indicate a stage. As for the attack by the Acharnians on Dicaeopolis, which he also quotes, the latter probably led his procession into the orchestra and was attacked there.

18. Presumably the parallel scene in the *Diktyoulkoi* of Aeschylus,

involving the drawing of the trunk containing Perseus and Danae, was engineered in the same way, see D. L. Page, *Greek Literary Papyri*, Harvard (1941, 3rd edn 1950), H. J. Mette, *Die Fragmente der Tragödien des Aischylos*, Berlin (1959), pp. 169ff.

19. *PCTh* p. 61.

20. *MTS* GVi; see H. Bulle, *Eine Skenographie*, Berlin (1934), cf. A. Rumpf, 'Malerei u. Zeichnung', *Handb. d. Arch.* 4 (1953), 136, J. H. Jongkees, '*Scaenae Frons*', *B.V.A.B.* 32 (1957), 50ff.

21. Eg. *PCTh* fig. 7, Bulle-Wirsing, *Szenenbilder zum Griechischen Theater*, Berlin (1950).

22. See M. Bieber, 'The Entrances and Exits of Actors and Chorus in Greek Plays', *AJA* 58 (1954), 277, pl. 52.

23. Oropus 2.68m (length 12.30m), Priene 2.723m (length 21m), Sikyon 3.10m (length 23.75m). The Athenian *skene* was 28m long.

24. K. J. Dover, 'The *Skene* in Aristophanes', *PCPhS* 192 (1966), 2ff.

25. A. M. Dale, 'An Interpretation of Ar. *Vesp.* 136–210, and its consequence for the stage of Aristophanes', *JHS* 77 (1957), 205ff. She has found little support: M. Platnauer ed., *Peace*, Oxford (1964), p. xii is not convinced; H. J. Newiger, 'Retraktionem zu Aristophanes' "Frieden"', *Rh.M.* 108 (1965), 229ff. has qualms about the *Peace*; K. J. Dover, op. cit., while accepting that consecutive scenes can be staged before one door, rejects the hypothesis of the single door.

26. *Peace* 728 is the only clear exception if, in fact, Trygaeus walks in through the central door to return to earth but, on arrival there, reappears through the *parodos*.

27. A. M. Dale, *JHS* 77 (1957), 205ff.

28. *PCPhS* 192 (1966), 2ff.

29. See p. 65.

30. Ed. *Clouds*, Oxford (1968), on 125.

31. Cf. Soph. *O.C.* 877, where a cry for help brings somebody from off stage; Eur. *Hippolytus* 902, where Hippolytus rushes in on hearing his father's moans.

32. 'Uber die *Wespen* des Aristophanes' in *Kleine Schriften* I, p. 308.

33. For a discussion of all the arguments see W. Beare, *The Roman Stage*[3] (1964), pp. 287ff. For the latest archaeological evidence, R. Kyllingstad and E. Sjögvist, 'Hellenistic Doorways and Thresholds from Morgantina', in *Acta ad Archaeologium et Artium Pertinenta, Institutum Romanum Norvegiae*, vol. ii, Rome (1965), 23ff.

34. *Ion* 184ff., 205ff., *I.T.* 113, 128, 405, *Helen* 70, 430, *Ba.* 591ff., 1214, *Or.* 1569, 1620. frag. 764.

35. See *MTS* TV 3, 4, 5, 6, 8, 9, 10, 12, 14, 16, 17. Many of these are by a single painter and refer to the theatre at Tarentum.

36. See T. B. L. Webster, 'South Italian Vases and Attic Drama', *CQ*. 42 (1948), 15ff.

37. See A. D. Trendall, *The Red Figure Vases of Lucania, Campania, and Sicily*, Oxford (1967), no. 917.

38. The actual number remains unclear; Dover ad loc. suggests three,

including Socrates. On the problems of MS. attributions see J. C. B. Lowe, 'The Manuscript Evidence for Changes of Speaker in Aristophanes', *BICS* 9 (1962), 27ff.

39. R. G. Ussher, 'The Staging of the *Ecclesiazousae*', *Hermes* 97 (1969), 34 claims that it strains audience credulity if the neighbour can see Blepyrus from the window and remark on the colour of his dress when he has just emphasized it is night time. I do not find this convincing.

40. The suggestion of E. Fraenkel, 'Dramaturgical Problems in the *Ecclesiazousae*' in *Greek Poetry and Life*, Oxford (1936), pp. 257ff., that the scene was enacted on the roof, is surely wrong.

CHAPTER III

1. See *IG* XI, 199, A64. The paintings in the Stoa Poikile were fastened in a similar manner, see R. G. Wycherley, 'The Painted Stoa', *Phoenix* 7 (1953), 24.

2. Arist. *Po.* 1449a 18. G. F. Else, *Aristotle's Poetics*, Cambridge, Mass. (1957), p. 166.

3. See A. Rumpf, 'Classical and Post Classical Greek Painting', *JHS* 67 (1947), 10ff.

4. Pliny *NH* xxxv, 65. 'In scaenam' probably means 'up to the *skene*' although the meaning 'scene in the picture' is possible. Plut. *Pericles* 13 suggests that Zeuxis and Agatharchus were contemporaries; schol. Ar. *Ach.* 992 refers the line to a painting by Zeuxis in the temple of Aphrodite, which, if correct, would provide a firm date for him.

5. See Achilles' painter's representation of Mount Helicon, J. D. Beazley, *Attic White Lekythoi*, Oxford (1938), pl. 3, 2 and cf. Paus. X, 25–31 in his remarks on landscape while describing Polygnotus' painting in the Lesche. For the Alexander mosaic see M. H. Swindler, *Ancient Painting*, New Haven (1929), figs. 451–4; for the Odyssey frescoes see T. B. L. Webster, *Hellenistic Art*, London (1967), pp. 138, 139.

6. *IG* XI, 158, A67; XI, 199, A95 and Sifakis, pp. 49ff.

7. *PCTh* figs. 89–91, Webster, *Hellenistic Art*, op. cit. pp. 133, 135.

8. *Boundaries of Dionysus*, Harvard (1963), p. 16.

9. Eg. *Clouds* 326, *Peace* 174, *Birds* 296, *Thesm.* 96, frag. 388.

10. For a good discussion of the problem see R. T. Weissinger, *A Study of Act Divisions in Classical Drama*, Iowa Studies in Classical Philology (1940).

11. S. Srebrny, *Studia Scaenica*, Warsaw (1960), p. 93.

12. Cf. Eur. *Phoenissae* 1–87, *Medea* 1ff. Tragedy has an advantage in that the location and identity of the main character are often well known, see Antiphanes *Poesis* 1–5, Arist. *Po.* 1451b 19.

13. 'Dramaturgical problems in the *Ecclesiazousae*', in *Greek Poetry and Life*, Oxford (1936), pp. 257ff.

14. W. Beare, 'The Element of *opsis* in Theatrical Production', *Phoenix* 7 (1953), 77ff.; A. M. Dale, 'Seen and Unseen on the Greek Stage', *WS* 69 (1956), 96ff.; L. H. G. Greenwood, 'On the absence of realism and illusion in Greek Tragic Performance' (Summary), *PCPhS* 179 (1946–7), 5f.

15. Heraklides Pontikos frag. 170 (ed. F. Wehrli, *Die Schule des Aristoteles VII*, Basel (1953).

16. Other gods occasionally connected with the altar include Zeus cf. Soph. *Athamas* (schol. Ar. *Clouds* 257), Eur. *Heracl.* 238, *H.F.* 48, and Thetis cf. Eur. *Andr.* 565.

17. The *Suda*, which quotes this fragment, claims it is used metaphorically, thereby precluding its use as evidence for sacrifice on the stage.

18. Arnott p. 49f. J. D. Denniston argues that he carries it out and puts it down, cf. *Greek Particles*, 2nd edn, Oxford (1934), p. 251.

19. See E. G. Turner, *POxy* 2654, (Menander *Karchedonios*) for possible Ἄπολλον ὦ πάροικ' ἄναξ.

20. See M. Bieber, 'Entrances and Exits in Greek Plays', *AJA* 58 (1954), 282ff.

21. Arnott pp. 66ff. where the examples relevant to tragedy are set out.

22. See p. 24.

23. MSS *KVA* see Dover, ed. *Clouds*, ad loc.

CHAPTER IV

1. 'The Function of the *Prothyron* in the Production of Greek Plays', *CPh* 10 (1915), 117ff.

2. *BHT* pp. 76ff.; E. Bethe, '*Ekkyklema* und *Thyroma*', *RhM* 83 (1934), 21ff.

3. P. 49. A second-century B.C. papyrus from Oxyrhyncus records the first letters of the *parepigraphe*, see *PSI* II, 1194, (Pack, 154).

4. *PCTh* pp. 115ff. gives a convenient list.

5. See Hourmouziades p. 97.

6. *IG* XI, 2, 199, A94ff. See Sifakis p. 51.

7. A. Fossum, 'The *Eiskyklema* in the Eretrian Theatre', *AJA* 2 (1898), 187ff.

8. C. Exon, 'A New Theory of the *Eccyclema*', Hermathena 26 (1900), 132ff.; A. C. M. Mahr, *The Origins of the Greek Tragic Form*, New York (1938), pp. 101ff.

9. *BRL* 42 (1959–60), 502ff.; see above p. 11.

10. *PCTh* p. 102.

11. See, however, Webster *GTP* p. 39 and E. W. Handley and J. Rea, *The Telephus of Euripides*, *BICS* sup. 5 (1957), 29.

12. Arnott p. 83.

13. Bethe, op. cit. 25ff.; A. M. Dale, *WS* 69 (1956), 100ff.; and cf. Men. *Dysk.* 690ff.

14. For various interpretations of the first Hippolytus see W. S. Barrett, ed. *Hippolytus*, Oxford (1964), pp. 15ff.; B. Snell, *Scenes from Greek Drama*, California (1964), pp. 23ff.; Webster *Tragedies* pp. 64ff.

15. P. 52.

16. Op. cit. pp. 299ff.

17. Op. cit. pp. 27ff.

18. The tablets were hung 'round' rather than 'on' the statue as has been

assumed from Aesch. *Supp.* 463. For an illustration see Agora Kantharos P 6878, T. B. L. Webster, *Hellenistic Poetry and Art*, London (1964), pl. ii. For other evidence see Herodas IV, 19.

19. See E. W. Handley and J. Rea, *The Telephus of Euripides*, *BICS* sup. 5 (1957).

20. Webster *Tragedies* p. 193.

21. See A. D. Trendall and T. B. L. Webster, *Illustrations of Greek Drama*, London (1971), pp. 78ff.; cf. the discussion of Sophocles' *Andromeda* (pp. 63ff.) where the heroine was apparently bound to a stake or stakes *on stage*.

22. *MTS* AV34.

23. *POxy* 2161, Page, *Lit. Pap.* no. 2.

24. *Peace*, Oxford (1964), p. xiii.

25. *PCTh* p. 63. This is a completely unnecessary supposition, for the statue would be out of sight of the audience at this point, cf. R. Vallois, 'L'Antre de la Paix', *REA* 49 (1947), 58ff.

26. E. Buschor, 'Feldmäuse', *SBAW* (1937), 1 Heft, 32ff.

27. *Pace* the fantasies of J. E. Harrison, 'Sophocles' *Ichneutae*, Col. ix 1–7', in *Essays and Studies for William Ridgeway*, Cambridge (1913), p. 136 for there is no evidence for the *Charonian Klimakes* in Athens at this date, cf. *PCTh* p. 51. For the problem of the dancer(s) see R. J. Walker, *The Ichneutae of Sophocles*, London (1919), p. 463.

28. See Soph. *Ajax* 344, Eur. *Hipp.* 808, *H.F.* 1029; but cf. Eur. *Med.* 1314, *I.T.* 1304, where there is certainly no reference to the *ekkyklema*.

29. A. M. Dale, *JHS* 77 (1957), 205ff. There seems little reason for the introduction of the bed here except for a joke of this kind.

30. *Clouds*, p. lxxv.

31. Dover, ed. *Clouds*, pp. xciiff.

32. I have discussed this scene in *Mnemosyne* 23 (1970), 17ff.

33. Arnott p. 102.

34. T. G. Tucker, *Ranae* (1906), suggests rollers, *PCTh* p. 67 that it was rowed or rolled, *GTP* p. 57 that it was wheeled, Flickinger p. 89 favours 'a trundle-boat', H. Bulle-Wirsing, *Szenenbilder zum Griechischen Theater*, Berlin (1950), p. 50 shows it being paddled.

35. *BHT* pp. 37, 70.

36. P.15.

37. *Die Ritter des Aristophanes*, Berlin (1867); cf. S. Srebrny, *Studia Scaenica*, Warsaw (1960), pp. 87ff.

38. See A. M. Dale reviewing G. W. Bond, *Hypsipyle*, in *JHS* 84 (1964), 166.

39. In Eretria the cost was 600 drachmae, see *IG* XII, 9, 207, 21; cf. the 'Pronomos' vase named after the Theban flute-player, which suggests he too would be expensive to hire.

40. Hourmouziades p. 93ff.

CHAPTER V

1. *POxy* xxv, 2742.

2. *BHT* pp. 67ff.; H. Bulle, *Untersuchungen en Griechischen Theatern*, Munich (1928), pp. 77ff.

3. P. 32.

4. See A. G. Drachmann, *The Mechanical Technology of Greek and Roman Antiquity*, Copenhagen (1963).

5. See Georges Daux, 'Chroniques de Fouilles 1964', *BCH* 89 (1965), 776 for the remains of a machine discovered in the *Necyomanteia* at Ephyra in Epirus which may have worked in a manner similar to the *mechane*.

6. Op. cit. p. 155.

7. See Platnauer, Van Leeuwen on *Peace* 109ff.

8. Attempts have been made, with little success, to refer the whole scene to the *Stheneboia*, cf. the reconstruction of both plays in Webster *Tragedies* pp. 87ff., 109ff.

9. See, however, *POxy* 2742 where two further examples mentioning the engineer suggest that such a reference may have been fairly commonplace.

10. Webster *Tragedies* p. 4.

11. Hourmouziades pp. 151ff.

12. For some suggestions cf. B. B. Rogers ed. *Birds* on 1199.

13. See Page, *Lit. Pap.*, no. 6. It is just possible, though unlikely, that the remarks of the scholiast on *Birds* 1203 direct attention to the *Inachus* (frag. 251N) because he knew this was the source of the parody.

14. *Tragodumenon Libri Tres*, Krakau (1925), p. 232; Webster *Tragedies* pp. 4, 163ff.

15. Webster *Tragedies* p. 226; for a bibliography of work on the play, see ibid. p. 220.

16. For the possible meanings of ταρρός see Dover ed. *Clouds* on 226.

17. See A. D. Trendall and T. B. L. Webster, *Illustrations of Greek Drama*, London (1971), pp. 78f.; cf. also P. E. Arias, 'Una Nuova Scena del Mito di Perseo e di Andromeda', *Dioniso* 36 (1962), 50ff.

18. T. B. L. Webster, 'The *Andromeda* of Euripides', *BICS* 12 (1965), 29ff.; Webster *Tragedies* p. 195; Hourmouziades p. 154. *POxy* 2742 seems to show that Cratinus (?) wrote paroemiacs for delivery from the *mechane*, in which case it may be incorrect to argue solely on the basis of the presence or absence of anapaests.

19. 'Andromeda' op. cit. p. 30. *Thesm.* 1016 = *Andr.* frag. 117N. Cf. W. Mitsdörffer, 'Des Mnesilochoslied in Aristophanes' *Thesmophoriazusen*', *Philologus* 98 (1954), 66ff. Similarly Rogers, Tyrwhitt and others.

20. J. M. Edmonds, *Attic Comic Fragments*, Leyden (1957), vol. i, p. 625. He dates the play to 414 B.C., and assumes a plot inspired by the Sicilian expedition with Icarus/Alcibiades as one of the main characters. Kock, on the other hand, thinks Zeus was here portrayed.

21. Webster *Tragedies* p. 32; P. Geissler, *Chronologie der Altattischen Komödie*, Berlin (1925), p. 45.

CHAPTER VI

1. *The So Called Rule of Three Actors in Classical Drama*, Chicago (1908).
2. 'Silence in Tragedy and the Three Actor Rule', *CPh* 25 (1930), 230ff.; 'The Ins and Outs of the Three Actor Rule', *CPh* 28 (1933), 176ff.
3. This objection was met by E. B. Ceadel, 'The Division of the Parts among the Actors in Sophocles' *Oedipus Coloneus*', *CQ* 35 (1941), 139ff.
4. For a discussion see O. J. Todd, '*Tritagonistes*: a Reconsideration', *CQ* 32 (1938), 30ff.; G. F. Else, 'The Case of the Third Actor', *TAPA* 76 (1945), 1ff., and 'The Origin of *Tragoidia*', *Hermes* 85 (1957), 17ff.; A. C. Schlesinger, 'Three Actors and Poetry', *CPh* 46 (1951), 32ff.
5. See schol. Aesch. *Cho.* 899, Horace *A.P.* 192, Tzetzes *On Comedy* 16 (Kaibel p. 18), schol. Ar. *Frogs* 570 who remarks on four people speaking as if it were unusual; Sifakis p. 74 and his references.
6. Cantarella p. 37.
7. At least after 449 B.C., see *IG* II² 2318.
8. *Ach.* 959ff., *Clouds* 889ff., *Wasps* 1416ff., *Peace* 1240ff., *Birds* 1565ff., *Lys.* 81ff., 829ff., 1216ff., *Thesm.* 443ff., *Frogs* 549ff., 830ff.
9. The introduction of three gods at this point is presumably to allow a majority verdict while permitting Heracles and Poseidon to express conflicting opinions.
10. It has been generally held that Socrates too is present, but see Dover ed. *Clouds* on 1105.
11. The attribution of the OCT at this point is surely incorrect. Kinesias must remain on stage for the conversation with the Herald, as the schol. R on 1014 realized. The speech 1007ff. probably misled a copyist into assuming that the character delivering it held an official position, so that he ascribed the part to a magistrate. There is no opportunity for Kinesias to leave the stage, nor does he make any excuse for doing so, as would be normal. For a fuller discussion see Russo pp. 269ff.

CHAPTER VII

1. For a selective history of the chorus see E. Roos, *Die Tragische Orchestik im Zerrbild der Altattischen Komödie*, Lund (1951); R. T. Weissinger, *A Study of Act Divisions in Classical Drama*, Iowa (1940); A. M. Dale, 'The Chorus in the action of Greek Tragedy', in *Classical Drama and its Influence*, London (1965), pp. 15ff.; T. B. L. Webster, *The Greek Chorus*, London (1970).
2. For a discussion of XOPOY and its implications see E. W. Handley, 'XOPOY in *Plutus*', *CQ* NS 3 (1953), 55ff.; W. Beare, 'The Meaning of XOPOY', *Hermathena* 84 (1954), 93ff. For New Comedy see Men. *Dysk.* 230ff. and E. W. Handley ad loc., *Epitr.* 33ff., *Periker.* 71–6. For the *komos* see *PCDith* pp. 132ff.
3. Platon. (Cantarella p. 23), schol. Dionysius Thrax (Cantarella p. 28), *Vita Aristophanis* (Dindorf p. 36). For chorus numbers see *PCF* p. 236, Sifakis p. 72.
4. The scholiasts attribute the change to economic conditions exemplified

by the ending of the *synchoregia*, but cf. K. J. Maidment, 'The Later Comic Chorus', *CQ* 29 (1935), 1ff.

5. *The Greek Chorus* p. 181.

6. *PCDith* pp. 194ff.

7. The absence of choral odes can be traced back as far as the *Vita Aristophanis* (Dindorf p. 36) where an attempt is made to explain it.

8. Fragments of an *Oineus* of the fourth century B.C. contain XOPOY M⟨ΕΛΟΣ⟩; XOPOY is found in a fragment of a *Medea* by Nicophron (?), cf. Euripides' *Hippolytus* ed. W. S. Barrett, Oxford (1964), p. 438 n. 2; Flickinger pp. 144–6.

9. *Frogs* 85 suggests c. 405 B.C. for his death; P. Lévêque, *Agathon*, Paris (1955), pp. 74ff. argues for a date between 405 and 399, preferring the later date. *Thesm.* was produced in 411.

10. See Pollux IV, 109; schol. Ar. *Birds* 297; *Ach.* 211; Bekk. *Anecd.* p. 746; Tzetzes schol. in Lycophr. (Cantarella p. 46).

11. For individual introduction cf. also Eupolis' *Cities, Kolakes*; Ar. *Islands.*

12. W. E. Blake, 'The Aristophanic Bird Chorus—A Riddle', *AJPh* 64 (1943), 87ff.; *PCF* p. 238.

13. *Frogs* 315ff. All participles and adjectives are masculine—385, 395 etc. but cf. 415, 447.

14. For formation see Tzetzes schol. in Lycophr. (Cantarella p. 46); Bekk. *Anecd.* p. 746, *Vita Aristophanis* (Dindorf p. 36); Pollux IV, 108, 109. For the position of the dancers see schol. Aristid. iii, (Dindorf p. 535): for the military character of the training Athen. p. 628.

15. As an indication of the cost cf. the pay received in Eretria, *IG* XII, 9, 207.

16. See p. 107.

17. L. B. Lawler, 'Four Dancers in the Birds of Aristophanes', *TAPA* 73 (1942), 58ff.; H. L. Crosby, 'The Bird Riddle Re-examined', *Hesp.* sup. 8 (1949), 75ff.; E. Fraenkel, 'Some Notes on the Hoopoe's Song', *Eranos* 48 (1950), 75ff. argues they were merely intended to look 'pretty and exotic'.

18. Anon. de Com. (Dindorf p. 29), *Vita Aristophanis* (ibid. p. 36).

19. *Ach.* 626, *Knights* 498, *Clouds* 510, *Wasps* 1009, *Peace* 729.

20. *Attic Theatre* (3rd edn) p. 308.

21. The flute-player normally led out the chorus, see schol. Ar. *Wasps* 582, cf. *MOMC* AS 3.

22. Cf. Aesch. *Eum.* 231, Soph. *Ajax* 814, Eur. *Alc.* 746, *Hel.* 385, *Rh.* 564.

23. See *BHT* fig. 180. L. B. Lawler, *The Dance in Ancient Greece*, London (1964), fig. 34.

24. See L. B. Lawler, *The Dance in the Ancient Greek Theatre*, University of Iowa (1964), and the following articles: *TAPA* 76 (1945), 59ff.; 79 (1948), 254ff.; 80 (1949), 230ff.; 81 (1950), 78ff.; 82 (1951), 62ff.; Webster, *The Greek Chorus.*

25. *Ach.* 627, *Peace* 729, *Wasps* 408, *Lys.* 637, 662, 686, *Thesm.* 656; Alexis frag. 237K.

26. See p. 120.

27. See K. Rees, 'The Meaning of the *Parachoregema*', *CPh* 2 (1907), 387ff. For the initial cost of a chorus cf. *Lys. Or.* xxi, 1–5. Periods of war or financial stringency do not seem to affect the provision of extra dancers.

28. *The Greek Chorus* p. 188.

29. See E. K. Borthwick, 'Dances of Philocleon in Aristophanes' *Wasps*', *CQ* NS 18 (1968), 44ff., Webster, *The Greek Chorus* pp. 184ff.

30. E. Roos, 'De exodi *Ecclesiazusarum* fabulae ratione et consilio', *Eranos* 49 (1951), 5ff.

31. *Ass.* 1158 shows that this section was added after the lots had been drawn to determine the order of performance.

CHAPTER VIII

1. W. Beare, 'The Costume of the Actors in Aristophanic Comedy', *CQ* NS 4 (1954), 64ff.; see also T. B. L. Webster, 'The Costume of the Actors in Aristophanic Comedy', *CQ* NS 5 (1955), 94ff.; Beare, 'Aristophanic Costume Again', *CQ* NS 7 (1957), 184ff. and Webster's note in reply; *PCF* p. 221 now seems to incline to Webster's interpretation; J. F. Killeen, 'The Comic Costume Controversy', *CQ* NS 21 (1971), 51 accepts Aristophanes' statement at its face value; Iris Brooke, *Costume in Greek Classic Drama*, London (1962); T. B. L. Webster, 'Attic Comic Costume—A Re-examination', 'Αρχ. 'Εφ. (1953–4), 192ff.

2. *MOMC* AS 3, AS 4, AT 1 etc. short, AT 52, AT 114, AT 115 etc. long.

3. See W. K. Pritchett, 'The Attic Stelai II', *Hesp* 25 (1956), 178ff.

4. Used by men on *MOMC* AT 1, AT 12 etc., by women on AT 8, AT 22; AT 83 affords a good illustration of Praxagora's remark that the women would have to bare their right shoulders to vote.

5. *MOMC* AT 40 perhaps illustrates the type; certainly the cloak is short and skimped.

6. Probably *MOMC* AT 11, BT 4, KT 6 etc.

7. For the *sagma* see, possibly, *MOMC* AT 42; for cloaks which fall straight and indicate heavy material see *MOMC* AT 2, BT 3 possibly examples of these types.

8. *MOMC* AS 3.

9. *MOMC* TT 7, where the clay retains the original pigment and depicts a pink *himation* that may be a *chlanis*. For the *xustis* see the Delphi charioteer, Delphi inv. 3484, see R. Lullies and M. Hirmer, *Greek Sculpture*, London (1960), pls. 102–4.

10. *MOMC* AT 10. AT 14, AT 21 etc.

11. *MOMC* AT 74. Certainly this garment is larger than the *himation* on AT 73.

12. For the *mitra* see *MOMC* GV 13, GV 15, GV 16 etc.: for the *kalumma* *MOMC* AT 9, AT 15 etc.

13. *MOMC* AT 18.

14. There is no evidence that this is to be taken literally. If it is not, then *Ach.* 435ff. may be a parody of quasi-realism in tragedy. Certainly the problem of exactly when Dicaeopolis removes his rags would disappear if

the rags were not real, for they would cease to be rags as soon as they ceased to be termed such.

15. See Andromeda krater in Berlin, *MTS* AV34, *BHT* fig. 110, T. B. L. Webster and A. D. Trendall, *Illustrations of Greek Drama*, London (1971) s.v. Hermes in the general index.

16. P. 70.

17. See *British Museum Catalogue* III E 65, Webster and Trendall, *Illustrations*, pp. 92, 104.

18. B.M. B509, *BHT* fig 123; Berlin Museum *BHT* fig 124 cf. B/f. vase from Boston *BHT* fig 125b. For a discussion of theriomorphic choruses see G. M. Sifakis, *Parabasis and Animal Choruses*, London (1971), Part II *passim*.

19. *BHT* fig 126; Webster and Trendall, *Illustrations*, p. 21.

20. *PCDith* pl. 6b, *MTS* AV 37.

CHAPTER IX

1. See C. Robert, *Die Masken der neueren attischen Komödie*, Halle (1911), p. 60. The fact that he knows the *onkos* mask but not the thick-soled *cothurnos* would suggest his source is an Alexandrian scholar. Pollux is less helpful than he might be in his descriptions, see *MNC* p. 6.

2. Schol. *Knights* 230, *Clouds* 146 (see Dover ad loc.), Aelian *V.H.* ii, 13.

3. K. J. Dover, 'Portrait Masks in Aristophanes', in *Komoidotragemata*, Amsterdam (1967), pp. 16ff.

4. *V.H.* ii, 13 cf. Xen. *Conviv.* V 1–10.

5. See T. B. L. Webster, 'Grave relief of an Athenian Poet', in *Studies Presented to D. M. Robinson*, St Louis (1951), vol. i, pp. 590ff.

6. See p. 181, n. 11.

7. I.e. First Old Man, Second Old Man, First and Second Hermonian—Hermon was an actor in Aristophanes' time and presumably introduced the mask, see T. B. L. Webster, 'The Masks of Greek Comedy', *BRL* 32 (1949), 118ff.

8. See W. G. Arnott, 'Studies in Comedy I: Alexis and the Parasite's Name', *GRBS* 9 (1968), 161. The parasite was a character in Epicharmus' comedy, and Eupolis' *Kolakes*, produced in 420 B.C., had a chorus of parasites, but the single parasite is much more common in the fourth century.

9. *MOMC* AT 18 shows a beardless man and is dated before 348 B.C., see *GTP* p. 60.

10. *MOMC* AT 8–14 possibly illustrate a performance of the *Auge*, see T. B. L. Webster, 'Greek Comic Costume', *BRL* 36 (1954), 565.

11. See also *Wasps* and McDowell's comments, edn Oxford (1970), p. 9.

12. For illustrations see S. Charitonidis, R. Ginouvès and L. Kahil, *Les Mosaïques de la Maison du Ménandre à Mytilene*, *Ant. K* Beiheft 6 (1970), pl. 5.

13. See J. C. B. Lowe, *BICS* 9 (1962), 37. The *Dyskolos* is possibly our earliest example.

INDEX LOCORUM

(Figures in brackets refer to notes)

Aelian, *V.H.* ii. 13: 123, 190 (4)
Aeschines, *in Ctes.* 43: 180 (8)
Aeschylus, *Choephoroe* 899 schol: 187
 (5)
Diktyoulkoi: 62, 181 (18)
Eumenides 34ff.: 50
 64: 52
 231: 188 (22)
Seven against Thebes 42ff.: 47
Suppliant Maidens 463: 185 (18)
Alexis, *Lebes*: 75
 fr. 237k: 188 (25)
Anon de Comoedia: 33, 87, 188 (18)
Antiphanes, fr. 19k: 113
 fr. 191k: 75, 76, 183 (12)
Aristides, *on rhetoric* ii, p. 2 (Dindorf):
 180 (13)
Aristophanes, *Acharnians*: 143ff:
 20: 43, 44
 20–173: 71
 23: 44
 40: 44
 43: 44
 54: 44
 56: 44
 61: 44
 110ff.: 91
 124: 44
 133: 41, 44
 156: 94
 172: 44
 173: 44
 175: 41
 202: 43, 44
 211: 188 (10)
 241: 43
 395: 54

395ff.: 93
395–479: 55ff.
408: 6, 52
408–79: 6, 72
435ff.: 189 (14)
502ff.: 7, 180 (8)
504ff.: 5
572: 28, 43
626: 188 (19)
627: 109, 188 (25)
719: 180 (17)
729: 41
732: 6, 14
955ff.: 89
959: 28
959ff.: 187 (8)
1007ff.: 26
1047ff.: 26
1070ff.: 26
1072: 28
1139: 114
1142: 41
1143–73: 28
1174ff.: 28
1190: 28, 41
1198: 41
Birds: 162ff.
 49ff.: 15
 56: 21
 84ff.: 93
 207–66: 71ff.
 209ff.: 107
 227ff.: 107
 291: 119
 295–6: 106
 296: 11, 180 (18)
 297 schol: 188 (10)

Aristophanes, *Birds* (*cont.*)
  343ff.: 17
  493: 115
  675: 21
  786ff.: 180 (9)
  793–5: 11
  848: 48
  850: 95
  859ff.: 47
  922: 42
  933: 115
  944: 116
  973: 117
  1056: 48
  1090: 115
  1170ff.: 119
  1198–261: 79ff.
  1297 schol: 186 (13)
  1514ff.: 42
  1565ff.: 88, 118, 187 (8)
  1567: 115
  1574: 118
  1614: 118
  1638: 118
  1693: 115
  1708: 21
  1743–52: 180 (18)
Clouds: 151ff.
  1ff.: 46, 51
  1–89: 64ff.
  5: 43
  70: 115
  83: 49
  89: 27
  125: 28
  146: 190 (2)
  181–509: 65ff.
  217–68: 81ff.
  292: 180 (18)
  326: 11, 180 (18), 183 (9)
  510: 188 (19)
  537ff.: 111ff.
  540: 108
  543: 112
  653: 112
  669: 49
  719: 117

  734: 112
  803: 28
  858: 117
  870: 115
  886: 89
  889: 187 (8)
  889–1104: 67ff., 89, 95
  990: 89
  1146: 49
  1201: 181 (5)
  1238: 113
  1301: 24
  1353: 109
  1473: 24, 49
  1475: 24
  1478ff.: 24, 49
  1485ff.: 30
  1508: 49
Frogs: 172ff.
  22: 118
  38ff.: 118
  46ff.: 116
  47: 118
  85: 188 (9)
  170–9: 43
  172ff.: 89
  180–270: 67ff.
  193–5: 12
  200: 113
  297: 118 (5)
  315ff.: 188 (13)
  460–674: 93
  549ff.: 89, 187 (8)
  557: 118
  570 schol: 187 (5)
  605ff.: 118
  738–813: 95
  783: 181 (5)
  784: 119
  830ff.: 47, 187 (8)
  830–1481: 69ff.
  849 schol: 85
  888: 47
  897 schol: 108
  1061ff.: 118
  1067: 114
  1500–14: 89

Knights: 148ff.
146–7: 25
148: 93, 95
149: 6, 114
149 schol: 14, 181 (4)
154: 93
163: 11
169: 14, 181 (15)
230 schol: 190 (2)
235: 93
498: 188 (19)
516: 106
523: 120
589 schol: 106
595ff.: 120
749: 21
751: 44
763–1252: 70ff.
783: 44
882: 114
997–8: 25
1109: 44
1110: 25
1136: 44
1151: 25
1249: 22
1326: 21, 44
1404: 44
1407: 22
Lysistrata: 166ff.
45: 116
48: 114, 116
81ff.: 90, 187 (8)
150: 114
185ff.: 47
250: 43
253: 22
254ff.: 15
286ff.: 14
428: 43
437ff.: 11
439: 90
457: 133
467ff.: 105
530: 116
586: 115
637: 188 (25)

662: 114, 188 (25)
668: 188 (25)
829: 30
829ff.: 90, 187 (8)
864: 95
873: 30
883–4: 30
884: 31
889: 31
904ff.: 22
933: 115
987: 115
987ff.: 111
1044ff.: 104
1107: 95
1188: 95
1216–323: 43
1216ff.: 90, 95, 187 (8)
1271: 95
Peace: 158ff.
1ff.: 126
43: 77
54ff.: 77
82: 95
82–180: 77ff.
174: 183 (9)
178: 45
180ff.: 118
233: 118
234: 69
289–728: 62ff.
296ff.: 16
361: 118
661ff.: 24
726: 49, 52
728: 26, 180 (18)
729: 188 (19, 25)
731: 18, 32, 180 (18)
871: 11
872: 180 (18)
937: 47, 48
938ff.: 47
942: 47, 48
Wasps: 155ff.
74ff.: 181 (5)
103: 117
135ff.: 93, 95

Aristophanes,
Wasps (cont.)
　136ff.: 29
　140ff.: 30
　198ff.: 30
　230ff.: 105
　275: 117
　379ff.: 31
　398: 31
　403ff.: 17
　408: 109, 120, 188 (25)
　447: 117
　582 schol: 188 (21)
　738: 115
　875: 46, 49
　1009: 188 (19)
　1031ff.: 130
　1122–1264: 73
　1137: 115
　1142: 115
　1158: 117
　1341: 6, 14
　1343: 111
　1416ff.: 89, 187 (8)
　1482–537: 108
　1500ff.: 110
Wealth: 177ff.
　257ff.: 105
　530: 114
　714: 115
　770ff.: 91ff.
　823: 94
　850ff.: 135
　913: 129, 130 (3)
　953 schol: 180 (15)
　982: 115
Women at the Thesmophoria: 169ff.
　1ff.: 46
　39–70: 54
　70ff.: 93
　95ff.: 54, 55
　95–265: 57ff.
　96: 183 (9)
　101ff.: 103
　142: 115, 117
　214: 115
　249ff.: 114

　250: 115
　253: 116
　257: 116
　265ff.: 45
　277: 52, 53
　278–946: 60ff.
　279ff.: 17
　280–458: 90
　395: 11
　443ff.: 187 (8)
　643ff.: 111
　656: 188 (25)
　748: 46
　885: 47
　929ff.: 91
　953ff.: 108
　1001–231: 61ff.
　1010ff.: 82ff.
　1016: 186 (19)
　1172ff.: 110
　1194: 118
Women in Assembly: 174ff.
　73ff.: 114
　268: 114
　279: 17
　283: 43
　284: 96
　310: 108
　327ff.: 27, 31
　332: 116
　372: 25
　416: 115
　477: 25
　504: 96
　535ff.: 115
　536: 116
　727: 96
　728–9: 25
　877ff.: 23
　976ff.: 91
　989: 23
　990: 23
　1093: 25
　1152: 6, 14
　1158: 189 (31)
Fragments, 8: 114
　54: 115

188: 84ff.
245: 47
253: 119
365: 47
388: 11, 183 (9)
491: 115
Aristotle, *Eth Nic* 1123a 23: 32, 34
   181 (4)
Poetics 1449a 18: 86, 183 (2)
   1449a 37: 2
   1449b 3: 87
   1451a 10: 4
   1451b 19: 183 (12)
   1452b 22: 34
   1454b 1: 75
   1456a 29: 103
Athenaeus, 217a, b: 180 (2)
   628: 188 (14)

Bekker, *Anecd* p. 746: 188 (10, 14)

Cosmas Indicopleustes, *top. Christ*
   V 204a: 33, 36
Cratinus, fr. 71k: 123
   111k: 123

Demosthenes, *De Corona* 129, 209,
   262, 265: 87
   in Meid 17: 18, 32
   74: 180 (8)
Diogenes Laertius, V, 26: 180 (6)

Euboulos, fr. 30k: 113
Eupolis, fr. 42k: 20
Euripides, *Alcestis* 746: 188 (22)
   Andromache 43: 48
   563: 184 (16)
   1226ff.: 80
   Bacchae 591ff., 1214: 182 (34)
   Helen 70: 182 (34)
   385: 188 (22)
   430: 182 (34)
   437ff.: 171
   H.F. 48: 184 (16)
   822ff.: 81
   1028ff.: 50
   1029: 185 (28)

Heracl. 238: 184 (16)
Hippolytus 171: 52
   178ff.: 59
   808: 185 (28)
   902: 182 (31)
Ion 184ff.: 182 (34)
   205ff.: 182 (34)
Medea 1ff.: 183 (12)
   1314: 185 (28)
Orestes 1569, 1620: 182 (34)
Phoen. 1–87: 183 (12)
Rhesus 564: 188 (22)
Suppl. 104: 48
frags. 123N: 83
   125N: 83
   132N: 70
   308N: 79
   309N: 79
   665N: 79
   764N: 182 (34)
   781N: 81
Eustathius, II, 976, 19: 52

Gregory of Nyssa, *ep* ix: 33, 34, 36

Harpocration, s.v. ἀγυιᾶς: 46
Heraklides Pontikos, fr. 170 (Wehr-
   li): 184 (15)
Herodas, IV, 19: 185 (18)
Hesychius, s.v. κραδή: 76
Horace, *A.P.* 192: 187 (5)
IG, II², 2318: 180 (1), 187 (7)
   II², 2325: 180 (1)
   XI 105–34: 180 (7)
   XI 158 A67: 183 (6)
   XI 163 A38: 181 (8)
   XI 199 A64: 183 (1)
   XI 199 A95: 183 (6), 184 (6)
   XII 9, 207, 21: 185 (39), 188 (15)

Lysias, *Or* xxi 1–5: 189 (27)

Menander, *Dyskolos* 230ff.: 187 (2)
   257: 115
   659: 47
   690ff.: 184 (13)
   Epitr. 33ff.: 187 (2)

Menander *(cont.)*
  Periker. 71–6: 187 (2)
  Samia 444 (Austin): 47
  frags. 303K: 115
    684K: 34
    801K: 47
    811K: 46

Pausanias, x, 25–31: 183 (5)
Pherecrates, fr. 185K: 119
Photius, s.v. ἴκρια: 2
Plato, *Apology* 19c schol: 63
  Clit. 407a: 75
  Crat. 425d: 75
  Symp. 173a: 180 (1)
Plato Comicus, fr. 188K: 135 (1)
  229K: 114
Platonius, *On Comedy*, Cantarella
  p. 23: 187 (3)
Plautus, *Rud* 429: 113
Pliny, *N.H.* xxxv, 65: 183 (4)
Plutarch, *Moralia* 805d: 181 (4)
  Pericles 13: 183 (4)
  Phok. 30: 180 (15)
Pollux, IV 108: 181 (4), 188 (14)
  IV 109: 188 (10, 14)
  IV 110: 94
  IV 115ff.: 110
  IV 122: 34, 181 (3)
  IV 123: 46
  IV 126: 36
  IV 128ff.: 52, 75
  IV 131: 76ff.

IV 133ff.: 122
IV 141ff.: 128, 138, 142
IV 143: 134
POxy, 2161: 185 (23)
  2654: 184 (19)
  2737: 180 (1)
  2742: 76, 79, 186 (1, 9, 18)
PSI, II, 1194 (Pack 154): 184 (3)

Scholiast on Dionysius Thrax (Cantarella p. 28): 187 (3)
  on Aristid iii (Dindf. p. 535): 188
  (14)
Seneca, *Phaedra* 387ff.: 59
Sophocles, *Ajax* 344ff.: 50, 185 (28)
  814: 188 (22)
  O.C. 877: 182 (31)
Suda, s.v. *paraskenia*: 18
  s.v. *Phormis*: 33, 34

Thucydides, VIII, 28: 181 (21)
Tzetzes, *On Comedy* 16 (Kaibel p.
  18): 187 (5)
  schol in Lycophr. (Cantarella p.
  46): 188 (10, 14)

Vita Aristophanis (Dindf. p. 36):
  187 (3), 188 (7, 14, 18)
Vitruvius, V vi, 9: 40
  VII praef., 11: 38, 39

Xenophon, *Conviv* V, 1–10: 190 (2)
  Cyr vi, i, 52–4: 19

INDEX OF MONUMENTS

(Figures in brackets refer to notes)

MOMC

AB 1: 114, 129, 130, 134, 140, 141
AS 1: 123
   3: 119, 130, 135, 138, 139, 188
    (21), 189 (2, 8)
   4: 119
AT 1: 189 (2, 4)
   2: 189 (7)
   8: 189 (4)
   8–14: 125, 190 (10)
   9: 131, 189 (12)
   10: 136, 138, 189 (10)
   11: 189 (6)
   12: 131, 189 (4)
   14: 189 (10)
   15: 140 (1), 189 (12)
   16: 140 (1)
   17: 128, 131, 132
   18: 189 (13), 190 (9)
   20: 128, 131, 134, 139
   21: 189 (10)
   22: 189 (4)
   23: 128, 129
   29: 141, 142
   35: 129, 130, 134
   40: 189 (5)
   42: 189 (7)
   49: 128, 129, 137
   52: 189 (2)
   57: 128, 131, 142
   60: 132
   61: 130
   74: 189 (11)
   77: 129, 142
   82: 139
   83: 141, 189 (4)
   114: 189 (2)
   115: 189 (2)
BT 1: 128, 131, 141
   3: 189 (9)

   4: 189 (6)
CT 1: 135
   8: 134, 135
GV 1: 133
   9: 141
   13: 189 (12)
   15: 189 (12)
   16: 189 (12)
IT 9: 134, 138
KT 5: 141
   6: 189 (6)
ST 17: 133
TT 7: 189 (9)
MTS
AV 34: 139, 185 (22), 190 (15)
GV 1: 182 (20)
TV 3–6, 8–10, 12, 14, 16–17: 182
   (35)
PV
Ph 1: 13, 36, 181 (10, 11)
   4: 128, 131
   5: 127
   6: 112, 119, 136, 141, 142
   7: 140, 141
   9: 119
   10: 141
   13: 138
   14: 125
   17: 135
   20: 138, 139
   23: 138
   28: 133
   37: 40
   58: 181 (11)
   79: 131
   80: 31
   84: 128, 129, 131, 139, 140
   95: 134
   139: 138

GENERAL INDEX

(Figures in brackets refer to notes)

Acharnians, 8, 29, 95, 96–7, 103, 104, 108, 125, 143ff.; chorus, 106; masks, 130; *see also* Index Locorum

Aeschylus, 1, 38, 39, 46; revival of plays, 62; as character, 89, 93, 99ff., 173ff.; mask, 138

Acropolis, 6, 14, 90, 151, 166

Actors, 86ff., arrival, 107; as women, 111; change of role, 68, 91; division of roles between, 96–100; dummy substituted, 89; extras, 89, 91, 94ff.; four actors, 92ff.; Hermon, 190 (7); number of, 67, 86ff.; silent actors, 86ff., 94ff., 127, 164; state supplies, 87; three actor rule, 86, 88–92, 94; with chorus, 16–18, 105

Actors' contest, 2, 87; at Lenaea, 88

Actors' texts, 52

Aedicula, 29ff.

Agatharchus, 38–9, 183 (4)

Agathon, 56, 57ff., 99, 103–4, 115, 117, 169ff., 180 (2), 188 (9); mask, 124, 140

Agon, 69, 89, 102, 178

Agyieus, 46, 48

Alexis, 75, 188 (25), 190 (8)

Altar, *see* Stage Altar

Analemmata, 12, 181 (6)

Anapaests, 77–8, 80, 82–3, 108, 159, 186 (18); in defence of poet, 102

Antepirrhema, 102

Archaeological remains, 9ff., 18

Aristophanes of Byzantium, 51, 122

Aristotle, 4, 13, 38; *Physiognomonika*, 122; *see also* Index Locorum

Arnott, P., 14, 47, 48, 49, 68, 181 (12, 13, 17), 184 (18, 21, 12), 185 (33)

Audibility, 54, 84

Audience, 3, 5, 11–12, 45, 101, 102, 145, 177

Auletes, 72, 106–7, 164, 188 (21)

Bdelykleon, 17, 21, 30–1, 73, 89, 83, 95, 98, 104, 155ff.; costume, 177; mask, 132

Beare, W., 111ff., 182 (33), 183 (14), 187 (2), 189 (1)

Bellerophon, 57, 70, 75, 77, 79

Bethe, E., 51, 60, 184 (2, 13, 17)

Bieber, M., 51, 68, 181 (10), 182 (22), 184 (20, 2), 185 (35), 186 (2), 188 (23), 190 (15, 18, 19)

Birds, 21, 85, 95, 98ff., 101, 102–3, 106, 109, 162ff.; chorus, 107, 119, 136; *see also* Index Locorum

Blepyrus, 27, 31, 96, 100, 175ff.; mask, 141

Boulē, 11, 149, 160–1

Bouleutic seats, 6, 11, 181 (3)

Broken Greek, 89, 90

Bulle, H., 185 (34), 186 (2)

Cantarella, R., 187 (6, 3)

Cario, 91, 96, 100, 105, 177ff.; costume, 115; mask, 141

Character, chief, 94ff.; absence of, 95–6; supported by chorus, 104

Charonian Klimakes, 185 (27)

Charon's boat, 15, 67ff.

Children in plays, 94, 96–100; lack of masks for, 127

Chiton, 114–17, 119–20, 150, 164

Chlamys, 115, 189 (8)

Chlaina, 115, 189 (6)

Chlanis, 115, 189 (9)

Choregus, 5, 48, 94, 109, 110, 161

Chorus, 58ff., 60, 64, 94, 101ff.; of boys, 94; *chorou*, 103, 105, 188 (8); cost of, 189 (27); costume of, 119ff.; dancing of, 108; decline of, 101, 103; delivery of *parabasis*, 107; extra choruses, 109; in New Comedy, 101; *parodos*, 101; plural titles, 105; semi-chorus, 90, 105, 108–9, 166ff.; size and arrangement of, 105ff.; splitting of chorus, 95, 102; supplementary chorus, 94

Choral ode, 67, 71, 89, 95, 104, 153; abandoning of, 103; absence of actors, 95; *embolima*, 103

Chremes, 25, 96, 100, 176; mask, 141

Chremylus, 21, 92, 96, 100, 105, 177ff.; mask, 142

City Dionysia, 1ff., 3ff., 87, 180 (3), 181 (21)

Clement of Alexandria, 52

Clouds, 8, 97, 102–3, 108, 112, 113, 151ff.; chorus of, 106, 151ff.; masks, 125, 132; *see also* Index Locorum

Comedy, introduction of, 20; early history, 2; origins of, 102

Contest of comic poets, 1, 87

Conventions in theatre, 41

Coryphaeus, 105, 107, 108; solo speaking, 107–8; *coryphaei*, 108

Costume, 107, 111ff.; change of, 93; decency in, 113; guide to character, 125; of Gods, 117ff.; of Heracles, 118ff.; of tragic characters, 117ff., 145; of women, 116ff.; rags, 189 (14); wearing of phallus, padding, tights, 110ff.

Cothurnos, 117

Cratinus, 46, 75, 123

Curtains in theatre, 32–4, 36

Dale, A. M., 20, 24, 28–9, 66, 182 (25, 27), 183 (14), 184 (13), 185 (29, 38), 187 (1)

Dancers, speciality, 107, 109ff., 177; extras, 189 (27)

Dances, 108ff.; dancing during action, 109; *kordax*, 108; round dance, 108

Delos, theatre, 2, 38, 40

Delphic Soteria, 105–6

Demetrius of Phalerum, 113

Demus, 21, 22, 44, 71, 97, 148ff.; mask, 130

Dicaeopolis, 7, 27–8, 41, 54, 55ff., 89, 91, 93, 96, 104, 114, 143ff.; mask, 128

Didymus, 18

Dinos, 24, 49, 154

Dionysus, 47, 68, 89, 93, 99, 105, 113, 172ff.; costume, 116, 118; mask, 138

Dionysus Eleuthereus, 1ff.

Diphthera, 116, 189 (10)

Dithyrambic competitions, 94

Dochmiacs, 101

Doors, number of, 19ff.; audibility through, 54; central door, 22, 24, 26, 50, 72ff., 182 (26); change of ownership, 22, 24; house doors, 182 (33); in Tragedy, 20, 29; 'knocking', 23; size of, 29, 54; three doors, 29; two doors needed at once, 26ff.

Dover, K. J., 7, 20, 23, 24, 28, 65, 66, 89, 123, 131 (1), 180 (19), 182 (24, 25, 28, 30, 38), 184 (23), 185 (31), 186 (16), 187 (10), 190 (2, 3)

Dramatic competitions, 1ff., 3ff.

Dressing room, 37

Dummy, substituted, 89

Echo, 83ff.

Edmonds, J. M., 84ff., 115, 186 (20)

Eisodoi, 12, 18

Ekkyklema, 6, 11, 15, 16, 22, 27, 40–42, 44, 45, 48, 50ff., 79, 82, 145,

Ekkyklema (*cont.*)
150ff., 160ff., 162ff., 169ff., 172, 174; size of, 54, 60, 66
Embas, 117
Engkuklon, 116, 189 (11)
Epirrhema, 102
Eretria, theatre, 53
Erinyes, 59, 178
Euelpides, 15, 21, 72, 95, 98, 104, 162ff.; mask, 135
Eupolis, 20, 188 (11), 190 (8); *see also* Index Locorum
Euripides, poet, 4, 55, 57, 102; *Andromeda*, 61, 82, 171; *Cresphontes*, 65; *Cretans*, 85; *Daedalus*, 85; *Palamedes*, 61, 170; *Telephus*, 61; *Trojan Women*, 81; *see also* Index Locorum
Character, 47, 54, 55–7, 57–62, 72, 82–4, 89, 91, 93, 97, 99, 100, 104, 145, 169ff.; costume, 118; mask, 128, 139, 140 (1)
Exodos, 108
Exōmis, 114
Exostra, 53

Fantasy, move from, 101
Fasti, 180 (1)
Festivals, nature of, 1ff, 75, 87; organization, 3
Flickinger, R., 103, 185 (34)
Flute-player, 72, 106–7, 164, 188 (21); cues for, 108; costume, 120; cost of, 185 (39)
Fossum, A., 184 (7)
Frogs, 6, 8, 45, 96, 99, 101, 102, 105–106, 106, 113, 172ff.; chorus, 69, 105, 106, 109; costume, 120; mask, 139; *see also* Index Locorum
Geranos, 77
Geissler, P., 85, 186 (21)

'H', 9, 11, 18, 32, 76, 181 (2)
Haigh, A. E., 108, 188 (20)
Handley, E. W., 184 (11), 185 (19), 187 (2)
Harness, *see mechane*

Hellenistic theatre, 19
Heracles, 172; costume, 118; mask, 125, 138
Herm, 24
Hetaira, 124, 174
Himation, 109, 114, 116, 119, 120, 150, 156, 165; cost of, 115; in tragedy, 117
Hoopoe, 21, 72ff., 99, 107, 120, 162ff.; mask, 136
Hourmouziades, N. C., 13, 18, 77, 83, 180 (14), 184 (5), 185 (40), 186 (6, 11)

Iambic, chorus in dialogue, 105
Icarus, 84
Ikria, 1ff., 11
Inconsistency in plays, 112
Iris, 80ff., 98, 164ff.; costume of, 119; mask, 135

Jongkees, J. H., 19, 182 (20)

Kalumma, 116, 189 (12)
Kaunakes, 115
Kekruphalos, 116
Kleon, 7, 8, 22, 25, 27, 70, 93, 97, 104, 109, 120, 123, 148ff., 157, 161; mask, 130
Knights, 8, 25, 27, 95, 97, 102, 103, 104, 123, 148ff.; chorus, 106; costume, 120; mask, 131; *see also* Index Locorum
Komos, 101, 102
Kordax, see Dances
κραδή, 76
krokōtos, 116

Laconian shoes, 117, 158
Lamachus, 26, 27, 29, 97, 145ff.; mask, 128; son of, 88, 94, 98, 110; mask of son of, 134
Lawler, L. B., 108, 188 (17, 23, 24)
Lenaea, 1, 2, 4–7, 88, 180 (3); attribution of plays to, 8ff.; domestic nature of, 5, 7; introduction of comedy, 1ff.; of tragedy, 180 (1)

Lenaion, 25
Lightning machine, 180 (18)
Logoi, 67, 89, 95, 98, 99, 151ff.;
    masks, 131ff., 132 (1)
Lycurgan theatre, 3, 5, 18, 19, 34
Lyric poetry, in dialogue, 104; in
    parody, 102
Lysistrata, 8, 22, 43, 95, 99, 102, 104,
    106, 108, 109, 117, 166ff.; charac-
    ter, 15, 22, 30, 90, 95, 99, 109,
    116; mask, 137; costume of chorus,
    114, 117; mask of chorus, 138; *see
    also* Index Locorum

Mahr, A. C. M., 53, 184 (8)
Manuscripts, 60, 168, 176, 178, 183
    (38), 184 (23); *chorou*, 176, 177,
    179; codex R, 60; codex V, 67,
    78; dramatis personae, 127; Ox-
    ford MS., 28; wrong attributions,
    187 (11)
Marmor Parium, 2
Masks, 40, 122ff.; bird, 119; beard-
    less, 124; change of, 92, 132 (2),
    154; descriptions, 126ff.; Her-
    monian, 190 (7); in Old Comedy,
    124ff.; *onkos*, 190 (1); portrait,
    123, 131 (1), 190 (3); special,
    120, 124ff.; standard, 126ff.; two
    actors in same mask, 126
Mechane, 6, 11, 40, 53, 66, 75ff., 152,
    159, 164ff., 171; drum, 77, 84;
    harness, 77, 83, 85; hook, 76; in-
    dicating flight, 77–80, 85; length
    of jib, 83; mechanics of, 186 (5);
    paroemics delivered from, 186
    (18)
Mechanopoios, 76, 78–9, 159, 186
Metre, 101
Menander, 101, 127; *see also* Index
    Locorum
Middle Comedy, 101, 105, 113;
    evidence for masks, 122
Mitra, 116, 189 (2)
Mnesilochus, 17, 26, 46, 57–62, 82–
    84, 90, 91, 99, 104, 111, 114,
    169ff.; costume, 116–17; mask, 139

Mutes, *see* actors
Mystae, 102, 105, 106

New Comedy, 40, 46, 101, 130 (3),
    187 (2); dress in, 113; masks, 122–
    124
Nightingale, 72, 107, 163ff.; costume,
    120

Old Comedy, 101; masks, 124, 127
Orchestra, 16, 57, 64, 68, 144, 147,
    149, 153, 156, 158, 161–6, 168,
    170, 174–7, 179
Orthostadion, 116

Padding, 111, 113, 120; disappear-
    ance of, 113
Parabasis, 41–2, 44, 45, 102, 103,
    112, 120, 146, 149, 151, 152–3, 157,
    158, 161, 164, 171, 173; absence
    of actors, 95; decline of, 103;
    second production because of,
    102; independent of plot, 103;
    position of chorus, 107
Parachoregema, 94, 189 (27)
Paraskenia, 18ff., 40, 175
Parepigraphe, 52, 53, 60
Parodos, 12–15, 19, 21, 26, 28–9,
    32ff., 34, 36, 48, 67–9, 76, 83ff.,
    106, 107, 142, 144, 146–7, 149,
    153–5, 158, 160–2, 164–6, 168,
    169–78; *parodos* of chorus, 101,
    102, 106, 108; *parodos* in New
    Comedy, 36
Pedila, 117
Paroemiacs, 186 (18)
Peace, 8, 45, 94, 95, 98, 102–3, 104,
    120, 124, 127, 158ff.; *see also*
    Index Locorum
Peisthetairus, 15, 21, 72, 80, 95, 104,
    162ff.; mask, 135
Peloponnesian War, 3–5
Perseus, 13, 75, 83, 84
Peplos, 116
Performance, length of, 3ff., 180 (11);
    order of, 189 (31)
Periaktoi, 53

Pericles, 123

Petasos, 117–18

Phallus, 41, 106, 111ff., 120; elimination from comedy, 112–13; hidden, 112; not worn by chorus, 119; tied up, 112–13

Pheidippides, 24, 27–8, 64ff., 89, 97, 109, 151ff.; mask, 131

Philokleon, 17, 21, 30, 73, 93, 95, 98, 104, 111, 155ff.; costume, 117; mask, 133

Pickard-Cambridge, A. W., 9, 13, 51, 55, 57, 58, 63, 64ff., 96, 180 (2, 5, 8, 11, 16), 181 (1, 2, 3, 11, 13), 182 (19, 21), 183 (7), 184 (4, 10), 185 (25, 27, 34), 187 (1, 2), 188 (6), 190 (20)

Pilos, 117

Place, unrealistic, 44ff., 65; change of, 44ff.

Pluto, 69ff., 89, 100, 174; costume, 119; mask, 139

Pnyx, 21, 22, 43, 44, 70ff., 143, 150

Pratinas, 1

Praxagora, 43, 96, 100, 104–5, 111, 114, 116, 117, 174ff.; mask, 140

Propylaea, 21, 22, 41

Prothyron, 19, 29ff., 51ff., 64

Prytaneion, 22, 44, 144

Prytanis, 44, 91, 97, 99, 129, 140, 143, 170ff., 175; mask, 129

Realism in plays, 101; lack of, 41ff., 65, 102; quasi-realism in tragedy, 189 (14)

Rees K., 51ff., 54, 64, 86ff., 184 (1), 187 (1)

Rehearsals, 4

Rogers, B. B., 59, 80, 90, 155, 156, 186 (12)

Roof, use of, 24, 30ff., 76, 93, 155–6, 167ff., 183 (40)

Rural Dionysia, 5

Rumpf, A., 19, 39, 182 (20), 183 (3)

Russo, C. F., 5, 6, 7, 60, 96, 180 (17), 184 (16), 187 (11)

Sagma, 115, 189 (7)

Sausage-Seller, 14, 21, 22, 25, 27, 44, 70, 93, 95, 97, 104, 148ff., 181 (15); mask, 130

Scaenae frons, 15

Scene painting, 38ff.; in comedy, 39; stock sets, 40

Scenery, 4, 6ff., 14, 38ff.; cost of at Delos, 40

Scene setting, 42ff., 147, 148, 151; audience's imagination in, 45ff.; change of, 44ff.

Schlesinger, A. C., 86, 187 (2, 4)

Screens, 65, 67

Scythian Archer, 26, 62, 82, 99, 118, 171; mask, 137, 140

Sifakis, G. M., 180 (7), 183 (6), 184 (6), 187 (5, 3), 190 (18)

Singers, speciality, 110

Sisura, 115

Skene, 3–5, 9, 11, 15–16, 18, 31, 38ff., 49–50, 54, 56, 66, 68–9, 72, 77, 79, 159, 183 (4); early development of, 3; front, 19, 20, 30; height of, 19, 182 (23)

Smoke hole, 30, 155

Socrates, 24, 28, 66, 82, 85, 89, 97, 152ff.; costume, 115; mask, 123

Sophocles, *Athamas*, 184 (16); *Daedalus*, 85; *Ichneutae*, 63ff.; *Inachus*, 81, 186 (13); *Laocoon*, 46; *O.T.*, 142; *see also* Index Locorum

Speciality dancers, *see* Dancers

Spolas, 115ff., 164, 189 (10)

Stage, 6, 13ff., 68, 144, 147, 148, 166, 169, 175, 176, 179, 181 (15); absence of, 17; height, 18; low stage, 13ff.; steps up to, 13

Stage altar, 17, 46ff., 59, 61, 148, 155, 161, 170

Stage hands, 127

Stage properties, 18, 46ff., 66, 71

Statues, 48ff., 61, 63, 150, 155, 169

Stilts, 160

Stone Bearer, 12

Stone of Withering, 12

Strepsiades, 24, 27–8, 64ff., 82, 89, 97, 109, 112, 151ff.; costume, 117; mask, 131
Strophion, 116
Suda, 52, 184 (17); *see also* Index Locorum
Susarion, 2
Synchoregia, 188 (4)

'T', 9, 11, 18, 19, 32, 54, 75ff.
Tableau, 51, 54, 66
Technitae, 87
Telephus, 57, 145, 161, 184 (11)
Terracottas, evidence for costume, 115; for masks, 124ff.
Theoris, 46
Theomophorion, 59, 60
Thespis, 1, 180 (1)
Thunder machine, 180 (18)
Thymele, 106
Time, unrealistic, 41ff.; passage of, 165
Tragedy, 1ff., 20, 101, 103; at City Dionysia, 2; at Lenaea, 180 (1); competitions, 4; decline of chorus, 101
Trendall, A. D., 13, 182 (37), 185 (21), 186 (17), 190 (15, 19)
Tribōn, 115, 189 (5)
Tritagonistes, 87
Trygaeus, 11, 14, 16, 26, 47, 49, 77ff., 98, 110, 118, 159ff.; mask 134

Van Daele, 58
Van Leeuwen, 73, 90, 156, 181 (9), 186 (7)

Vase paintings, evidence for stage, 13ff.; for theatre, 13, 30, 181 (11)
Victor lists, 1ff.

Wasps, 8, 21, 43, 94, 95, 98, 102–3, 104, 108, 155ff.; costume of chorus, 119ff.; masks, 133; *see also* Index Locorum
Wealth, 7, 8, 21, 96, 100, 101, 103–4, 105, 117, 124, 177ff.; *see also* Index Locorum
Webster T. B. L., 4, 9, 11, 29, 54, 72, 81, 84, 85, 101, 109, 111, 112, 133 (1), 180 (10, 12), 181 (11), 182 (36), 183 (7), 184 (11, 14) 185 (18, 20, 21, 34), 186 (8, 10, 14, 15, 17, 18, 19, 21), 187 (1), 188 (5, 24), 189 (28, 29, 1), 190 (15, 19, 5, 7, 9, 10)
Wilamowitz-Moellendorf, V. von, 29, 90, 112
Window, 27, 31ff., 40, 155, 156, 175, 176, 183 (39)
Women at the Thesmophoria, 7, 8, 26, 96, 99, 102, 104, 169ff.; *see also* Index Locorum
Women in Assembly, 7, 8, 96, 100, 101, 103–5, 108, 110, 174ff.; chorus, 106; *see also* Index Locorum

χορυ, *see* Chorus
Xustis, 115, 116, 189 (9)

Zeus, 81, 123, 159, 177, 179, 184 (16), 186 (20)
Zeuxis, 39, 183 (4)
Zielinski, Th., 81, 186 (14)